THE PALESTINIANS

FRANK H. EPP

THE PALESTINIANS
Portrait of a People in Conflict

PHOTOGRAPHS BY JOHN GODDARD

HERALD PRESS
Scottdale, Pennsylvania

To those who speak
And to those who still listen

It has frequently been charged in the West, especially after
commando bombings, airplane hijackings, and Munich massacres,
that the Palestinian Arabs can speak only the language of violence.
Such accusations are at least partly misdirected; for rarely has a
people suffered so much injustice so passively for so long, waiting
for the powers-that-be to redress the inflicted wrong. It is probably
more true that violence is the only language the West understands.
As fellow Westerners, we have not accepted our deafness as
complete or as incurable. We believe that there is among us some
capacity for hearing, for understanding, and for a wiser
statesmanship. To those who speak in this Portrait and to those
who can still hear, we dedicate this book.
                                    – Frank H. Epp and John Goddard.

Contents

Tables

Maps

Credits

All photographs by John Goddard unless otherwise noted.
Cartography by A.E. Hildebrand.

PREFACE

This portrait of the Palestinians arose from annual research trips to the Middle East beginning in the summer of 1968, the year after the Seven Day War. Its specific content is based on interviews with 172 Palestinians in the summers of 1971 and 1974, in other words before and after the October War of 1973. These interviews produced over 2,500 pages of text, transcribed from tapes, and hundreds of pages of notes, in cases where taping was not possible for one reason or another.

The interviewees are identified in the source section of the book, including their names, real and fictitious (if pseudonyms were requested), their occupational or residential identity, their Palestinian origin, and their location at the time of our meeting.

In every instance the main goal of the interviews was to elicit the freest possible story-telling and the truest expressions of feeling. Anonymity was granted where requested. While many facts were sought and uncovered, such research was not the primary purpose. A people without a home are rarely a people of exact record anyway. The first intention was to get at the most fundamental fact of all, so often overlooked by chroniclers and diplomats, namely how the people themselves perceive and feel about their past experience, their present situation, and future prospects. For this reason also the words of the Palestinians themselves are richly employed in this portrait.

The production of this volume, and particularly the field work, was made possible by the cooperation of many persons, too many to list here. I am especially indebted to certain people in the Arab League Information Service (Ottawa and Cairo), the Near East Ecumenical Bureau of Information and Interpretation (Beirut), the Palestine Liberation Organization (Cairo, Beirut, and Damascus), UNRWA (Beirut and Amman), the Fifth of June Society now merged with the Lebanese Association for Information on Palestine (Beirut), the Jordan Information Ministry (Amman), St. George's Cathedral (Jerusalem), the Near East Council of Churches Committee for Refugee Work (Gaza), Americans for Middle East Understanding (New York), and Mennonite Central Committee (Winnipeg, Akron, Amman, and Jerusalem). Helen Epp and Anna Ens transcribed most of the interviews. My assistants on the two research trips were John Goddard (1971) and our daughters Marianne and Esther (1974). Goddard followed up our 1971 trip with another photographic mission in 1973, a few months after the last war. Secretaries Pauline Bauman, Miriam Jantzi, and Joan Weber were also of great assistance.

None of the individuals or organizations and their staffs can, of course, be held accountable for any part of this portrait. That responsibility is mine. For any misreading of the Palestinians, however small, I apologize. It was not intentional. I am deeply grateful that they accepted the risk of sharing their lives with us so that, hopefully, we could share them with the rest of the world. The portrait is not as complete as I had hoped, but as complete as it could be in the face of some restricted access and otherwise difficult circumstances. The reader may be surprised that we did not enjoy the full confidence of all the Palestinians wherever we went, but in the face of their many disappointments with Westerners, we accept the fact that trust must be earned.

We also acknowledge that our Jewish friends may by this effort be shaken in their trust. Be the outcome of that as it may be, we intend also to listen to the Israelis and produce an empathetic portrait also of that people, likewise caught in conflict. In Israel also the people have not been heard sufficiently through the din of war and the propaganda of officialdom.

Peace, we believe, lies in the direction of deep, sensitive, and prolonged listening to the peoples on both sides, from both sides and by both sides. Such listening will reveal that justice for the Palestinian, security for the Israeli, and peace and fulfilment for both, are all a part of each other. Neither side can pursue and achieve only one goal without the other.

Thus, we present this portrait of the Palestinians without apology to the Jewish people. We intend also to complete our portrait of the Israelis without apology to the Palestinians. We want the world to hear both of them and both of them to hear each other. The Palestinians come first because, in our humble opinion, they have been heard the least.

Frank H. Epp
Conrad Grebel College
University of Waterloo
Ontario, Canada

Chapter 1

Giving a People a Hearing

"No one hears our quiet cries for justice. Perhaps they will hear when the bombs explode."

— *Ahmad Fariah*

The people most neglected in the international dialogue about the Middle East conflict are the Palestinian Arabs (hereafter simply known as Palestinians). There are over three million of them, and half are outside their homeland. Our first discovery of these people and their need to be heard was after the Seven-Day War, which made many of them refugees for the second time.

Annual research trips reconfirmed this need, and we resolved to do something about it. Twice we went to the Middle East for the specific purpose of interviewing Palestinians. It was our desire to have the Palestinians' story told as completely as possible, using their own words.

Giving a hearing to a people like the Palestinians means first of all coming to terms with the causes of Western ignorance and apathy concerning their plight. It also requires a resolution, or at least a suspension, of the biases of the "average" Westerner, whose empathies tend to lie with the Israelis. Conversely, it is necessary to deal with Palestinians' suspicion and mistrust, on the one hand, and with their eagerness to get the story told and told right, on the other. Finally, the fact that the people are scattered into many regions with rather diverse settings complicates not only the task of understanding but also the problem of contact.

There are three main reasons why the Palestinians and their cause are not known in the West, all of them related to the chief methods of exposure: tourism, the mass media, and governmental communications.

Let's take tourism first. The homeland of the Palestinians is the so-called "holy land" to which millions of pilgrims and tourists have travelled through the centuries. Today, tourism is conducted on a massive scale with great potential for increased understanding among peoples. However, it is the historic places rather than the contemporary people to which most tourists are exposed.

Hundreds of thousands of Christian pilgrims return to Europe and North America each year with millions of coloured slides of stones and shrines, graphically depicting where Jesus once walked, but with very little feeling for the helpless and homeless peoples among whom he might walk today.

Tourists look with awe on the Jericho road, a trail where once two thousand years ago a man fell among thieves; but they rarely see it as the modern highway along which thousands of Palestinian refugees have been driven downhill by tanks and jets to the bridge of no return. Indeed, many tours are designed not only to distort the Palestinian reality, but also to hide it. Rather than introducing the traveller to the Palestinian Arab agricultural genius, still evident in hundreds of olive orchards and vine-yards clinging to barren and rocky hillsides, false images of laziness, inepti-tude, and sluggishness are perpetuated.

Likewise, the mass media have, by and large, so closely identified Pales-tinians with terrorists as to make the two terms synonymous. It is true, of course, that terrorist acts have been perpetrated by people identified as Palestinians. The acknowledgement of that objective fact must, however, be accompanied by a similar acknowledgement of another terrorism, lest an unfair onus be placed on one group of people. The other terrorism is the terrorism of dispossession and displacement forced upon the Palestinians for nearly three decades; the terrorism of refugee camps – cold and fright-ening by night and in the winds of winter, hot and parching by day and in the scorching heat of summer; and last but not least the terrorism of gov-ernments and states. As in Vietnam so in the Middle East, the Western press has always seen greater terror in guerilla grenades than in bombs and flaming napalm dropped by state authority on villages and camps. How-ever, terrorism meted out by the Palestinians, regrettable as it is, is minute by comparison with that which has been inflicted on them. The mass media have failed to make that point adequately.

Where Palestinians have not been identified as terrorists they have been called refugees. The latter term, or at least the intention of its users, is undoubtedly positive. But distortion sets in when the word "refugee" evokes a humanitarian response that includes blankets and food, but not the main requirement – justice. And when descriptions of camps overlook the tens of thousands who have gone forth to provide an independent existence for themselves and their families. Palestinians are not only refu-gees with needs, but human beings with rights.

Finally, governmental communications. The Palestinians themselves are rarely heard in international communications; their voices are drowned out by government and official spokesmen. For the leaders the microphones are always ready, even when the speakers are known to be lying, while the masses cry in vain to be heard. The truth of Indo-China could have been known much earlier if the West could have heard the people of Vietnam, as well as their governments. The same is true in the Middle East. The voices of the people have been drowned out by official communiqués from within and without the area.

Beyond the failures of tourism, the mass media and governmental communications lie some deeper reasons for the faulty Western perception. Long historical conditioning has shaped both the cognitive and affective responses of the West to the Middle East. Locked in by a given frame of reference and by a psychological bent, it is not simple for Western people to break through their preconceptions.

John Goddard and I are, or rather were, good examples of this phenomenon. As typical North Americans, our earliest and strongest impressions about the Middle East conflict were those common to most of our countrymen. We empathized most strongly with the Israelis. In the 1967 War, and even later, both of us believed that once again the Arab Goliath had been slain with a sling-shot – a jet-age sling-shot to be sure – and with the help of God – by the Israeli David. In the aftermath of that war John Goddard signed up for a summer in an Israeli kibbutz.

My own linkage to the Jewish people has a very special history. The Mennonite people have often been likened to the Jews, both by themselves and by outsiders. Mennonites, like Jews, have been a wandering minority, often persecuted by both church and state, though the Mennonite story is much briefer, dating back only to 1525. And its tales of martyrdom, however horrible in Stalinist Russia in the twentieth century and in the Holy Roman Empire in the sixteenth, are surpassed in magnitude by the Nazi holocaust. Yet there are strong parallels, and every time *Fiddler on the Roof* visits our community I see not only Jewish exiles escaping the tsarist pogroms, but also thousands of my own people, including father and mother, driven from their homes by the Communist revolution, by the ensuing civil war, and by the collectivization in the Soviet era.

My own very personal and particular empathy for the Jews emerged from three separate experiences. The religious, already referred to, received a strong push in the eschatological teachings of my church high school in the early 1940s. I was taught then that God wanted the Jews to return to Palestine, and that the parts of the new temple were ready in London and New York, waiting for war's end and transport to Jerusalem! Throughout the 1950s and 1960s I never seriously questioned these teachings, although I also did not pursue them. At the conclusion of the 1967 War I felt, with most North Americans, that Israel was on the side of God and God on the side of Israel.

13

The second source was an academic experience. My doctoral dissertation at the University of Minnesota (1965) was an examination of Germanist and National Socialist influence among Canadian minority groups. Deeply disturbed by the extent to which pro-Germanism and anti-Communism had led also to anti-Semitism, I resolved to do battle with this vicious syndrome.

The third source was the common political experience of the campaigns against the Vietnam war and capital punishment. In the loneliness of the early protests (1965-68) one could count on the loyalty and friendship of Jews when it came to taking an unpopular stand. I can, therefore, never forget the common cause we were privileged to share with such morally sensitive and courageous Jewish people as Cy Gonick in Winnipeg, Helen and Gilbert Levine in Ottawa, Irwin Cotler now in Montreal, and last but not least, Rabbi Abraham Feinberg at Holy Blossom Temple in Toronto.

It was, therefore, not an easy matter to adjust my thinking on the Middle East when, beginning in 1968, I realized that I had been exposed to only one side of the story. Several facts became clearer as time went on, and consequently unavoidable, namely that Israel was no longer a David, that the Arabs were not yet a Goliath, that a great injustice had been done to the Palestinians, and that a religious Zionism, quite properly desiring a homeland, had largely been replaced by a political Zionism dependent on militarism and seeking an empire.

I also became convinced that the mass media of North America and the thousands of Christian tourists who visited the Holy Land were doing very little to bring about a balance of information and a more adequate understanding of the heart of the Middle East conflict. Not surprisingly, the Palestinians were turning to bombings, hijackings, and massacres to make their voice heard in the world. It became imperative, therefore, to tell their story in another way, thereby hastening the end of violence and the day of justice and peace.

It was easier, however, to declare our intention than to execute it. Although the organizations and their leaders knew about us, their trust and confidence, as well as that of the common people who did not know us, had to be won. And this winning could not be superficial. The depth of feeling expressed and the extent of personal exposure is directly related to the degree of trust extended to those who listen.

Establishing contact with a reasonably representative group of Palestinians became a formidable undertaking. The estimated 3,500,000 Palestinians are today mostly outside of the boundaries of their former homeland (see Table 1) including Israel, Gaza, and the West Bank. We could not visit them everywhere they are found, but our goal to talk to a repre-

TABLE I

THE LOCATION OF THE PALESTINIANS*

Region	Number				
	Refugees Registered by UNRWA				
	In Camp	Not in Camp	Total Refugees	Non–Refugee	Total
Egypt (UAR)	–	–	–	40, 000	40, 000
Gaza Strip	200, 000	125, 000	325, 000	75, 000	400, 000
Israel	–	–	–	375, 000	375, 000
West Bank	75, 00	225, 000	300, 000	450, 000	750, 000
Jordan (East)	200, 000	400, 000	600, 000	400, 000	1, 000, 000
Syria	50, 000	125, 000	175, 000	15, 000	190, 000
Lebanon	100, 000	100, 000	200, 000	85, 000	285, 000
Persian Gulf & Other Arab States	–	–	–	225, 000	225, 000
Europe, North & South America	–	–	–	235, 000	235, 000
Total	**625, 000**	**975, 000**	**1, 600, 000**	**1, 900, 000**	**3, 500, 000**

*Compiled and estimated from various sources, including UNRWA, Institute of Palestinian Studies, and Palestine Research Center.

sentative group of people within the homeland and in the Arab lands bordering it was achieved to our satisfaction thanks to the people and organizations referred to in the Preface.

They helped us to move as freely as we did in Egypt, Lebanon, Syria, Jordan (East), the Occupied Territories (West Bank including East Jerusalem and Gaza Strip), and Israel. The 172 Palestinians listened to on two separate research trips (1971 and 1974) broke down into age, geography, and sex categories as illustrated in Tables 2-5.

Almost every one of the conversations with the Palestinians began with an explanation of our mission, and with the questions: Would they talk to us? Could we talk to them? Some were eager, some not at all. Coming from Canada helped to open doors. Claiming refugee parentage and belonging to a large family were also very useful. Empathetic and patient listening helped most of all. Thus suspicion and mistrust often turned into an eagerness to use this new possibility of getting a story told. Even so, quite a number considered our mission useless, since they had talked many times before to journalists to no good effect. Their own words give the reasons best. They also express their many conflicting feelings, including love and anger, hope and despair, determination and surrender, trust and distrust, encouragement and disappointment.

ABDUL-RAHMAN RA'II, muktar from Hebron now in an East Bank refugee camp: "Many, many missions and broadcasting teams have already come and interviewed us. There is no use in all this, because by now everyone should know the case, the Palestinian case. No matter how many billions of dollars America will pay to settle us in any other country, even in America, we won't accept anything but our land. We want our land, and sooner or later we will be back in our land."

NIMREH TANNOUS ES-SAID, Jordanian director of emergency refugee program: "We don't need blankets, we don't need tents. We need understanding. We don't even need sympathy. Hypocritical sympathy we don't need. We want you to hear us and know us, hear both sides and then decide for yourself. God has given you all the wisdom to see and think and find the truth. That is all."

NE'MEH SIMA'AN, Catholic bishop from Nazareth: "The people here cannot believe what the Western people are saying or declaring. There is mistrust. They mistrust the whole Christian church. I will be glad if you can try to give at least truth to the people, because we need it now in the world."

MUSA ABU TALEP, a tourist guide: "I hope this will help, because there were many reports, many articles written, many speeches, but I don't know whether such things help or not."

16

TABLE 2

LOCATION OF PALESTINIANS INTERVIEWED

Location	Israel	Occupied Palestine	Jordan	Lebanon	Syria	Egypt	North America	Total
Number	7	55	51	47	3	6	3	172

TABLE 3

AGE OF PALESTINIANS INTERVIEWED

Age	Teens	Twenties	Thirties	Forties	Fifties	Sixties & Over	Total
Number	8	31	41	41	28	23	172

TABLE 4

SEX OF PALESTINIANS INTERVIEWED

Sex	Male	Female	Total
Number	129	43	172

TABLE 5

YEAR OF FIRST INTERVIEWS

Year	1971	1974	Total
Number	140	32	172

*Numerous 1974 interviews, not included here, were repeats with people listened to first in 1971.

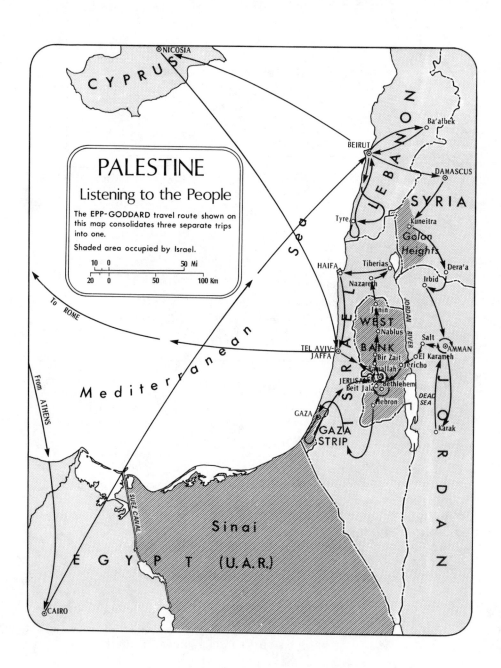

PALESTINE

Listening to the People

The EPP-GODDARD travel route shown on this map consolidates three separate trips into one.

Shaded area occupied by Israel.

10 0   50 Mi
20 0   50   100 Km

MUHAMMAD ALAZEH, a refugee camp director: "I don't expect you to solve the problem. But what I ask from you is that you give a very clear idea to the people. I don't expect more. I only want you to communicate what you see."

HAJJA ANDALIB AMAD, leader of women's movement in Nablus: "The problem of the Palestine people is one the civilized world does not understand."

NAJIB NASSAR, father of imprisoned commando: "We can explain, but the West doesn't understand. I talked for six hours to a group of clergymen, but they couldn't accept."

LINA AWEIDA, a student: "We want them to know that we are not terrorists. We are freedom fighters. We fight only to have a just peace in Palestine, where everyone can live as a Jew, as a Muslim, or as a Christian."

SALEH ABDEL-JEHIL, teenager in orphanage: "I hope you and all our friends in Canada, in Europe, and all over the world will understand our situation well, and be sure that we, the Palestinians, have decided to carry on our struggle until victory."

SAID DIRAWI, camp resident in Lebanon: "We are pleased to see you here to take a good picture to the United States about our living here, and I hope you tell the true thing. The thing which I am going to tell you about our life – we are living a miserable life now."

TARAK, a commando in refugee camp: "The problem of the Palestinian people is one the civilized world does not understand."

ELIAS FREIJ, a Bethlehem businessman: "I just want to thank you for your coming, and I hope you will help me because your people have better lives and more prosperity, and we pray that you will have peace and that the Christian communities in America will remember Bethlehem, not remember it in various Christmas cards, but to remember it in fact and deed."

ISSAT AL-ATAWNEH, a Bedouin sheikh from Hebron: "I want this to be announced in the Canadian radio. The Arabs are not in favour of bloodshed. All that we want is to live as brothers in this Holy Land. Jews, Christians, and Muslims without discrimination. And the country is rich enough, but discrimination, the spirit of hitlerism should cease."

SAMIR, a military camp leader: "You shouldn't say that you came here and that you had help from us, because even the leadership doesn't know what education I have, that I was in Germany. So please when you go there don't say that you have been here. Otherwise I will be punished, you know."

NAJIB, a commando: "Now whether you are a Zionist or not, I don't care. The point is that at this very moment you are not subjecting me to your Zionism. You are not part of the Zionist state, and at least, you are ready to listen to my point of view."

RHOUI EL-KHATIB, Jerusalem mayor in exile: "I wish to request you and your colleague to convey to your people, to the Canadians, our love and hope that they continue their stand in the case of Jerusalem for a peaceful Jerusalem, for a holy Jerusalem, not to allow its changes, to stand bravely, to oppose any changes in the character, whether spiritual or architectural, of Jerusalem. We have a great faith in your people and please convey to every citizen the blessing of our good wishes."

HUDA SAID, from Jerusalem: "We would like the North American woman to try to understand our problem and to be at least neutral, not to listen to one side."

NAJLA KANAZEH, a homemaker from Haifa: "For an American woman it is as simple as this: Would she like to be displaced from her house and be thrown out, for somebody to come and live in her house? Would she accept this fact? I don't think she would. Our case is as simple as this: We were thrown out of our houses, our country. We want back our country. We want to live in our country."

HALDA DAJANI, a high school student: "If I could go on a tour and visit the high schools of North America, and talk to girls and boys my age, I would explain to them the real case of Palestine. They know the case through the Jews, not through the Palestinians, not through the Arabs. They don't know the other side of the story."

YOUNES ASA'S, a camp doctor: "Medical-officers should have a campaign against wars, against every war in the world, not only to treat the patients but to prevent them from the wars. For example, when a soldier is injured we treat them in order to live, but what happens? We treat him so that he can go back to die in the war. That's all. The doctors in the world, in the whole world, should fight peacefully against what happens here. Everyone in the world should have the right to live as others in spite of his colour, in spite of his faith. In that time, when it comes, there will be no Jews, no Arabs, no Europeans. They will all be human beings."

MUNZEV, an engineer in occupied Palestine: "We are living in the age of computers and space travel, where men are conquering the universe. Instead, they should try to improve the standards of the present world on earth and understanding between nations. The engineer is a seeker of truth. The nations must take some time away from technology to look at the problems of the earth. Please tell your engineers."

MAHA AL-ATAWNEH, a school teacher of Bedouin ancestry: "Please tell the teachers to teach the students to love all the humanities, how to be kind to all, and how to hate the war and to love."

"AN ARAB IN ISRAEL," from Tiberias: "Who are you? Twelve years ago a writer like you came. He came to me like a lamb. Three hours we talked. He wrote two anti-Arab books. All I got was a full report from the military authorities in Israel. I was interrogated for every word I said."

* * *

In the end very few Palestinians turned us away, and most ended up talking longer than expected and introducing us to others who also had things to say. The telling was often a repetition of what we had already heard. But so urgent was their story and so overdue its hearing that there remained no doubt about our own calling to record this sad human drama.

Chapter 2

The Longest Memory on Earth

"The people here lived on this very same piece of land for thousands of years, generation after generation, without changing localities, without even changing homes. Our identity with the land and our memories go back thousands of years."

— *Leila Nasser*

Westerners have relatively short histories and memories. In their interpretation of world events, such as Vietnam and Middle East, they tend to go back not to the beginning but only to the most recent wars, or battles, or bombing strikes. It isn't so with the peoples of the Middle East, particularly the two main Semitic peoples: the Arabs and the Jews. Their histories go back thousands of years, and their memories reach into antiquity – especially those parts of antiquity that are favourable to their story. For the Arabs, specifically the Palestinian Arabs, it is unacceptable to interpret the Middle East conflict or to attempt a settlement only in terms of 1967 and on the basis of what has happened since then.

Their memories go back at least to 1947 and the United Nations Resolution (No. 181-11, November 29), by which the General Assembly approved the partitioning of Palestine to allow for an Arab state, a Jewish state, and an international zone for Jerusalem. As the Palestinians remember it, that action of the United Nations was a contravention of its own charter because the majority affected by it was opposed to it. But even if the resolution wasn't against the charter, the Palestinians know that the state of Israel was not an implementation by the United Nations but a unilateral act of the Israelis.

They also remember 1917, the year the British government issued the famous Balfour Declaration, which promised British help in establishing a homeland for the Jews in Palestine. The declaration was a by-product of the war. Britain had designs on parts of the Middle East, which had for many years been controlled by Turkey. The Jews were interested in Palestine. Both needed the help of each other in achieving their goals. Britain was particularly interested in obtaining the support of American Jews and of America itself. When the British succeeded in entering Palestine and in

23

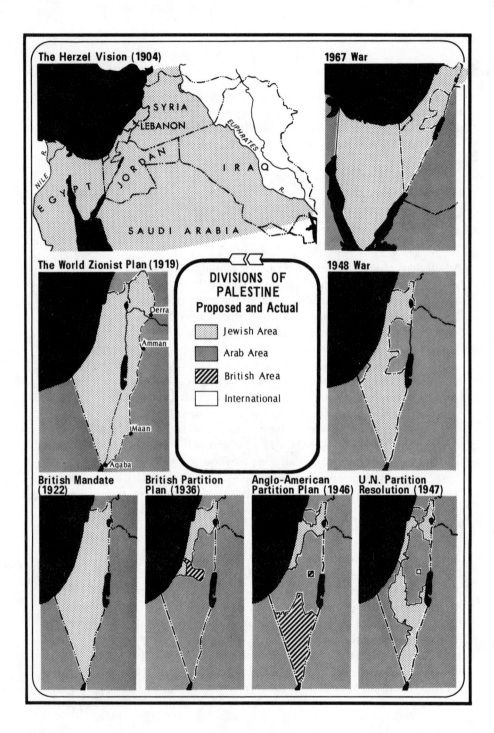

The Herzel Vision (1904)

SYRIA

LEBANON

EUPHRATES

JORDAN

IRAQ

NILE R.

R.

EGYPT

SAUDI ARABIA

1967 War

The World Zionist Plan (1919)

Derra

Amman

Maan

Aqaba

DIVISIONS OF
PALESTINE
Proposed and Actual

Jewish Area

Arab Area

British Area

International

1948 War

British Mandate
(1922)

British Partition
Plan (1936)

Anglo-American
Partition Plan (1946)

U.N. Partition
Resolution (1947)

24

obtaining the League of Nations mandate for Palestine, the Jewish Agency was given a relatively free hand in Palestinian affairs.

The Arabs also remember their own "Balfour Declaration." In 1916 the British promised them independence as a nation, if they would side with them rather than with the Turks in the Great War. The Turks were aligned with the so-called Central Powers (Austria-Hungary, Germany, and Bulgaria) against Great Britain and other Allied Powers (Belgium, France, Russia, Serbia, Italy, Rumania, and after 1917 the United States). For a while the Arabs weren't sure which alignment might offer them their best hope for the future. In the end most of them sided with the British, only to discover that total independence for the Arabs was not really on the British mind.

Some of them remember 1897 and the first World Zionist Congress, after which the Jews and leading world powers began to negotiate the possession of a land without asking the people who lived there. The slogan was "A people without land to a land without people," but the Palestinians knew that at least half of that statement was false. They were inhabiting the land that others said was empty.

Their historians remember 1517 and the conquest of Arab lands, including Palestine, by the Turks, and the long struggle of the subordinated people to regain the glory and the unity which they had when they overcame the Christian crusaders and destroyed the Kingdom of Jerusalem. They remember Muhammed and his two main achievements: first, the creation, through the religion of Islam, of a synthesis of Judaism, Christianity, and later "prophecies"; and second, through a "holy war," the unification of the many Semitic tribes.

They remember Jesus and they remember Abraham, whom many Palestinian Arabs call their father, some emphasizing the physical ancestry through Ishmael, some the spiritual ancestry through the prophets and Jesus. They remember the City of the Jebusites and that memory lays claim to the first stones that are the foundation of ancient Jerusalem. Their memories, like those of all peoples, are not always completely and exactly matched to the historical unfolding, but the long unfolding itself has not been forgotten. Those who seek peace in the Middle East do well to share a forgotten people's memories, memories that again and again reach back to the times of beginnings.

Most vivid, of course, is the twentieth-century background to the present conflict, which began with the end of the Turkish era and the coming of the British and the British Mandate government. Two Palestinians who were born in the nineteenth century remember those years. They are Aref Al-Aref, deceased since he told us his story in 1971, and Issat G. Tannous.

Aref Al-Aref, the renowned Palestinian historian, fought with the

Turks on the Russian front. He did so mostly against his will, but also because it was said that Palestinian independence lay in that direction. He became a Russian prisoner of war. Upon his release his Palestinian nationalism got him in trouble with the British, who sentenced him to death. He escaped, but his nationalism again got him into trouble, first with the Jordanian king and still later with the Israeli rulers. From 1967 he lived in the West Bank town of Ramallah under Israeli occupation. This is his story:

AREF AL-AREF: "I am a Jerusalemite. I was born in Jerusalem. I finished my elementary study in Jerusalem. Then I had to go to Constantinople for my higher study. I finished the University of Constantinople in political economy. That was in 1914 when the First World War was declared. I was sent to the Caucasus front where I had to fight with the Turkish army against the Russians. I lived in the Caucasus for about eight months. Then, in a big battle that took place between the Turks and the Russians I was taken prisoner of war. All our battalion was smashed. From the whole battalion eleven persons remained alive. Fortunately I was one of the eleven.

"The Russians took me prisoner of war. I was sent to Siberia where I saw Omsk, Tomsk, and other cities. I was kept in a detention camp as prisoner of war for three years. During these three years I met the Germans, and from them I learned some German. I also learned some Russian. I published a paper, a comic paper to entertain my fellow prisoners. Then I heard about the Arab revolution in Arabia against the Turks. Being an Arab nationalist, I sought release from prison in Siberia in order to join the Arab revolutionary army against the Turks. In the beginning of the war I had no choice. The Turks conscripted all graduates of the Turkish University in Constantinople, and I was one of them.

"I managed to escape from Vladivostok with the help of the British Consulate. I was sent in a British ship to Arabia. So we left Vladivostok, went to Japan, to China, to Colombo, and then came back to Arabia. On the way armistice was declared. That was on the eleventh of November, 1918, remember? Although there was no need for any more fighting, I had to come back to my birthplace, which is Jerusalem, and I was sadly disappointed to see the Union Jack, the English flag, in Palestine, because we had been promised independence if we would fight with the British against the Turks.

"When I returned to Jerusalem I was expecting to see it under Arab rule. Unfortunately I found the contrary to be true. I found the British occupation and, what is worse in my opinion, Zionism and the Balfour Declaration. I was disappointed. I was an Arab nationalist. I didn't want any foreign occupation. Being a young man with no money and no work, I thought: What am I to do to help my country? I decided to publish a newspaper. With the help of a friend, I published a local Arabic paper with the aim of fighting both the British occupation and the Jewish national home business.

"My paper was closed seven times. I was put seven times in prison by the British because of my strong criticism against the administration. And when the first clash took place between Arabs and Jews, the British considered me to be the spearhead of the trouble and they arrested me. Then they released me on bail. Then a military court was convened. I was sent from Cairo to Jerusalem. Having heard about the military court, I left Jerusalem and went to the Transjordan around the Dead Sea. Then I went to Damascus. I was elected to represent Jerusalemites in the Syrian Congress which declared Syria, including Palestine, to be one state.

"When I was in Damascus I was notified that the military court in Jerusalem had sentenced me to death. That death sentence was commuted by the high commissioner to ten years in prison. And they, the British, asked King Feisal of the Syrian government to extradite me. But he refused to do it, saying that I was not an ordinary criminal but a political criminal. So he refused to hand me over to the British authority in Jerusalem. I left Damascus and went to Transjordan, where I had to live for a couple of months with Bedouin tribes.

"The first high commissioner for Palestine came to Transjordan and declared a British mandate in the Transjordan area. All Bedouin sheikhs went to see him and asked him to pardon me, which he did. So I returned to Palestine. I was appointed governor to southern districts in Palestine, during which time I wrote many books. I have so far written eighteen books, mostly on history. Eight of my books were translated into English, French, and German. And two of them were translated into Hebrew. And now I am busy writing about what happened from the sixth of June, 1967 until today. I am keeping a day-by-day account of what happened. I hope to be able to publish this new book of mine very shortly.

"Now this is a short history of my life. I was mayor of Jerusalem from 1950 until 1955. I was first appointed as mayor, then I was elected by my people to be mayor, and at the end of the first election in 1955 I was re-elected. Then I was asked to be minister by King Hussein until I differed from him regarding the so-called Baghdad Pact. I was against that pact. The prime minister was for it. So we differed in opinion, and I was obliged to resign because I didn't agree with him. When I submitted my resignation, five other ministers followed my steps. We all signed the resignation and so the cabinet fell.

"From 1955 to 1966 I was on pension. In 1966 I was appointed by the Jordan government to be director-general of the Palestine archaeological museum in Jerusalem, in which position I remained until the Israelis occupied Jerusalem on June 7, 1967. From that time until now I am on pension, writing new books."

* * *

Isaat G. Tannous was trained as a medical doctor, but was later called to be a Palestinian diplomat. He is spending his old age in Beirut. We were among the fortunate few who could be admitted to the home of the frequently ill, but always visionary, Arab statesman. It might be noted that in the Palestinian Arab world, medical doctors frequently become leaders of a variety of causes, including, as in the case of Tannous, national and international politics. This is his story as it was told to us:

ISAAT G. TANNOUS: "I was born of Christian parents in Nablus in 1897. My parents knew how to read and write. They were Anglican. When I was about seven years old, I was sent to Jerusalem to study at St. George's school. After 1911 I taught there for three years. During that time I prepared myself to come to the American University of Beirut, then called the Syrian Protestant College. It was the only English-speaking college that you could go to.

"I studied medicine, graduating in 1918. I went back to Jerusalem where I stayed most of my life. There were very few doctors there as the British occupation started. I was very much interested in children. So in 1928 I went to London to specialize in paediatrics. During these two years in England I was struck with the way the British people were attached to the throne. We, of course, were under British occupation. Although it was a mandate, it was not really a mandate, because we had the Balfour Declaration and were not as stupid as other mandate territories. England was obliged under the Balfour Declaration to allow as many Jews as possible to immigrate to Palestine.

"So we could never have the same privileges that Syria or Lebanon had, for instance, because they didn't have anything of that sort. Whenever we wanted to become really independent, the Balfour Declaration came into the way. The British couldn't enforce the Balfour Declaration, except by force, against us Palestinians. As an Anglican I could have been quite sympathetic to the coming of the British. And we were very sympathetic. Before the British came to Palestine, the whole population, Muslim, Anglican, Catholic, everybody was happy that the Allies were coming.

"We thought the Allies would adopt democratic rules and help us to become independent. Therefore, when we saw that the British came to execute a policy against the Arabs, we had many riots and disturbances every two or three years. When I saw that British people were free and we were not free, I thought of giving all my time for my country. In 1929 there was a riot, the riot of the Wailing Wall, which is a Muslim sanctuary.* The Jews tried to make it into a synagogue. And, of course, the Muslims objected to that. So I joined them, and since that time I have devoted all my time to the Palestine question.

"The British interest in Palestine? The Jewish influence in England was very strong. Whenever the government wanted to be a little bit more on the Arab side, the Jews had so much power and so much influence that they could not do very much. In one year we had 80,000 Jews come to Palestine. So in 1936 we had a great strike. The whole Arab population went on strike. And they said we will not stop striking unless this immigration stops, even temporarily. And this strike went on for six months and the British government could do nothing.

"We were all part of this strike. It started on April 19, 1936. In June I was asked to go with a delegation to London to see the colonial secretary in order to stop the immigration, at least temporarily. Three of us went to London. We stayed five months and met the colonial secretary about fifteen or twenty times. We asked him just to stop immigration temporarily, and he wouldn't do it. It just happened that he was the liaison officer in 1918 between the Zionist commission and the British government. So he was really a Zionist through and through.

"However, we were able to make many speeches, and we also published a little pamphlet explaining our case. That had little effect. We had many friends in London at that time, including a committee of sixty members of Parliament. Mostly they were Conservatives. The Jews had wonderful means of propaganda and communication, which we did not have. So the committee of parliamentarians asked me to open an office in London. I accepted for the next four years, until 1939. When the war started I had to go back. During that time I worked a great deal for the 1939 British White Paper.

"You see, in 1937 when the strike was over, the British sent a royal commission under Lord Peel to Jerusalem. Of course, the Arabs boycotted it. We had had commissions before this: the Shore Commission and the Simpson Commission. Many commissions came and the result was always the same. We appeared before the commission, and the commission went, and they decided to divide Palestine into an Arab section and a Jewish section, an Arab state and a Jewish state. That to my mind, of course, was the most criminal of all solutions. At that time the Arabs were about 1,300,000, the Jews were only 600,000 and they assigned them half of our

* The Wailing Wall, now also called the Western Wall (of the Herodian temple), is a more sacred place for Jews than for Muslims, but the area above and below the wall, which Tannous probably has in mind, is the site of two of Islam's most holy mosques.

land, these newcomers. Before the First World War they were no more than 60,000 and they became 600,000.*

"So about 500,000 were newcomers, and we originally were in the land. They gave them the better part of the land, the more fertile part. And a little bit more than half, and they gave the original people of the country less than half the country and mostly unarable land. So, of course, the Arabs refused partition. The British government, however, adopted the partition plan as its policy as soon as the commission gave out its report. So during my time in London, I got in contact with the colonial secretary, and I tried to convince him that partition would not work. There would never be peace in Palestine as long as the partition was there.

"In the House of Lords we worked with Malcolm Macdonald, a young man, only twenty-nine years old. His father was the Liberal Prime Minister. But he was also a Zionist in his thought. I got in contact with him, and I had two years of talks with him. I showed him how partition of Palestine would destroy the country with unending fighting between the Arabs and the Jews. He was finally convinced, although he was really of Zionist inclinations. After so many talks he was very much on our side. Even in the House of Commons he often gave statements that showed that he really understood the Palestine problem from the Arab point of view. Then one day, he came and told me he was convinced that partition would not work. So a special committee was sent to find out whether partition was practical or not.

"This commission stayed about six weeks in Palestine. And then they came back and reported that partition was not practical at all. So on November 9, 1938, they gave up the partition. Now what was the next thing to be done? We came to an understanding, he and I, that we should call a conference and ask Palestinians to come to the conference. They would have a conference with the Jews all alone. I insisted that other Arab states should come along with the Palestinians. And so in December 1938, we had a great conference in London. We stayed three months and, of course, the British met with the Arabs first and then they met with the Jews. When the Jews saw that the policy of the government was the independence of Palestine, they had only one meeting. They never had any others, but the Arabs continued with their meetings until March.

"And then the White Paper came, and they stopped immigration, except for a quota of 75,000 for the next five years. They also stopped the land sales. It was really a great White Paper. It called for a Palestine with both Arabs and Jews, with two-thirds Arabs and one-third Jews, to be independent within ten years. The Arabs were very happy with this. Of course, the Jews fought against it. They made war against it.

* Tannous is speaking about the British partition plan of 1937. The population statistics, however, are those of a decade later.

"Unfortunately we had World War II in 1939, so the White Paper was put on the shelf. After the war, you know, the Jews started with Hagana and Stern guerilla forces, and England couldn't implement the White Paper. So they sent the Anglo-American commission. The commission allowed for more immigrants. Finally there was such a row in Palestine, disturbances both by Jews and Arabs, that England gave its mandate to the United Nations. The United Nations sent another, the UNSCOP Commission. And it also recommended partitioning Palestine. And since the United Nations approved partition of Palestine you know what the result is. There have been fights. There have been quarrels. There has been war until today.

"How was such a decision possible in the United Nations? You see, you are speaking of 1947. And that was only two years after the formation of the United Nations. During that time we didn't have many friends. There were only forty-seven nations in the United Nations. At that time America was the supreme power. Whatever America wanted in the United Nations at that time, they could have. And you know that Truman wanted to help the Jews, and that is how their wishes were approved.

"During the time of the Mandate, the Jewish Agency had a special relationship with the government. They were a government within a government. There was nothing equivalent within the Arab world. Nothing at all. The Arabs really felt that the Zionist Agency had no place there. The role of the Arab hierarchy? I was with them most of the time. The powers against us were very, very many. We made our mistakes, I quite agree. I don't think we did everything quite right. We tried our best. We are a people who wanted to learn, and we wanted a power like Great Britain to teach us, not to come and to subjugate us."

* * *

Few colonies or mandates of the British Empire turned as sour on that empire as did Palestine. In the end, the British found themselves hated by the Jews, who felt that immigration was restricted far too much, as well as by the Palestinian Arabs, who thought that the British policies were much too liberal toward the Jews. Other Palestinian voices reinforce this impression.

RHOUI EL-KHATIB, former mayor of Arab Jerusalem: "Who bears the blame for the whole state of affairs in Palestine? Number one, the Britishers, who gave the Balfour Declaration and who paved the way for the Israeli immigration. Number two, the League of Nations, who approved the Mandate, and the United Nations, who decided to partition Palestine and who continued to play the game until we reached the present catastrophe of dispersion."

ALBERT HADAWI, graduate student in Canada from Jerusalem: "Of course, the Israelis themselves base their existence on three cornerstones: the Bible, the British Balfour Declaration, and the UN. Now if you take every one of them separately, you will find out that there is absolutely no legal justification or no argument whatsoever that could justify the existence of that state. Take, for example, the Balfour Declaration. It was given at a time when the British desperately needed Jewish world support. There was only one way to get the U.S. to join the war: enlist the help of all Jews all over the world by promising them Palestine. And they in turn would help to railroad the U.S. into the First World War on the side of the Allies."

WADIE TLEEL, oil company representative: "The British during the Mandate contributed towards establishing the Jewish state."

NE'MEH SIMA'AN, Palestinian church leader relocated to Jordan: "The Palestinian problem was a human tragedy from the very beginning, because it was based on injustice through the Balfour Declaration."

HUSSAM AL-KHATEEB, PLO leader in Syria: "Palestinians will never forgive Mr. Balfour. No, Balfour I will never forget in my whole life. Since I was a kid, six, seven years old, I know that Balfour has given the declaration to the Palestinian Jews to have their national home in Palestine."

MUSA AYOUB, camp chauffeur from Beersheba: "I think the big mistake was made by the British government. They had no right to let Jewish immigrants come to the country, no right at all."

GHANEM DAJANI, radio producer from Jaffa: "We can't save the British from the blame that they did everything they could to create the state of Israel. They had promised to stop immigration, but at the same time they were keeping them coming in by the thousands. Be sure of one thing. We did not invite the British to come to make a Mandate out of Palestine. It was decided for us."

NAHIDA DAJANI, radio announcer in Lebanon: "The British were on the other side. It was a well-known fact for all people. The English people are good. We like them. We have many things from them. We go there every year. We live with them. We communicate well. But politics is something else."

WADIE GUMRI, chartered accountant from Jerusalem: "I like the British, but I don't think they were fair in their policy. Yes, they gave good government to Palestine those twenty-five years, except that we always felt that there was something special made in favour of the Jews. They allowed the Jewish Agency, which was a sort of a government within the government, and they put the regulations in such a way as to aid and help the building

up of a Jewish rule. What we thought was a Jewish home in Palestine for Jews came to mean giving all of Palestine to the Jews and that is how it was implemented. They knew what they were doing, but why they did it, ask another. I am told that the Jews promised a lot of help to the British during the First World War. Some kind of help, financial or otherwise, and I think they wanted their influence in America. There are a lot of things of which I am not quite sure. But I know the effect.

"Right from the start the British should not have given the Balfour Declaration. They had no right to offer something which was not their property. They offered Palestine, which is for the Palestinians, to the Jews of Central Europe. They could have stopped what they termed in their own reports illegal immigration. But I have a feeling that the Mandate was worked in such a way as to help the influx of the Jews into Palestine. We were brought up with Americans and with the British. We have a Western education, and we used to like them so much, but after our bad case, I really do not like them at all. I will never forgive them. And we are stupid to continue working with them."

SAID NASRALLA, a businessman from Haifa: "It was before May before the British Mandate finished. At that time I was still working with the British army and my post was in a camp which is in a Lydda railway station. I saw trains come and go all the time with troops, with soldiers from Haifa. I asked one officer why they were leaving Haifa. The trains were going to Suez where there were British camps. This officer told me they had orders to leave Haifa. All the soldiers had to leave Haifa.

"The British made a big mistake and cheated the people. They should have stayed till the Mandate finished. We were unhappy with the British. The British in the 1920s and the 1930s were with the Jews. In my opinion the British should not have evacuated before getting the matter settled with Palestine. The UN determined that Palestine should be divided into governments. Of course, the Arabs did not agree, but the British should not have left before things were settled."

ELIYA KHOURY, deported priest: "The problem was created firstly by England, then by the United Nations and the Americans, and lastly by the Jews."

* * *

Whenever the Palestinians think of their loss, they remember, in addition to the actions of the British, the rulings of the United Nations, the take-over by the Israelis, and their own sentimental attachments to the soil of their ancestors. It is widely believed in the West that the State of Israel was created or at least sanctioned by the United Nations. Most Palestinians do not accept that view. Even if they do, they say that the United Nations acted against its own charter. Most articulate on this matter is Fouad Atalla, a Palestinian who in 1971 was named World Lawyer of the Year by the World Peace Through World Law Conference. Others, including the former Jerusalem mayor-in-exile, share his view.

FOUD ATALLA: "The 1947 resolution, in my opinion, is against the charter. The United Nations cannot exercise jurisdiction in dividing one country into two or three parts. This is an internal matter. Moreover, it is against the principle of self-determination since the Arabs at the time were more than two-thirds of the population, and more than 90 per cent of the land of Palestine was Arab. There is no precedent in the world at all, where the minority should get the best part of the country and then separate and obtain the establishment of a government of their own against the will of the majority.

"I think the United Nations is becoming more conscious of the injustice that was inflicted in the Palestine Partition. But unfortunately, most of the resolutions are what you call 'advisory' and are not enforceable. They seem to be enforced only if the greater powers want it. And that is one thing we want to avoid in the future with our scheme of revising the United Nations charter and the whole constitution of the United Nations organization. I think they should enforce the resolution of the 22nd of November, 1967. Resolution 242. I think not to enforce it is a precedent that cannot be tolerated. Nearly four years have passed without its being enforced. And then the matter has been in the hands of the mediator now for about two years without any progress being made. What is the use of the United Nations if they are going to remain as helpless and as ineffective as they have been so far?"

RHOUI EL-KHATIB, former Jerusalem mayor: "Do I recognize the decision of the United Nations in 1947, referring to the partition of the land and the internationalizing of Jerusalem? No, no, no! The United Nations unlawfully made a decision over property which she did not own, without taking the opinion of the majority of the owners of the land. The United Nations has given a decision against the constitution of the United Nations itself. One of the principles of the United Nations is to give the citizens of every country their free right to determine their own life. I consider the action and the resolution of the United Nations to be against human rights and an illegal resolution. I do hope that the conscience of the United Nations may be awakened one day."

ALBERT HADAWI, psychologist from Jerusalem: "The United Nations? The General Assembly has the power to make recommendations, not the power to implement those recommendations. The General Assembly's recommendations are nothing more than recommendations. But the point is that the

United Nations General Assembly recommended partition, and the Jews in Palestine at that time took that recommendation as a legal tender and declared their independence. But what is also not known is that about six months after this recommendation, the Security Council regretted it out of hand, as it was unfair to the Palestinians."

* * *

The memories of past history live on perhaps because the consequences of that history are so real. Events and decisions of long ago, and also more recently both inside and outside the Middle East have left a bitter legacy for the Palestinians. At that point in history, when they were most ready for independence, their destiny was taken out of their hands and their land assigned to, and taken by, others. These losses, of course, duly intensified their desire to achieve self-determination and to win back their land.

Chapter 3

The Loss of a Homeland

"The land of Palestine seems to have a grip on its people that perhaps is unusual in history or geography. The West fully understands why after two thousand years the Jews should have this desire to go back to Palestine. Why isn't the same love for the land, the same grip of the land extended to the Palestinians, who have only been twenty years away, not two thousand? Most of them can still see it. Are the Palestinians less faithful to the land than the Jews?"

— Shakib A. Otaqui

In the search for peace in the Middle East, some people begin with the Suez Canal and its role as an "international" waterway, others with a new status for Jerusalem. Still others see peace primarily in the withdrawal by Israel in whole or in part from lands claimed by Egypt, Jordan, and Syria and occupied by Israel since 1967. The Palestinians begin with the loss of their own lands and their rights, lands which they held for hundreds of years and which were taken from them without their consent.

To them this is the central issue of the Middle East conflict. Their most articulate spokesman in this matter is Nabeel A. Shaath, a professor of public administration first in America and then in Lebanon and more recently an organizer for the Palestine Liberation Organization. We were fortunate to get an hour of his time between seminars and press interviews.

A young man in his early thirties, Shaath hails from the northern Galilee town of Safad to which he would like to return eventually as a school teacher. He impressed us as one who could some day be prime minister of, or foreign minister for, a new state of Palestine, should such a state come into being. We were not surprised that he was later chosen advance man for Yasir Arafat at the United Nations in the fall of 1974 and as the key interpreter of the Palestinian cause on the American television networks. He explained the fundamental issues as follows:

NABEEL A. SHAATH: "The issue now, as always, is the Palestinians exercising the right to self-determination in their own land. The Palestinians have been uprooted from Palestine. They have been forcibly thrown out of it. Those who have stayed have been treated as second-class citizens. They have become a subjugated, occupied, oppressed people in a state which is avowedly racist, colonialist, and also expansionist. When you have a state which combines these elements of colonialism, as well as ethnocentric racism with religious overtones, you have the worst kind of oppression.

"Therefore, the Palestinians are fighting a war of liberation. They are resisting their exile and occupation and are determined to continue in that struggle until Palestine is liberated. In lieu of an expansionist, racist, ethnocentric, closed state of Israel, they want to create a new land of Palestine, a democratic, non-sectarian, secular, open, multiple, plural state in which Jews, Christians, Muslims, Buddhists, atheists, those who belong and who believe in Palestine as an open non-exclusive society can share, work, cooperate, live together, and really create a modern state which is integrated in the Arab world of which it is a part.

"This is a long-term goal. In the process, the Palestinians find themselves not only oppressed by the Israelis, but also subjected increasingly to pressure and oppression from several Arab states around Israel which enjoy the "fruits" of American military aid, economic assistance, and political support. And this is what makes the Palestinian problem more severe and more difficult.

"Palestinians have been fighting a formidable enemy. The Israelis are no less powerful, comparatively, than England was in the nineteenth century. England in its nineteenth-century colonialism combined three things that Israel has: technology, economic resources (England got them from Indian gold and Israel gets them from American gold), and their ideology, their expansionist, colonialist ideology.

"When you have technology, ideology, and economic resources, your size is not important. The size of your population is not important. England was a very small territory. Yet she occupied almost all of the world at that time: America, Australia, the Indian sub-continent, Africa, the Arab world, etc. And Israel with that explosive trio – technology, economic resources and ideology – is similarly capable. She has already oppressed the Palestinians, taken their land, forced them out, occupied and kept the others under oppression, and is threatening to do the same to the Arab countries around her.

"If Arabs do not accept Arabs, how is the world to accept Arabs or how are Jews to accept Arabs? Nobody is asking anybody to accept us. We have a land. We have a home. We have a right. We are not asking for charity. We are asking for justice. We are not asking for somebody else's home. We have a home, well defined and in existence. And unlike any other people in the world that I know, we are not asking for our home by excluding those who occupied it. We are saying we want to share it, our home, with those people who have settled in it.

"Some of them came as invaders, but probably most came as exiles who thought that 'Palestine was a land without people' which should be given to 'a people without land.' This slogan, which the Zionists concocted, made a very deep impression in the mind of many Jews. They thought that their coming to Palestine was not doing injustice to anybody. Well, that stage is over. Every Israeli now knows that the Palestinians exist, and therefore our revolution must escalate until our right is achieved."

* * *

The forcefulness and precision with which Palestinians identify what to them is the fundamental issue is quite startling, especially for those who have heard the Middle East conflict defined in every other way except in terms of Palestinian losses and rights. Shaath spoke as an expert on public policy, but businessmen, engineers, and agricultural workers all offered the same understanding and communicated the same feeling.

WALLED BUKHARI, refugee at Allenby: "It's a Palestine problem. It's not an Arab problem. It's not a Middle East problem. It's not a Near East problem. It's not a world problem. It's a Palestine problem."

ALBERT HADAWI, a graduate student in psychology in Canada: "There is an erroneous conception in the minds of many in the West that the Israelis are giving concessions if they allow a few thousand refugees to come back to the occupied territories. Well, this is truth upside down. It's the Palestinians who are giving the biggest concession by allowing those alien Jews to come to our country, illegally and against our wishes. They took away our land, our homes, massacred our people, committed untold atrocities. The Arabs are always discriminated against. We are the bad guys. It's like a western movie. The Arabs are the guys with the black hats. The Jews are the guys with the white hats. It should be the other way around. We are the ones who are punched, kicked, down on our backs. We are bleeding, and if we try to get up and fend off the blows, we are called terrorists. But their action is called self-protection, self-survival."

FUAD SAHKNINI, a Baptist pastor in Nazareth: "It is a human case. It is a very simple case. It doesn't need an explanation at all. You bring a nation from outside, you want to put them in a land, uproot the people of that land, kick them out, and bring in immigrants in place of them. This is what is happening."

RAJA FARRAJ, a businessman from Jerusalem: "As far as the conflict between them and the Arab states, they represent it to the whole world as a conflict between three million Jews and a hundred million Arabs. It is between a country that is making the desert bloom and rich sheikhs who spend their money on luxuries. If they put it in this light they have the moral edge, but when they put it on the basis of a conflict between Israel and the Palestinians, that's another matter."

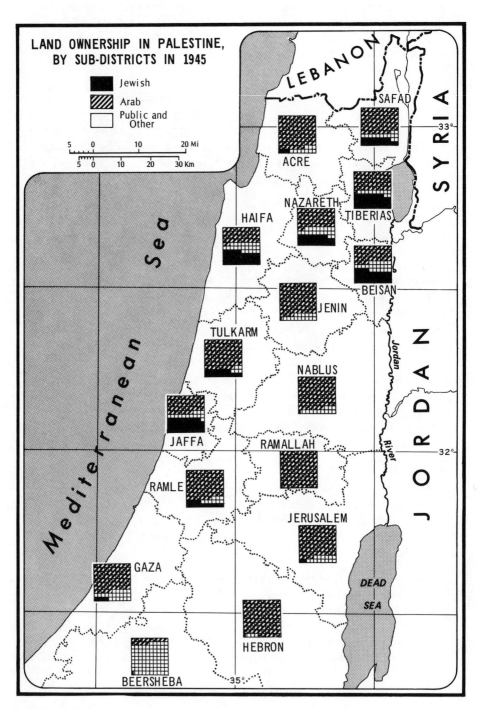

LAND OWNERSHIP IN PALESTINE,
BY SUB-DISTRICTS IN 1945

Jewish
Arab
Public and
Other

5 0   10   20 Mi
5 0   10   20   30 Km

LEBANON
SYRIA
JORDAN

SAFAD
ACRE
NAZARETH
HAIFA
TIBERIAS
BEISAN
JENIN
TULKARM
NABLUS
JAFFA
RAMALLAH
RAMLE
JERUSALEM
GAZA
HEBRON
BEERSHEBA

Mediterranean
Sea

Jordan
River

DEAD
SEA

33°
32°
35°

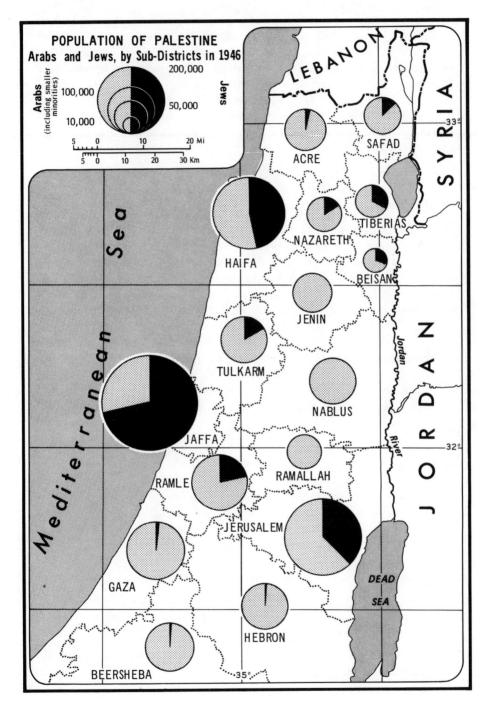

POPULATION OF PALESTINE
Arabs and Jews, by Sub-Districts in 1946

KHALED MOUAMMAR, who migrated to Canada from Nazareth and became a systems analyst with a computer company and president of the Canadian Arab Federation: "The peace talks are really evading the major issue, because if the Israelis are sincere about peace talks, they should first of all recognize the existence of the Palestinians. Yasir Arafat, the leader of the Palestinian Liberation Organization, which represents the Palestinian masses, has repeatedly asked Golda Meir to sit down with them and discuss the issues of the Palestine question. Israel has completely bypassed the Palestinians and has always tried to project the issue to the world as an issue of territorial boundaries between Israel and the Arab countries."

OMAR, a farmer from Jericho: "Our problem is very simple. A foreigner came and took our land, took our farms and our homes, and kicked us out. We have in mind to return."

EMILE TOUMA, an Arab editor in Haifa who attended university in Moscow: "To understand this problem as I see it, we have to remember that three forces met on this territory which is known as Palestine. First was the imperialist interest. In 1917 it was Britain, now it is the United States. The second thing is the Zionist movement. The Zionist movement is a new movement, a political movement of the last century. The third movement is the Arab National Liberation Movement. You have these three forces all the time very active. What makes the problem more complicated today than at any other time in history is that within the conflict of these three forces a new element has come in: the struggle between socialism and capitalism. Naturally I am giving you my concept of history and my concept of the world. These are the two main forces of our age."

* * *

There are several reasons for this deep attachment to the land. First, humanity has almost universally designated this land as holy or of high worth. Palestine has through millennia been a geographic, economic, cultural, and religious point of international focus. Secondly, and related to the former reason, the culture of the semitic peoples has since ancient times tied together land, people, ancestors, and deities. And finally, present-day Palestinian families have associations with the land in general, or with plots of ground in particular, that go back many centuries. Those from Jerusalem expressed themselves most intensely on this aspect of the land.

ELIAS BANDEK, mayor of Bethlehem: "How long has my family lived in Bethlehem? You can say so many centuries that I can be sure more than ten centuries."

NASR HASAM, a restaurant owner in Bethlehem: "Hundreds and hundreds of years. You can't trace back."

WADIE TLEEL, oil company representative in Jordan formerly from Jerusalem: "I think our family goes back four hundred years in Palestine. We have proof of this and there are records in the Greek Orthodox patriarchate in Jerusalem."

HAZIM MAHMOUD EL-KHALIDI of Jerusalem, formerly Jordanian tourism director: "All semitic people since time immemorial have been interested in their ancestry. It is known from Arab history and also from official records available for at least eight hundred years at the religious court, the Muslim religious court in Jerusalem."

SHAFIK FARAH, formerly from Galilea: "We were born in Palestine. Our parents are still there. Our brothers are still there. Our land and property is still there. We have been there ever since history, as far as we are concerned. That is our land, that is our country."

GAMAL EL-SOURANY, a diplomat of PLO in Egypt, formerly from Gaza: "The Arabs have lived in Palestine at least since five thousand years ago. Jerusalem, for instance, was built by the Jebusites, an Arab tribe. The Arabs were the first who erected this city. The Arabs were living in this part of the world at least five thousand years ago, before the Israelis and after the Israelis, before the Philistines and after the Philistines, before the Grecians and after the Grecians, before the Romans and after the Romans, before the Persians and after the Persians. The only time when Arab life stopped for the people of Jerusalem was during the Crusades. For eighty-seven years not a single Arab and not a single Jew lived in Jerusalem."

WADIE GUMRI, a chartered accountant from Jerusalem: "The Arabs have been there for hundreds and hundreds of years. The Russian Jew or Polish Jew has never seen or even smelled the Palestine air."

FAOUD SAID, businessman in Lebanon from Jaffa: "I am a Palestinian. I have been a Palestinian all my life. For the last five generations we have been Palestinians. We are very proud of being Palestinians. We love our country. It was most unfortunate for us to leave our country just overnight. I will never forget Jaffa and I am glad that my children feel the same way about it. So this country is very dear to our hearts. We will always think of it and always try to do our utmost to go back to our home. We have been there for the last five hundred years. I have documents stating my ancestry."

MARK OMAR, a student in Jerusalem: "I am proud to be a Palestinian from Jerusalem going back many centuries."

* * *

The expansion of Jewish landholdings in Palestine began with land purchases, often from absentee Arab landowners whose tenants were then evicted, and with the reclamation of swamp areas and other neglected lands. The big expansion, however, came through military conquest. In speaking about the take-over, the Palestinians refer sometimes to the total take-over, sometimes to different phases of the change in ownership. About one thing they are quite certain: that the land transfer happened for most illegally and, as far as they are concerned, involuntarily. Typical is the statement of Ahmed Ali, a medical doctor in Lebanon, who left Acre, just below the Lebanese border, as a sixteen-year-old. He knew that his family left behind well-developed lands.

AHMED ALI: "The Jews in Palestine did not get their land mainly by buying it. The statistics of the United Nations show that at the time the British left Palestine, the amount of land owned by the Jews in Palestine was a very, very small portion of land. It is often said that the other side really got their start by going into the swamps which no one wanted and into the desert which was barren. This is propaganda, of course. I can again talk about my immediate neighbourhood in Acre and of the areas that I knew as a child. Acre itself was not inhabited by Jews at all. It was purely Arab. But twenty miles north of Acre there was a purely Jewish settlement called Nahariya. This was on the seacoast, and the lands around Nahariya were very, very rich, but Arabs owned all of them. And most of the land my father owned was close to Nahariya. It had lovely orange groves. It was there before the Jews came. My grandfather had it, his grandfather had it, and so on."

GHANEM DAJANI, a radio producer in Lebanon from Jaffa: "The existence of the Jews in Palestine owes a lot to the British who gave them the Balfour Declaration. But after thirty years, when they felt that they were strong enough, they just kicked the British until they were leaping. I'm sure that the time is not very far when they will kick the Americans out from this area.

"The Israeli or the Jewish defence forces also killed many British military police. That is what they called their fight for independence. They went with the British as soon as the Mandate started. When they decided to have an independent state, they fought against the Britishers. The Jews used these defence forces beginning with their early settlements as a way of expanding them. They knew exactly what they were going to do. They knew that they had an unjust cause, and that they would have to force the Arabs off the land."

EMILE TOUMA, Arab editor in Haifa: "To those Zionist or Israeli leaders who tell us that they can't trust the Arabs, I tell them that the Arabs feel exactly the same. They can't trust the Jews, who said first of all that they wanted only a national home, they wouldn't throw the Arabs out, they wouldn't build a state. They built a state. They threw the Arabs out. Now they say they want a secure state."

BASAL EANAB, a refugee from Jaffa who became information director for UNRWA refugee camps in Jordan: "The only way to establish a Jewish state was to reduce the number of the Arabs. And they succeeded in that. Count Bernadotte was killed for the simple reason that he asked or he pressured the Israeli government to accept refugees back, and he included a strong recommendation in his report to the United Nations. The Jews wanted the Arabs to leave simply because they were afraid that they would not be able to establish their state."

NE'MEH SIMA'AN, a Catholic bishop in Jordan, formerly from Nazareth: "This national home after the Second World War became a national state. And now, through this Zionist political movement and expansion, it is becoming the national empire menacing the whole Middle East."

* * *

Some of the older people have vivid memories of the earliest flare-ups of the conflicts between Arabs and Jews. Wadie Gumri, Jerusalemite, recalls that in 1921 the Balfour Declaration was interpreted to the Palestinian Arabs with printed articles and public speeches. The meaning was clear, he says: "Little by little we got the feeling that it meant that the Jews were going to take our place." This awareness led to protests and demonstrations, in which even the children took part. Sami Khoury from Nablus, now a chest surgeon in exile in Jordan, remembers demonstrations which were characterized by the singing of Arab national songs: "I remember once I was given a licking in the police station because I went to such a demonstration." Said Nasralla, a businessman from Haifa, recalls that agitators drove wedges between Palestinian Muslims and Christians: "There was a difference in relationship between the Jews and the Christian Arabs on the one hand, and Muslim Arabs on the other hand. You see, the Jews were treating the Christians in a different way to make a separation between Christians and Muslims. They were showing kindness to Christians. So they excited the Muslims, you see?"

The reasons for, and the circumstances surrounding, the departure of the Palestinians from their homes and villages in 1948 and again in 1967 have been widely debated. There are basically two interpretations. The Israelis say the Palestinians left voluntarily, encouraged by the Arab leaders. The Palestinians, for the most part, feel that they were coerced, and not ungently. Fouad Yasin, originally from Shagara, later a radio announcer in Egypt, remembers that his village of about one thousand was emptied by a large force of Zionist soldiers. The departure from Acre, recalls Ahmed Ali, was due to shooting: "The people were really running away from terror more than anything else. A high-ranking British officer told us it would be better to leave. The weapons of the Jews were far more advanced. Every Jew was a fighter. They had artillery. They had everything. The government never allowed us to have a pistol. We could have been hanged. But it was totally different with the Jew."

Salwa Khuri Otaqui, one of the few Palestinian women medical workers, a Jerusalemite, remembers that people were enjoined to take the road down to Jericho: "Anyway, they were saying: 'People of Jerusalem, we have taken Jerusalem, the only way for you now is through Jericho and to Amman. The road to Amman is open. We advise you to go.' This we heard. My husband isn't here to testify, but my son and I heard it."

Tawfic Zananiri, a family patriarch, remembers the same thing: "We heard the loudspeakers here in Jerusalem. Leave, the fighting is coming. Go to Hussein."

Lily Tannous Gumri, a homemaker, knew that an exchange of populations was being forced: "We were outside of Haifa. The Jews were coming in to Palestine, and the Arabs were going out. The Arabs were being pushed into the sea."

Isolated instances of physical terrorism produced a psychological terrorism, which as much as actual violence and blood-letting contributed to the departures of the Palestinians. A one-time incident like Deir Yasin could produce many emotional Deir Yasins by either friend or foe only whispering the name of the fateful village.

Deir Yasin was a village of 400 to the west of Jerusalem, where on April 9, 1948, at least 250 men, women, and children were massacred in cold blood by Irgun, one of the Jewish guerilla groups. The massacre was confirmed and the bodies were counted by the head of the International Red Cross in Palestine. Menachim Begin, the leader of Irgun and later a minister in the Israeli cabinet, justified the massacre on the grounds that there would not have been a state of Israel without the victory at Deir Yasin.

In one instance, recalled Nadejda Georgieff, a seamstress, a "relative of ours had gone to get a doctor for his wife who was ill. The minute he left the house a shot was fired from a nearby Jewish house. The man was killed on the spot. Many people were frightened by that special accident, and this is why so many people left." Anita Damiani, a teacher from Nablus, remembered that an occasional sniper's bullet in a schoolyard and bombs planted or rumoured to have been planted were sufficient to set off panic.

Rape or the fear of rape was a big factor in the exodus. Hanan Toukan, secretary of a women's movement, estimated "that about 55 per cent of the people fled to save the honour of their women." Leila George Deeb, a refugee camp administrator, put it this way: "You know a professor of the American University of Beirut was here a couple of days ago, and we were talking about this in particular. He had found that 'women's honour' had a lot of bearing on the reason many people left Palestine in 1948. They were worried about the honour of their women, because the Zionists were known to use this as a weapon. He found that many of the families who left Palestine consisted mostly of young girls."

Others, like Faoud Said, remember the clashes between Hagana, a Jewish underground force, and Palestinian citizens, the rumours and the threats that Deir Yasin would repeat itself, the continuous shelling and bombing from Tel Aviv in some sectors of Jaffa, and the desire to get away, just for a little while, "to Lebanon until things were quiet again."

SAID NASRALLA, who subsequently became a businessman in Beirut, described the exodus from Lydda: "In about June or July, 1948, when Hagana conquered Lydda, they asked us to stay in our houses for the time, not to go out, not to move. The second day the soldiers searched every house. The third day they went around with loudspeakers telling everybody to gather near the church in the old city. I took my old mother and two sisters. They asked us to leave everything in the house as we might be in the church for only two days.

"We put a little clothing in a suitcase and walked. On the way, they told everybody to keep moving, a little further, and again a little further. Soon we were not in a church but out of town. Again they said, "Keep moving." They kept us moving in the valleys and over the mountains from Lydda to Ramallah. There was no water and nothing to eat. We had to keep walking for about three days. Children died from thirst. Old men and old women also died on the way. And then we arrived at Ramallah where the Jordanian government had trucks for people to go to Amman.

"I know that in Lydda at that time many, many people were begging the Hagana officers not to drive them out of their homes, but nobody listened. A friend of mine resisted and was killed in front of me. He had 400 Palestinian pounds in his pocket. On the way, I forgot to tell you, they also searched everybody, men and women, for money, for gold and anything. My friend refused. The soldiers took a revolver and shot him there."

FOUAD BAHNAN, leading Protestant churchman in the Middle East, recalls his Jerusalem experience: "What did the Hagana do? Well, to start with, it was six o'clock in the morning. All of a sudden we heard heavy shooting. Then a loudspeaker passed by, saying, 'We don't want to kill, but for your own sake please move out.' We were asked to pass through a line of armed people, young men who were carrying their rifles. We were driven out. I have never heard directly or indirectly of any Palestinian leader who has asked the Palestinians to leave. On the contrary, we were being urged daily by our leaders to stick it out and to remain where we were.

"My father was dead that morning, and I had to take care of his burial. That very afternoon our only sister was graduating in Ramallah. I carried my father when he was shot down. I took him over to the government hospital. I didn't tell my mother, but drove over to Ramallah, attended that afternoon the graduation of my sister, gave her a present, drove her from Ramallah to Nablus to our village, and then came back the following morning to pick up the rest of the family. As the eldest son, I took my mother and the three other brothers and drove them back from Jerusalem to the village next to Nablus, and then I broke the news to my mother that father had been killed. The shock of the situation and the impact of it broke me to pieces that day, you see, feeling torn between seeing my father dead, not breaking the news to a sister who was working so hard for so many years to graduate, and suddenly realizing that I was the responsible man in the family, a family already homeless. But we were very lucky. We still had the small piece of land and a house in the village next to Nablus where we could find shelter. Did we take anything with us? No, absolutely nothing. We were allowed to move out with the clothes that we had on. One of our next-door neighbours, an elderly man of about sixty, I still remember him, had to move out of his house with his pyjamas on."

NAJIB, a commando from Gaza: "My father had a trade in Jerusalem and Haifa. My newly born sister and my mother went to Iraq first. He followed them, thinking like all other Palestinians, that in two to three weeks everything would be settled by the big powers and no harm would come to the Palestinians. So they left everything."

WADIE GUMRI, a chartered accountant from Jerusalem: "All my assets we left, except my suitcase with two suits and two dresses for my mother, which we carried on our back."

* * *

Most of the departing Palestinians left behind them all their property. What was movable stayed put nonetheless, and what was immovable was not sold or rented. This fact alone says something about the nature and the speed of the departure. It also documents the intention to return and the rightful claim of the Palestinians all these years to return to that which was theirs. Their own words tell the story best:

ALI MOHAMMED, a cook from Beit Eksa: "I had a big family: four boys, four girls, one mother, one father. I leave everything, house, luggage, everything. No work for two months. I come to Amman. No job. No clothes. Whose fault? I don't know. I am little man. Big man make decision."

OTHMAN MAROUF, a camp resident from Acre: "No, we were not landowners. We left our furniture, but we didn't own our house or anything."

SAMIR, a military camp leader from Bel El-Shik: "We left our houses. We had two, one in the village and one in the mountain. We didn't take anything with us. We just escaped by ourselves, nothing more."

MARY NASRALLA, a language teacher from Nazareth: "In March, 1948, when the trouble was dangerous, my father agreed to leave Haifa. So we came by car to the South of Lebanon just for one week without anything, without even our clothes."

LILY TANNOUS GUMRI, from the famous Tannous family: "They said we were going back to Jerusalem, because we left all our furniture, everything. All our belongings. We had nothing except our clothes. If you go to Jerusalem you can see the Tannous Brothers Building in stone. We had property in Haifa, between Tel Aviv and Jaffa. In Jerusalem we owned land, lots of land, properties, also apple groves. Was he ever offered compensation? You answer me that? Did the Jews pay? They take everything for nothing, always."

ABDUL-RAHMAN RA'II, a muktar from Hebron in refugee camp: "The catastrophe of Palestine has not happened to any other nation in the world."

GEFFHAH NIGA, needlework lady from Jericho: "When we came to Amman we had nothing."

ABDUL-SALAM QAMHAWI, medical doctor from Jaffa: "The first misery I remember was in 1948. We had all our relatives coming from Jaffa and from Ramleh in very bad shape, coming only with their clothes and whatever. And that year I went to university. I come from a very well-to-do family, and I remember that year my father had to sell his car to support me because we lost really everything of value in the Palestine which was occupied. We had two groves, and we had some houses in Jaffa."

SALWA KHURI OTAQUI: "My husband lost his business in Jerusalem and, having no capital, for several years he couldn't find work. This is true of many Palestinian men, a terrible situation from 1948 until at least 1952. I was the earner and this is not easy. I think it's not easy anywhere in the world, but especially for an Arab because an Arab likes to keep his family."

49

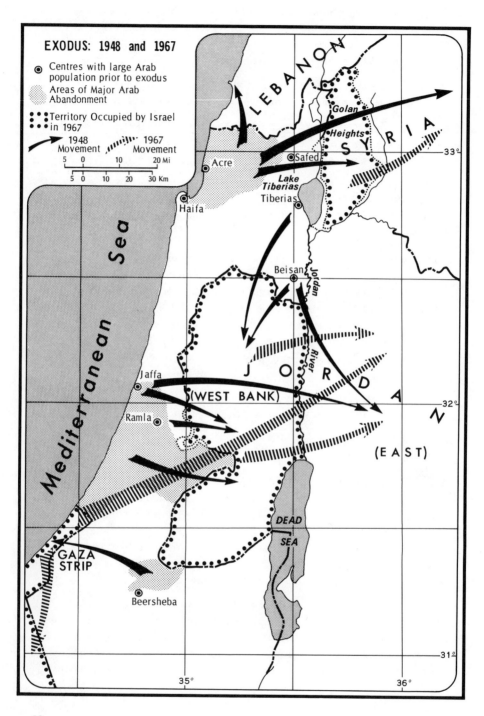

EXODUS: 1948 and 1967

⊙ Centres with large Arab
population prior to exodus
Areas of Major Arab
Abandonment
Territory Occupied by Israel
in 1967
1948   1967
Movement   Movement

5 0   10   20 Mi
5 0   10   20   30 Km

LEBANON

Golan

Heights

SYRIA

Acre

⊙ Safed

Lake
Tiberias

Haifa

Tiberias ⊙

Mediterranean Sea

Beisan

Jordan

JORDAN

Jaffa

River

(WEST BANK)

Ramla ⊙

(EAST)

DEAD

SEA

GAZA
STRIP

⊙ Beersheba

33°

32°

31°

35°   36°

AHMED ALI: "My uncle, my maternal uncle was one of the wealthiest men in northern Palestine. He left with everybody else, and he lost the land completely. As a matter of fact, his house in Acre was destroyed."

* * *

In most communities the debate about the merits of leaving were short, because most people expected to be back shortly. In retrospect many believe they left too soon. In the words of Nahida Dajani, a former Jerusalemite who became a Lebanese radio announcer: "If we could do it all over again, we would not leave. Definitely not. Definitely we would all stay." Anita Damiani, a college teacher, put it this way: "If people had realized at that time that they weren't coming back, they wouldn't have left. You see it was the first time anything like that had happened. My mother left everything. She left her clothes. She left her things to sew, the pictures, the paintings, photographs, everything like that. These are things people wouldn't leave behind if they didn't intend to return. And they thought it would be just a matter of time when the Arab government would conquer these few terrorist gangs. So we thought."

Not everybody left; some stayed because they couldn't get away; others stayed because their communities remained relatively untouched. At Ain Karem, for instance, recalls Sami El-Karami, now a statistician in Canada, "there were about 100 older women who couldn't leave or were sick." In Jerusalem one woman, with a baby of six months, left only because "there was nobody in the streets except cats." And why didn't the people of Nazareth leave at all? According to Mousour Kardosh, a businessman and political activist, repeatedly jailed by the Israelis: "For more than one reason. For one, the occupation of Nazareth happened to be at a later stage, and the people had already learned some lessons. Besides, Nazareth was always considered to be a pro-Catholic town and any conqueror would have to think twice before causing a mass expulsion which would involve the wrath of Rome."

Not all accounts of the Palestinians agree. The experiences were often highly subjective and traumatic (or the memories faulty), and occasionally witnesses described similar events but different times or places, which led to implied contradictions. Examples could be the following accounts from Haifa, Nazareth, and Tiberias:

MARY NASRALLA, a teacher: "Excuse me, in Haifa no one kicked us out, no one. We were afraid, but no one kicked us out. Because of the children we just left. They were young, it was better to leave for one week."

GEORGE J. KANEZEH, a businessman: "The Jewish mayor of Haifa had loudspeakers asking the Arabs not to leave, but that was about one week after Haifa was nearly empty."

HANNA ABOUMAR, professor: "What would make people who had homes and an established life and jobs, jump into the nearest boat and go to Beirut with nothing? There was some kind of terrorism there in Haifa. In Jaffa it was very much the same."

EMILE TOUMA, one of those who managed to stay: "The Arabs of Haifa had to go, because they couldn't do anything. The military Arab organizations were extremely weak and incompetent, and therefore the exodus started."

YOUSIF ABULLULA, a camp administrator from Tiberias: "All the town had fallen into the hands of the Jews, and the people there were obliged to leave."

* * *

As with all human beings the memories of crisis events in childhood became a bitter motivating force in the lives of the Palestinians. The last days in their homes, the sudden departure from them, and the flight to safety left indelible mnemonic markings in the young ones.

MUNZEV, an engineer from Jerusalem: "I was ten, but I remember every bitter step. Some parents left their dying children in the mountains and marched on."

GEFFHAH NIGA, from Jericho: "I was four, my brother three. They shot my father in our house."

CONSTANTINE DABBAGH, voluntary program administrator: "I was a child of nine in Haifa. We were in the lower part of the mountain. The Jews were in the high places. There was shooting in the street where we played."

FOUAD YASIN, a radio director from Shagara: "I remember the children screaming. I was about fourteen years old, but I noticed the tears in the eyes of our people. There was a bitter feeling in every heart. Some of the old men were willing to die fighting for our land. But they were without arms."

ANITA DAMIANI, teacher from Nablus: "Where you are born, you belong. I remember Jerusalem and its holy places, Tiberias where I learned to swim, Acre where I had friends, Birzait where I went to school, the sporting club where we learned to ride horses, and of course, Nablus, our home."

KHALED MOUAMMAR, of Nazareth and Haifa: "A train which passed our house was dynamited. The wounded were brought to our house."

NAHIDA DAJANI, radio announcer from Jerusalem: "We did not see our father at all for five years. My mother said he was in the mountains fighting against the Britishers and against the Jews. We were six children. My father was standing up for the liberation of Palestine, and he was killed on April 26, before the State of Israel was declared."

SHAKIB A. OTAQUI, graduate student from Jerusalem: "How can I remember? We have no family photographs or books pre-dating 1948. Everything was left."

FAOUD SAID, businessman from Jaffa: "I remember the day and the month. Jaffa was almost surrounded by the Israeli forces and my mother and father had to be somehow smuggled out. That was in July, 1948."

IBRAHIM AL-ABED, a research director from Saforia: "I remember the night when we left Palestine. We left our home in the village in May, 1948. I was less than six years old. The Israelis were bombarding the village. Some of the people in the village left. We stayed late in the evening. My eldest brother was a fighter in the defence unit of the village. He came to us late in the evening and he said, 'Why are you staying here? The village is occupied by Israelis. It's better for you if you leave.' So we left the house. We had nothing with us at all. We didn't take any blankets, food, nothing at all. We moved into the olive tree area. The Israelis were besieging the village from three sides and they left one side open for escape. We spent the whole time walking. Of course I couldn't walk, so my elder brother had to carry me. We had to sleep in the wilderness until finally we managed to reach Lebanon. And in Lebanon we also slept in the wilderness until they moved us into a village called Karoum."

* * *

The vivid memories of childhood, of adolescence, and of the adult years have been carried by the Palestinians with them into exile. In the story-telling of the refugee camps or wherever the homeless Palestinians have gathered to recall their past, these memories have been reinforced, and sometimes made more colourful. In later recollections, the experiences thus shared became the experiences of all. Not infrequently did it appear to us that the individual memories were really the biography of all the people and, vice versa, the common memory of all the people tended to become the biographies of individuals. In this transfer, accuracy of detail or lack of it, was superseded by the larger historical fact – a people's loss of their homeland.

Chapter 4

Refugee Camps and Faraway Countries

"We are now the gypsies of the twentieth century."

— Farah Al-Araj

At the time of its founding in 1948, the state of Israel proclaimed the law of return and the immigration of the exiles. The result was that Jewish people from all over the world, many with no ethnic relation to the holy land, came to make their home in historic Palestine, a land that they now called Israel. But Palestine as a name, a concept, and a homeland could not be easily erased from the minds of the Palestinians. For them, Palestine was not only a geographic term originating in ancient times, or a political term confirmed as such most recently under the British Mandate (1923-48), but a term that included all the emotion, identification, and attachment that is normally intended by "homeland." However, for the Palestinians now in other countries, there was no law of return. On the contrary, the Israeli law of return became for the Palestinians a law of *no* return. The Palestinians could not go back to their homeland.

There were some exceptions, to be sure, but they were comparatively few. After the 1967 War, a visitors' program was instituted, but it had the effect not of bringing people back to join their relatives permanently, but rather of getting some of the relatives to join their kinfolk in exile. Not that they too loved exile, but separation from their loved ones was an even worse alternative.

How the Palestinian exodus happened has been a matter of controversy from the beginning. Israel says the Palestinians left voluntarily, urged on by their leaders. The Palestinians say they left involuntarily, frightened by acts of terrorism, by threats to home, life, and property. Confusion, uncertainty, and mass psychology also contributed to the exodus. Whatever voluntarism there was, was conditioned by the assumption of an early return. Yet, those who left discovered that they could not come back, as they themselves explain.

HANNA KHAMIS, from Haifa: "In 1948 we were living in Jerusalem. We saw everybody leaving, and we went with them and settled in Salt. Then after two years we went back, but the Israelis had occupied our old home."

NADEJDA GEORGIEFF, from Jerusalem: "We left in 1948. All the family left. We left together. We thought it was for a while. In a short time we would go back. We came to Amman. At that time it was crowded with refugees. There was no place to spend the night. Some of our friends invited us. We were twenty-three persons in a room, but we could not go back."

LEILA BITAR, from Jaffa: "In 1948 we had to leave Jaffa. I was eleven years old then, and we had to go to Lebanon. My father was the mayor of Jaffa. At the time we left we had enough money for a year. We thought that we would be back in a month or two."

BASAL EANAB, from Jaffa: "When the Israeli government was accepted as a member in the United Nations it pledged that it would accept the refugees who were willing to live at peace in Israel. The Israeli government was accepted as a member in the United Nations, and yet it has not complied with its own pledge."

WADIE TLEEL, from Jerusalem: "I am a Palestinian. I was living in Jerusalem. I had to leave because of the Jewish problems there and the shooting. We had to leave at night, because our home was destroyed. I tried to go back to my home. It was occupied by the terrorists."

NIZAM NAZER, from Hebron: "I am a Palestinian from Hebron. I graduated from the medical school in Damascus in 1967. I was unable to go back to Hebron, so I settled in the east bank of Jordan and I worked with UNRWA."

ABDUL RAZZAH AL-ALAMI, from Jerusalem: "All of them wanted to return to their city, and they all asked me: 'Father, please can't we live with you. You are an old man, we want to be with you.' I said: 'What can I do? The government doesn't give me any permission for you to come back.' You know most of our family is divided now. I have two boys and two girls studying abroad, and I asked permission to bring them back to stay with me. I can't bring them back, as I asked. They did not give me permission. I'm an old man."

AHMED ALI, from Acre: "I left Palestine in 1946 when I came to the American University of Beirut. Because of what happened we never went back."

ABLA DAJANI, from Jaffa: "When I came from Jaffa in April 1948, my father was an architect. There was an Arab architects' conference in Cairo. We came with him. Unfortunately we couldn't return."

SHAFIK FARAH, from Shafa A'mr: "I left either March or April 1948. I was working with the Iraqi petroleum company as an accountant, and they transferred me to Lebanon. When I wanted to go back home it was already under Israeli occupation. My home is a town between Nazareth and Haifa, called Shafa A'mr. It had a population of eight thousand. A beautiful spot on a hill overlooking the sea. From some parts of it you can see the sea, olive groves and vineyards. I resigned my work with the International Petroleum Company to go into the ministry. I studied theology in Beirut. I was engaged to Leila in 1945. Since 1948 she was in Israel and I couldn't see her. I couldn't go back, and so we had to arrange for her to come out."

MARY NASRALLA, from Nazareth. "I was born in Nazareth, and we moved to Haifa in 1941. We lived in Haifa for seven years. We were a big family. My father, my mother, and seven children. We were living on a big street, which led to the Jews' street, and it was very dangerous. They were shelling. We couldn't leave the house. It was very, very dangerous. Our neighbours told us to leave for one week and then come back, for the sake of the children. So we left my father and my two elder brothers, and we came to the south of Lebanon. We couldn't go back."

GEORGE GIACAMAN, from Bethlehem: "No one is certain as to the future. Many West Bank people have relatives abroad, in the East Bank and outside, who can't come back."

* * *

A factor contributing to the immense physical and psychological suffering of the Palestinians was the uncertainty and insecurity of their destination. The flight from their homes was, for most of them, not a single migration. For many, the initial dispersion was the beginning of seemingly endless wanderings, in which some remarkable instances of courage and endurance were established.

GEFFHAH NIGA, from Jericho: "How did my mother raise seven children? My mother is very good. She is clever with needlework. She had two cows. When my father died she took them with her. And when we came to Jericho she made a special house for them, and also she bought some food for them, and she made milk. She sold it and she made some money."

SAMI EL-KARAMI, from Ain Karem: "We had to walk. I remember that very clearly. I had to walk from Ain Karem to Beit Jala, which is about ten or twelve miles across the height of mountains with my mom and dad and my little baby brother. We stopped in Beit Jala, then for a few days in Bethlehem, then to Jericho for a few months in the hot summer, and from Jericho southward for another few months where we stayed in a church. Then from Jericho we moved to Amman for another four to five months. From Amman we moved to Madaba, about thirty miles south of Amman, where we stayed most of the time."

WADIE GUMRI, from Jerusalem: "It is not once or twice that I carried my tents and moved from one place to another like Bedouins, but five times. Some people were taken by surprise by the attack on the 15th of May. They stayed in what became later the Israeli part of Jerusalem. They lived there for a number of years and ultimately they all left. Some stood it for one year, some stood it for two and some for three and four, but ultimately they walked out one by one."

SAMI SAYEGH, from Hebron: "I am from a village beside Hebron. In 1948 the Jews took our land and our house and they pushed us out. We stayed about three months in the mountains. We lived in the caves."

MUHAMMAD ALAZEH, from Beit Jibrin: "I am from Beit Jibrin, a village near Hebron. I have been a refugee since 1948. I have moved three times."

BASIL SAHAR, in occupied Palestine: "So we went to the Old City for six months. And then we went to Jericho. I lived in Jericho, and I worked for one hundred cents a day. This is the way I started."

SULEIMAN ABU GHUNEINI, from Jericho: "I am thirty-seven years old. In 1958 I was in Jericho. I was arrested for political activity and from 1958 to 1959 I was unemployed. I went to Saudi Arabia as a teacher, and then eventually came back and did my B.A. at Damascus in 1967. I have four children. I lived in Baqa camp and am a welfare officer."

LEILA FARAH, from Nazareth: "Those five years were difficult, very hard years, for the Arab minority there. We were still under much control, you know, military rule. We couldn't correspond. He was in the Arab world, and I was in Israel. We remained in touch from 1948 to 1953 through missionaries. Maybe every year we had a message from each other. That's why we called our first daughter Waffa, which means sincerity, fidelity."

* * *

The determination not to allow their circumstances to overcome them as a people is reflected in several outstanding cases, including that of a businessman and a doctor.

WADIE GUMRI, from Jerusalem: "My father-in-law is a man that I admire. He acquired quite a bit of wealth and property. The value of the property he left in 1948 was at least one million sterling pounds at the 1948 valuation, £ 2,800,000 today. And if you see my uncle now, and see his cheerful smile and laugh, you think he has no worries in the world. That is why I admire him. He is just over eighty now. He started up again in Amman, and now his business is almost as good as it was in Palestine. He has new agencies, besides General Motors. He has pharmaceutical products, household equipment, frigidaires, washing machines, cookers, and other things like that."

SAMI SALIM KHOURY, from Nablus: "He worked all his professional life as a doctor in government service in Palestine during the British Mandate. In 1948 when the hospital was about to close down because the British were ordered to leave Nablus, this man took over the hospital. He was about sixty-five then. He had lost every penny he had made in his life. He was living on twenty dinars, twenty pounds pension from the British government. This is a man who lived a Christian life, and his contribution to Nablus is that the hospital never closed down. It is still open."

* * *

Since the refugees could not return to their homeland – Israel prevented their return – emergency care was provided for them in refugee camps by the Red Cross, the American Friends Service Committee, and later the United Nations. Some of these camps were located in areas immediately adjacent to the areas of evacuation. In Gaza, for instance, eight camps sprang up, and twenty others were established in the West Bank, that part of Palestine which Israel had not taken in 1949 and which was then annexed by Jordan. Additional camps sprang up: four in East Jordan, six in Syria, and fifteen in Lebanon.

Since the refugees could not or would not be resettled, the camps became permanent, administered by the United Nations Relief and Works Agency (UNRWA). The tents were slowly replaced by huts made of tin, mud, or concrete blocks. In the 1967 War, the populations of numerous West Bank camps became refugees a second time and were "re-established" in fresh camps mostly on the East Bank of Jordan. At that point there were a total of fifty-three "established" camps with refugees from 1948, and ten new "emergency" camps with refugees of 1967, with total populations as illustrated in Table 6.

We visited twelve camps in Lebanon, Jordan, Gaza, and the West Bank, and listened to the Palestinians talk about their plight. The concept of "culture shock" has sometimes been used to describe a person's first exposure to a strange country and culture. The term is particularly applicable to our introduction to the refugee camps. Whether located on rocky and barren hillsides, in valleys or on plateaus, near urban centres or away from them, all the camps impressed us by their extremely crowded conditions. Tin huts or mud-brick houses, usually of one or two rooms each, had been put up in the very places where the first tents had stood. Now they were separated by narrow, for the most part winding, walkways which also served as surface sewers. The older camps, established in 1949, usually showed some growth of trees and plants and often took on the appearance of a crowded city slum area, where the poorest of the poor lived. The latest emergency camps, established since 1967, reflected a little more organization in that the tin huts, like the tents before them, were set in neat rows

TABLE 6

DISTRIBUTION OF TOTAL REGISTERED REFUGEE POPULATION AND OF CAMP POPULATION*

(As of June 30, 1974)

	Total registered population	Number of camps		Number of persons officially registered in established camps	Number of persons actually living in camps	
		Established	Emergency		Established	Emergency
East Jordan	599, 571	4	6	67, 415	88, 147	122, 975
West Bank	288, 021	20	–	71, 649	73, 736	–
Gaza	326, 089	8	–	187, 573	195, 216	–
Lebanon	191, 698	15	–	91, 896	97, 111	–
Syria	178, 267	6	4	28, 250	33, 229	18, 123
Total	1, 583, 646	53	10	446, 783	487, 489	141, 098
					628, 537	

*Based on UNRWA Reports

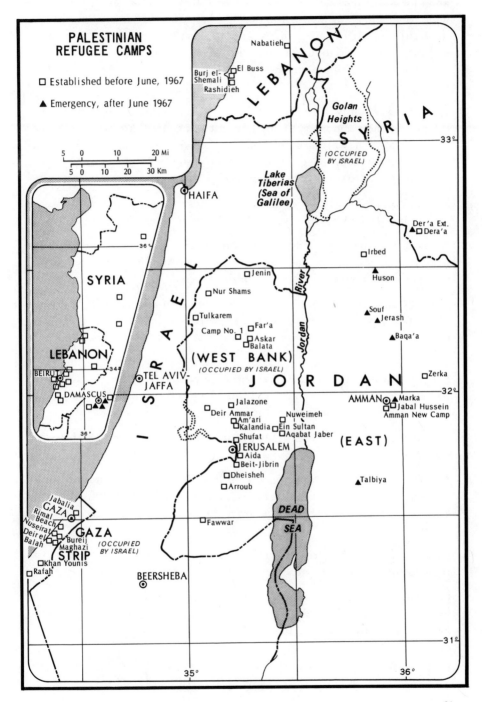

PALESTINIAN
REFUGEE CAMPS

☐ Established before June, 1967

▲ Emergency, after June 1967

Nabatieh

El Buss

Burj el-
Shemali
Rashidieh

LEBANON

Golan
Heights

SYRIA

33°

(OCCUPIED
BY ISRAEL)

5   0   10   20 Mi

5 0   10   20   30 Km

Lake
Tiberias
(Sea of
Galilee)

●HAIFA

36°

Der'a Ext.
☐▲Dera'a

☐Irbed

SYRIA

☐

☐Jenin

Jordan River

●Huson

☐Nur Shams

☐

☐Tulkarem

●Souf
▲Jerash

Camp No. 1 ☐Far'a

☐Askar
☐Balata

▲Baqa'a

LEBANON

34°

(WEST BANK)
(OCCUPIED BY ISRAEL)

JORDAN

BEIRUT●
●
●

●DAMASCUS ☐

●TEL AVIV-
JAFFA

I S R A E L

☐Zerka

32°

▲▲

36°

☐Jalazone

☐
Deir Ammar
☐Am'ari
☐Kalandia
☐Shufat

AMMAN●◉▲Marka
☐Jabal Hussein
Amman New Camp

Nuweimeh
☐Ein Sultan
☐Aqabat Jaber

(EAST)

◉JERUSALEM
☐Aida
☐Beit-Jibrin

☐Dheisheh

☐Arroub

▲Talbiya

Jaballa
GAZA☐
Rimal
Beach
Nuseirat
Deir el
Balah

◉

☐Fawwar

DEAD

SEA

☐Bureij
Maghazi

GAZA
(OCCUPIED
BY ISRAEL)

STRIP

☐Khan Younis

☐Rafah

BEERSHEBA
◉

31°

35°   36°

and blocks, the narrow passageways alternating with "streets" sufficiently wide for vehicles to pass through. All camps had schools, clinics, food distribution centres, small shops, and a central market where fruit and vegetables were sold to supplement the UNRWA rations.

How the Palestinians reacted to these camps is illustrated by the following comments.

INAM YASIN, from Nazareth: "Let me tell you why these people fight. It's because of their condition. They live in camps. They are not living like other people. They are tired of camps. I believe that if you would stay in camp for one week, you would be sick. You would feel that you had to fight your father, not to speak of fighting Israel."

SAMI SAYEGH: "Now I have only a small house, two metres by four metres. I cook in it, I sleep in it. I have guests in it. I read in it, everything in it."

SAMIR, a military camp leader: "As you can see, the small houses are not healthy. The poor light. The small sitting room. And the small kitchen. So much crowding with a family of six or seven people."

MARY NASRALLA: "Yes, we have been to the refugee camps lately. We were about thirty persons. We brought boxes with food, clothes, and games on Christmas. And really, we cried. We did not know that it was as bad as that."

SALAMA MAZEM, from Gaza: "We are nine people living in this hut. We have no electricity in the camp, so I think we sleep around nine hours, and get up around five o'clock in the morning."

FAIZEH SAKKIJHA, from Gaza: "My people live in tents. They lived there for twenty years."

MAHER THABET, from Ashkelon: "I am one of the people who left their lands over twenty years ago. We haven't seen our lands, and we live here in Gaza in very bad houses. I hope from the gods to live in peace and in liberty."

GEROUS ABOU RADANI, from Jaffa: "The school for this camp is in tents. All these twenty-three years it has been in tents."

GEFFHAH NIGA, from Jericho: "They give each family three gallons of water for the whole day. If we are seven people in the family, and we get three gallons, what are we going to do for washing, bath, dishes, and to drink, and to cook? It is very hard."

* * *

The psychological condition of refugees is as great a problem as their physical status:

AHMAD HAMZEH, from Jericho: "Am I hungry? No. Our greatest need? The real thing that we are in need of is to be settled, back in our own land."

SHAFIK FARAH: "I think what worries them most is that they don't feel secure. The emotional problem is much greater than the crowded conditions."

FOUAD YASIN, from Shagara: "Maybe I am living now in an apartment here, but I feel the camps in Egypt. I feel that I am in refuge, even if I am living in a palace. Psychologically, we are still refugees and in the camp."

LEILA BITAR, from Jaffa: "They think we want only food and water, but they do not know what we really feel."

IBRAHIM AL-ABED, from Saforia: "From the human point of view, our life in the camp was horrible. But this difficult life led to a counter-reaction. And this is why I was engaged in politics in my early childhood. I was head of the General Association of the Secondary Palestinian Students. And in the university I was the head of the General League of Palestine Students."

* * *

Despite the psychological depression and physical poverty, the camp residents do their best to maintain cleanliness, orderliness, and creativity. Health problems are kept to a minimum; venereal disease in most places is unknown; and friendly hospitality always greets the visitor. Making the best of a bad situation is a matter of human pride and everybody's responsibility.

SULEIMAN ABU GHUNEINI: "That man's suit is immaculate. His shirt is perfectly white. His shoes polished. His face is clean. It's amazing how some of them survive and thrive in impossible conditions."

SAMIR: "We are friends with all the people here. My work here in this camp is just to be director or a policeman, just to keep the safety of the people. We are keeping the protection in this camp, you know. There are no quarrels, no incidents."

MUHAMMAD ALAZEH: "There are a few policemen in charge in the camps, and sometimes a case may turn up when a policeman is needed, but on the whole everything goes smoothly. We still have our Arab traditions, and there is the tribal way of the people divided into families. Every family respects the other family, and that is why nothing of that sort turns up."

SAMI SAYEGH: "Hospitality is our custom. Guests maybe like food, maybe they like water, maybe they like coffee or tea."

HODA ABO RADANI, from Jaffa: "There is quite a bit of music in the camps. We have a little orchestra."

YOUNES ASA'S, from Jerusalem: "The chief medical problems in a camp like this? Really, overcrowding. We don't have infectious diseases here. I have been working twelve years in the camp. I haven't seen a single case of venereal disease. Not a single case."

* * *

Over the years a close relationship has developed between the Palestinians and UNRWA, the non-political organ of the United Nations General Assembly which provided relief for the refugees and a considerable range of technical services for their health, welfare, education, and training. The headquarters of UNRWA and its Commissioner-General are in Beirut. An Advisory Commission of nine UN member states aids the chief executive officer in administering and servicing the fifty-three camps, all of which are more or less self-contained communities. The closeness of UNRWA to the Palestinians produced a love-hate relationship. Some saw UNRWA as the salvation of the Palestinians; others say that without it the people would become more self-reliant.

GEROUS ABOU RADANI: "UNRWA helps us to get rations, and schooling for the children and medicine. We got clothing at one time, but not any more."

ELIAS ANDROUS DEEK, from Jaffa: "We could not easily get along without the United Nations agency. It is quite helpful. Education is free, and you know that in Lebanon here it is very costly to be educated. Also medical services."

SAID NASRALLA, from Haifa: "For one year we suffered very, very much. I was making very little money, but we were getting aid from the UNRWA, you know, flour, sugar, cheese, milk. After one year I had a better job. This aid stopped, because they stopped it for anybody who makes his living. And now I am manager of a department store."

BASAL EANAB: "What UNRWA offers the children, I mean the families, is not quite enough for the family, even if all the members of the family receive rations, because UNRWA gives only about ten kilograms of flour per person per month. That is not enough. Here in Jordan the people subsist on a minimum of fifteen kilograms of flour per person per month. So the UNRWA also gives some rice, some sugar, some oil and a barrel of salt for the camp population but not for people outside of the camps. So the quantities that

UNRWA gives to the people are not enough. A family who maybe ten years ago was getting for two persons about twenty kilograms of flour now has seven persons in their family and yet they still receive only twenty kilograms of flour. How do they live? Some of these people do earn some money and some of the children get education and start earning some money. Not all the families have an outside income."

NAZRI ZANANIRI: "UNRWA should stop. Let me give you the idea. If UNRWA should stop the ration for three months then everything would be cleared. People would then be busy with something else. That is my belief. Maybe you will find two hundred or four hundred who believe what I am saying. That ration, there is no need for it, because rations make us lazy."

INAM MUFTI, from Safad: "The UNRWA Women's Training Centre is one of the best projects UNRWA has ever established. Education and training benefit not only the individuals but, through the closeness of the Arab family, also the whole family and community. The people who work here are really dedicated."

ABU ALWALID, from El-Kabri: "There are five primary schools run by UNRWA and one preparatory school. Average class size is sixty to seventy. Some families deny themselves food in order to send children to other schools. Education is very important, and there are many first-class students. One fourteen-year-old, Radi Aljishi, was first in mathematics in Lebanon. He is now at the American University in Beirut. From this camp alone there are 150 doctors, some with PhDs, and eighty are medical doctors. Many teachers have been exported to other Arab countries. From 1960 on all the people in this camp are literate."

* * *

Hundreds of refugee children attended secondary schools and later entered university. A survey of the Palestinian university population was undertaken by the Institute of Palestine Studies in 1969-70. At that time it was assumed that a total of 50,000 Palestinians had graduated from universities. Of these about 10,000 or 20 per cent responded as is set out in Table 7. These statistics serve to illustrate a number of things: first that motivation, self-determination, and personal achievement had not been destroyed by the camps; second, that a multi-lingual leadership has been emerging as a result of training in other countries; and third, why the aggressive and enterprising Palestinians could be both liked and disliked in other Arab countries.

Finding a new homeland for the majority of the Palestinians was exceedingly difficult. The other Arab lands, each for its own reasons, are not

TABLE 7

SUMMARY OF PALESTINIAN UNIVERSITY GRADUATES

	B.A.	M.A.	Ph. D.	Post Doctorate
Humanities	2, 386	104	46	2
Social Sciences	2, 278	191	83	5
Education	95	43	5	—
Law	822	23	17	—
Engineering	1, 036	128	35	2
Agriculture	397	42	14	1
Medical Studies	246	25	651	91
Physical Sciences	737	116	90	4
Total	7, 997	672	941	105

willing to welcome them wholeheartedly. The situation is different in almost every Arab state, although most have in common the fact that they are newly independent. Lebanon has a very limited geography in which a delicate balance between Muslim and Christian Arabs has to be maintained. The East Bank of Jordan, like Saudi Arabia, is largely underdeveloped desert land, much of it inhabited by Bedouin tribes. Egypt has severe population problems of its own, without admitting new immigrants. The overriding factor, however, is the Palestinian insistence on returning to their own land. Again, Nabeel Shaath, the PLO spokesman, explains the situation.

NABEEL SHAATH: "I only wish to reiterate that it is very important that the world sees the Palestinian problem in its human context. We are people who have a yearning for an identity, a yearning for a home, which is a very important element of man's life. The feeling that I, my people, my mother and my father, have is one of uprootedness, of homelessness. It is a feeling many Jews must have felt. I am only saying that if you feel homeless, it behooves you to look for solutions not only for yourself but for other people. To make other people homeless in order to make a home for myself, this is something that I don't want to do. But this feeling is very important.

"I always have this nagging fear as most Palestinians have in Arab countries and otherwise. One day somebody will tell you that your visa has expired and you are out of a country. You have no rights, absolutely no rights. Your work permit expires, you can't work any more, not in the American University, not even as a grocer, not even as a day labourer, and out you go. In Cairo airport I saw four Palestinians who had been there for seventy-four days because they could not get visas to enter any country. They had just been in the airport. They had been thrown out of one Arab country, and no other Arab country would accept them. That in microcosm is just a symbol of the status of the Palestinians."

ABLA DAJANI, from Haifa: "Palestine was always open to everybody, but now it is closed. A Jew of any nationality, who comes from anywhere in the world, has all the rights of citizenship. But the Palestinians must have a permit from the Israelis to go home. We are living in the Arab countries. We work and we have homes but not our real home. We want everybody to know that we are Palestinians, and we want to be proud of our passport, our Palestinian passport. We don't want everybody to say that we are stateless, and that they don't recognize our passports. It is not that we want to find a better life, because here we find every hospitality. We have jobs, we have good salaries, we have nice rent, and good friends; but we can have all this still if we had our country."

ISMAIL SHAMOUT, from Lydda: "What do we ask? I live as you see in a very nice apartment. If I lived in Palestine I might not have a nice apartment like this. I do have nice children. I have a nice stereo. I have a car. I have everything. But this is nothing for me. There is something I need: I don't want to live in a place and to feel that I am a stranger. I have my land. I have my country. Why shouldn't I live there?"

SALWA KHURI OTAQUI, from Jerusalem: "I consider this a mental health problem in the broad sense. You know what happens to you when you feel that nobody cares and you're living on charity. It puts you in a special frame of mind."

AHMED ALI, from Acre: "Some of the Palestinians may be integrated into the Arab world, but I don't think it is fair to ask the Arab world to integrate all the Palestinians. And it is not right either. From any point of view, legal or humanitarian, where is the justification for a European Israeli to come and occupy my home and prevent me from going back if I want to?

"I married a foreigner. I married an American. We are Lebanese now. You see in 1961, we got our Lebanese citizenship. It is rather difficult for Palestinians to get citizenship. We were the last to get it. After we got it, after 1962, it has been impossible politically. I guess it is just the feeling of competition. More Palestinians are becoming Lebanese, and they are competing with the local population. This is one factor. Another factor, of course, is that the respective Arab governments do not want to dissolve the Palestinian entity by making every Palestinian Lebanese or Jordanian and so on."

LILY TANNOUS GUMRI, from Jerusalem: "About 300,000 to 350,000 refugees are staying here. This country is too small, they cannot afford to house them, to find jobs for them and to give them a good life. Lebanon can't afford this really. Lebanon is very small."

FOUAD OSMAN: "Lebanon was one of the best countries to these Palestinians, really. Lebanon treated these Palestinians the best."

BASAL EANAB: "I don't see how a country like Jordan can absorb half a million people who left their home in 1967. It's like asking the U.S.A. to absorb another 200 million or Canada another 20 million. But even then, it's much different, because Jordan is barren."

FOUAD BAHNAN, from Nusf-Jbeil: "I am speaking of the countries immediately surrounding the country of Palestine, where the bulk of the Palestinians are living. These countries have limited resources. But they have given the refugees all the facilities within their own resources. You don't expect a country like Lebanon with a population of a million and a half to take care of 400,000 people coming all of a sudden. That is a staggering problem for a country like Lebanon. The Lebanese or other Arab countries did not invite the Palestinians to come to their country, and that is why we cannot blame them for not wanting us. The Israelis have been inviting Jews to come, and this is a completely different picture. We came against the will of the Lebanese."

* * *

For them it was a very painful dispersion. They lost their self-determination after centuries of subjugation in Palestine, just when Arab independence was within sight and almost within reach. Their destiny had been decided without their participation or compliance by the United Nations, which by its charter claimed to be working for self-determination of subjugated peoples around the world. Palestinian feelings were further aggravated by their social tradition of family togetherness in the ancestral home. Finally, they were separated from the most desirable piece of real estate on earth, considered holy by three religions, fought over by many armies, and coveted by most of the big empires of history.

SHAKIB OTAQUI: "I wrote an article some time ago, which I called the 'New Diaspora.' There are Palestinians in West Africa, in Latin America, in North America. And they are becoming the new money class, in the same way as the Jews in mediaeval Europe. And they are looked on with the same suspicion – certainly in London. They are jealous because the Palestinians took the best jobs and are the best secretaries, the best bankers."

SAMI EL-KARAMI: "Most of my relatives are in South America, Honduras, Central America, California and Australia. As Palestinians we all remain united by our homeland. We are becoming the new 'Jews' of the diaspora, but we won't be gone two thousand years."

NAZRI ZANANIRI: "How many of my large family of seven hundred are still in Palestine? Well we have about four or five families, about forty or fifty persons. The rest? Some of them in Amman. Some of them are in Lebanon and Syria. Some in Iraq and Egypt also."

MUHAMMED ALAZEH: "Some are still in the West Bank. Others are in Kuwait, some in Iraq, in Amman, and in Irbid. They are scattered all over. This is what other nations wanted. To scatter them, the Palestinians, all over the world."

SAMI SALIM KHOURY: "Now think of this situation, how sad it is. A woman's sister-in-law is living in Ramallah. One daughter is married and living in Saudi Arabia. Another daughter is a doctor training in America. Another daughter is married in Ramallah. One son is a doctor training in the United States, and recently her last son went to America, too. So when you see her, she is really a very sad chapter in the whole tragedy."

ELIAS FREIJ, in Bethlehem: "The Christians have been leaving this area for almost 150 years, emigrating to South America, to Central America, to North America, to Australia, Russia, Europe, everywhere. I know there are at least a hundred young people from Bethlehem with PhDs now working in America. A few of them are now working on Apollo and other projects. One of my former secretaries here is now professor of mathematics in Bethlehem University, Bethlehem, Pennsylvania. They just want a better education and a better life. And they get it in America."

FARAH AL-ARAJ, in Beit Jala: "Many people have left over the years. Fifty thousand from this town (Beit Jala) are in Latin America: 25,000 in Chile, and 25,000 in Bolivia, Peru, Ecuador, Honduras, Nicaragua combined.*

* The mayor appears to be speaking figuratively, his intention being to emphasize that very many have left his town over the years for Latin America, and that they and their descendants number in the thousands.

Immigration started during the last reign of Turks. In Latin America, Americans are called Gringos, Palestinians are called Turkos. Parents and grandparents had Turkish certificates. Contact is still strong. The majority are prosperous and well-to-do. They send money back. I myself was in Honduras 1960-66. I went to work after loss of property on Jaffa Road: three buildings on Jaffa Road near Zion Square. I never saw my family during those six years. To earn for my children's education, I worked sixteen hours a day. My game was money-making."

* * *

The "diaspora" is turning the Palestinians into a multi-lingual people. They always knew many languages, because so many pilgrims and trades people, not to mention soldiers, came to them through the centuries from many parts of the world. But now multi-lingualism has become desirable and necessary on an even broader scale. The following conversations are typical:

With IBRAHIM SAMA'AN, from Haifa:
Q. "How many languages do you speak?"
A. "Three and some other quarters and halves."
Q. "Arabic?"
A. "Hebrew and English."
Q. "In that order?"
A. "Arabic, Hebrew and English."
Q. "And?"
A. "A few words of Yiddish maybe, a few words of German, a few words of Italian, but that doesn't really count."

HIKMAT, in Jerusalem: "I know Arabic, English, French, and have learned a little German, Spanish, and Italian. I was proud (God punished me for my pride, and then I started studying a little modern Greek), and then suddenly overnight we became illiterate. Everything is in Hebrew. They send us letters and forms we have to fill out in Hebrew. Everything is in Hebrew."

With SAMIR, of Bel El-Shik:
Q. "You speak Arabic and you speak English."
A. "And German."
Q. "Are any of the Arabs learning Hebrew?"
A. "Yes, many of them."
Q. "Palestinians?"
A. "Yes. Many, many of them have learned Hebrew."

NAZRI ZANANIRI, from Jerusalem: "The Palestinians are clever people and, as I said, I wish we had the chance to work with our own business. We are more clever than other people. We understand English, we understand French, we understand German, we understand all kinds of languages; if not me then my brother; if not my brother, my friend. If we are not clever people, we would not survive twenty-five years in camps."

* * *

A quarter-century of camp life has been a precarious middle ground for the Palestinians. On the one hand, they couldn't help but look back to their homeland, so near to them and yet so far, and educate their children about its significance. On the other hand, they were also forced to look to their future in countries far away, most of all because they learn to accept the fact that at least part of the struggle to return would take place on foreign soil.

Chapter 5

Living Under Occupation

*"An occupation is an occupation. You never get used to it. To be sure,
some walls have been torn down and Jerusalem is 'united' but the
human walls are much higher than ever."*

— *Basil Sahar*

Not all Palestinians are living outside their homeland. About one half, or
1,500,000, are within the borders of what they knew to be Palestine. They
are, however, under Israeli rule in various ways and to varying degrees.
Israeli occupation of the land the Palestinians consider theirs started with
the establishment of the state of Israel and with the war that accompanied
that event. The 1949 armistice agreements between Israel and the various
Arab states resulted in demarcation lines, which in most maps became the
boundaries for the new state. Enclosed within these boundaries was 77.4
per cent of the total land area of Palestine, compared to the 56.47 per cent
allotted to the Jewish state under the UN partition plan. The other 22.6 per
cent remained Arab and included Gaza, East Jerusalem, and the West
Bank.

Of the approximately 700,000 Palestinian Arabs living in the land area
which became Israel, most became refugees in 1949. Only 120,000 remained, and they became citizens of the new state. In their opinion, they
always remained second-class citizens, and Arab representation in the
Israeli Knesset (Parliament) was seen as tokenism. By 1975 these Arab
citizens in Israel had experienced a natural increase to over 350,000. Their
main concentrations are in such cities as Haifa, which became a predominantly Jewish city, and Nazareth, which remained predominantly Arab.
The Palestinian Arabs in Israel are citizens of Israel, but they find their
possibilities for the future constantly shrinking. Not only are they handicapped in their educational and vocational advancement, but they experience a constant Israeli coveting of their remaining lands.

A person may come to Israel from anywhere in the world, identify
himself as a Jew, and immediately upon landing have more rights than an
Arab whose ancestry in his own land goes back hundreds of years. All
Arabs in Israel feel keenly the dilemma of being loyal to a state whose
interests are felt to be against their people. However, at least one Arab
Israeli feels that his people can obtain respect and dignity if they insist on

it. Ibrahim Sama'an, a Baptist layman and journalist, formerly of Nazareth and now of Haifa, explained this possibility when we visited his home.

IBRAHIM SAMA'AN: "We are sometimes called dirty Arabs or Arab donkeys. This is the mentality concerning the minorities. I don't think that an Arab should feel so depressed that he agrees to be called a second-class citizen. To a certain extent I blame the Arabs themselves, because if a man insists that he is a man of dignity, other people will have to respect him.

"I give you an example. One time I was in a bus and there was an Arab with a full Arab dress. The police came right to him at the check post and asked for his papers. The man gave them, and the policeman did not try to see any others. The policeman wanted to get off the bus. I held out my arm to stop the policeman. I said: 'Would you like to see my identity card too?' He said: 'I did not ask you for it.' I said: 'But I want you to see it, because I'm Arab too and I'm not ashamed to admit it. Secondly, I don't want this man to become angry because you gave him a bad feeling. Only because he's wearing the Arab dress you are checking him. And this is humiliating, and I don't like it, and I want him to continue to be a full Israeli like yourself and myself. So please check my card, and if you will see two or three others, that would be excellent. Please check a Jew or two, just to show him that he has not been singled out.' The policeman was able to understand it, and he did it.

"If you accept to be humiliated, I don't think you will have difficulty in having people humiliate you. But if you insist that you want to live with your own dignity, I think people will come to the point of understanding you and respecting you."

* * *

Dignity, however, is hard to come by where there is a basic inequality felt and experienced in many different ways – politics, business, job opportunities, language – as is indicated by the following testimonials from widely different individuals: a businessman, bishop, author, medical doctor, teacher, lawyer, pastor.

MONSOUR KARDOSH, a businessman and political activist: "As long as Zionism is connected with expansion, the treatment of the Arabs cannot be equal. As long as this is the general aspiration of Zionism and of the majority of the people of Israel, there is no way of equality between Jews and Arabs. Every day we realize that the long-declared ideas of Zionism are being implemented in one way or another. They occupied Nazareth. Then afterward they occupied upper Galilee. This was considered the first occupation. In 1967 there was another occupation, and in 1975 maybe there will be a third occupation.

"We wanted to form a list to take part in an election campaign. The election committee refused our application. We applied to the high courts. The high court ruled that our intentions were to make unauthorized activities afterwards if we take part in the parliamentary life of the state of Israel.

"The *New Outlook* magazine recently made much of the fact that an Arab had been appointed deputy minister of health. He is a friend of mine, but I told you that his party is not with the Zionist movement. He is taken in the coalition. What is written in the *New Outlook* is meant for foreign consumption. What can a deputy minister do? He has no power."

NE'MEH SIMA'AN, a church bishop: "You find discrimination in identity cards. All Jews have a card, a type A card. Why does the Arab living in Israel twenty-two years still have identity card type B? And discrimination in business! An Arab businessman cannot import from outside directly: he has to buy whatever he needs from a Jewish big store. There is discrimination among employees, and especially discrimination in science.

"An Israeli Arab asked a policeman how long he would be considered a second-category citizen here. And the police officer told him, you are not a second-category citizen. You are a fifth-category citizen. The first-category citizens are Jews coming from East Europe. Second-category citizens are Jews coming from Western Europe and America, and third-category citizens are Jews born in Palestine. Fourth-category citizens are the Jews from Arab states and North Africa. And the fifth-category are you, the Arab in Israel."

ADLA AWAD, an author: "We lived seventeen years in Haifa. My world was very narrow in a closed Arab community. I wrote three or four books and in 1948 was one of the top Palestinian writers. I was approached by Israelis to write in papers, but thought better of it. We were a very crushed people. I'm a stranger in my country. I have a complex about going to Israel proper even though I have many relatives there. All the intellectuals were put under the Communist wing. I couldn't accept everything, but they defended the Arab cause in Israel proper.

"Is life easier in Israel? If easiness is food, maybe . . . but again there has been much confiscation of property and there are all kinds of permits. Occupation of the West Bank was mild compared to occupation of Arabs in Israel. They experienced change of social status from agriculture to a working class. Israel needed the hard labour. It needed second-class citizens."

ABBRA JABBOUD, a medical doctor: "In elections you have to vote. If you don't they make a red mark. They stamp the identity card. If the mark isn't there it means that you aren't a very good citizen. So I go to get my card stamped, but I don't really vote."

* * *

The Arab problem of conflicting loyalties in a Jewish state is experienced differently by different people. Some are so committed to an egalitarian society in which Jewish and Arab identities are secondary to human community and solidarity that they could easily feel good about the state of Israel if it submerged Jewishness. This tends to be the view of communist Arabs in Israel. Others think highly of the state and of the need to be obedient to it. This view, however, militates against the equally strong identification with the Arab peoples. This tends to be the view of the Christian Arab in Israel.

Fuad Sahknini, a pastor: "We as Arabs have a divided loyalty. As I expressed it one time, I think I am 100 per cent loyal to the state of Israel and I try to be a good citizen, but I cannot identify myself completely with the state of Israel. I think there is the identification and there is the loyalty. As a Christian I am bound to be a loyal citizen. But I cannot identify myself completely with the state of Israel and with the Jews. I have a mixed feeling. I am an Arab who lives in Israel. I am a loyal citizen, but at the same time I cannot say amen to everything Israel does or to everything the Arab countries do to Israel. This is where I try to be neutral. I will give my moral support at least with my limited way to the right whenever the right is found."

"An Arab in Israel", a lawyer and teacher: "The Arabs in Israel should be law abiding. As an Arab in Israel I have my own inhibitions. I belong to various societies working for peace. I'm a pacifist, but I believe in self-defence. I am for confederation but against imperial interference. I am critical of great powers, but feel I should be grateful for some."

Ibrahim Sama'an: "I feel that I'm an integral part of the country, and I think that I should be loyal to the state of Israel, but still I feel that no power in the world whatsoever can cause me or force me to carry arms and kill my Arab brothers even if I wasn't a pacifist, which I am. And the only thing that I can do is to work for peace because my own people, my own nation, is fighting my own state. We Arabs in Israel have quite a dilemma when our own government is fighting against our own people. At the same time our compatriots don't consider us a part of them. Our own people see us as agents and traitors."

Ibrahim Salem, a student: "I am an Arab from the West side but not from Israel. I'm not Egyptian and not Jordanian. I'm a Palestinian."

* * *

In 1967, the portion of Palestinian land that remained after 1949 was occupied. The West Bank and East Jerusalem were taken from the Hashemite Kingdom of Jordan, which had annexed these areas in 1949; Gaza, which since that time had been under Egyptian administration, was, along with the whole of the Sinai, taken from Egypt. The Golan Heights were taken from Syria. East Jerusalem, with its 60,000 Arabs, was almost immediately annexed to the rest of Jerusalem and incorporated into the state of Israel, though its Arab inhabitants had a different status than other Arabs in Israel. The West Bank, with 600,000 inhabitants, and Gaza, with nearly 400,000, most of them 1948 refugees, were placed under military governors. Of the two occupied territories, Gaza experienced the greater authoritarianism, which Israel exercised to keep the seething refugee unrest and the resulting commando action under control. The pressures for the Palestinians to leave both areas were sometimes subtle, sometimes very direct. Deportation of leading Palestinian nationalists has continued to this day.

The Palestinians we talked to in the West Bank, in East Jerusalem, and north of Jerusalem had some positive things to say about the occupation, as an occupation. Leila Nasser, a needlework director, said that the people "did benefit from Israeli medicine," and other social policies were approved. But most had only negative things to say about everyday things, in all of which they experienced loss of freedom.

SIMON, a hotel employee: "There is in Ramallah no pressure to leave, and if there is, we will never leave. Many of our young men are in prison, some for resistance, some just for accusations. We all have resistance in the heart."

AYOUB, a retired school teacher: "Jerusalem was the nicest place on the earth. Everything holy has been desecrated. I don't think there is another race that can demoralize like this one. Our young men are all in prison. Everything is being done to make people sick and to leave. You feel the strain, the suppression. I was dismissed in 1967. I was too patriotic. It didn't matter much, because if I couldn't teach according to my heart's desire, I did not want to teach."

SINA MONSOUR, a teacher: "I started off with a Jordanian passport. I was an immigrant to the United States. I needed a visa to come back to visit my parents and work here. I needed a special permit to stay in my country. I had to fill out seven applications. They gave me a visa for a month and now it's being extended for a year, hopefully."

MUNZEV, an engineer: "I left teaching voluntarily in 1967. I can't teach that Palestine was always Jewish and that we are parasites. They wanted us to teach that our prophet was a liar, a distortion of all Middle East history."

BISHARA AWAD, a teacher: "There is no leadership in West Bank. No single leader. The best people have been deported. Palestinians in exile would definitely come back to build up the state. If there was a free choice, a minority would stay with Israel, say 10 per cent (merchants and people selling land to Jews); a minority would stay with Jordan, say 40 per cent (government employees, workers). The majority would want a Palestinian state. They are more educated now."

RHOUI EL-KHATIB, Jerusalem mayor-in-exile: "Tell me, did the French people accept the Nazis during World War II, even though the Nazis did not throw them out of their homes and did not confiscate their land and properties? Would the Belgians, the Dutch, the Norwegians, any Europeans invaded by the Germans in the Second World War, have accepted and lived with the invading Nazis? This is the same case. Why do you expect us actually to do less in looking after our own rights than other people?"

AMIN MAJIJ, a medical doctor: "Like all occupations, it's miserable. Nothing that you do you enjoy. For three months I locked myself into my bedroom. All of us feel the same. It might be the most enlightened occupation in history, but how can it be enlightened and occupation at the same time? This is the most comfortable prison you ever saw."

ISSA FARIS: "Demonstrations have been crushed ruthlessly. Strikes have been stopped with threats of shop closures. Even the ladies have been taken by force by the police. The schools are threatened. Anyone who protests is threatened. If you don't find people protesting, it is not because they don't want to protest, but because they fear harsh treatment. There is no tranquility in the West Bank. People are afraid."

FARAH AL-ARAJ, a mayor: "Occupation governments are something natural for us. We have never had our independence. After partition in 1948, Palestinians revolted and asked for help from Arab governments. Egypt, Iraq, Jordan sent forces to help Palestinians. There was fighting for nearly one year. Iraqis withdrew. Egypt withdrew and kept enclave of Gaza. Jordan stayed. At that time in those circumstances it was the only outlet for our people. We needed an outlet to the Arab world. The Jordanian army was protecting the borders. Israel would have taken more. The Jordanian army defended East Jerusalem most courageously."

BASIL SAHAR, a school principal: "Occupation is an occupation. You never get used to it. They pulled walls down, but the human walls are much

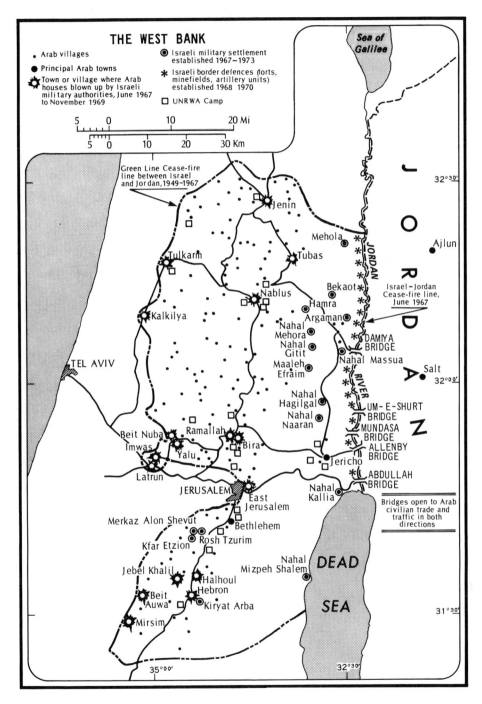

THE WEST BANK

- • Arab villages
- ● Principal Arab towns
- ✹ Town or village where Arab houses blown up by Israeli military authorities, June 1967 to November 1969
- ◉ Israeli military settlement established 1967–1973
- ✳ Israeli border defences (forts, minefields, artillery units) established 1968 1970
- ☐ UNRWA Camp

5   0   10   20 Mi

5   0   10   20   30 Km

Green Line Cease-fire line between Israel and Jordan, 1949–1967

Sea of Galilee

J O R D A N

32°30'

Jenin

Mehola ✳

Ajlun ●

Tulkarm ✹   Tubas ✹

Bekaot ✳

Israel–Jordan Cease-fire line, June 1967

Nablus

Hamra ◉

Kalkilya ✹   Argaman ◉

Nahal Mehora ◉   ✳ DAMYA BRIDGE

Nahal Gitit ◉

TEL AVIV   Maaleh Efraim ◉   Nahal Massua ◉

Salt ●

32°00'

Nahal Hagilgal ◉   UM- E- SHURT BRIDGE ✳

Nahal Naaran ◉   MUNDASA BRIDGE ✳

Beit Nuba   Ramallah ✹   ALLENBY BRIDGE

Imwas   Bira   Jericho ☐

Yalu   ✳ ABDULLAH BRIDGE

Latrun   Nahal Kallia ◉

JERUSALEM   East Jerusalem   Bridges open to Arab civilian trade and traffic in both directions

Merkaz Alon Shevut   Bethlehem

Kfar Etzion ◉◉   Rosh Tzurim ☐

Nahal Mizpeh Shalem ◉   DEAD

Jebel Khalil ✹   SEA

Halhoul ✹

Hebron

Beit Auwa ✹   Kiryat Arba ◉

31°30'

Mirsim ✹

35°00'   32°30'

79

higher. We cater to two different tastes altogether. Arabs are more reserved. We did not have prostitution in Old City. Now, according to Israeli Social Welfare Statistics three hundred Jewish prostitutes are working in Old Jerusalem every night. Many of them are under sixteen years of age. Earn about three hundred Israeli pounds every night. Why should they work in factory? Now they are asking not for money but for hashish. So the new generation of Arab young people are being corrupted."

HANNA NASIR, a college president: "The discriminations of occupation are many and they are subtle. The licences of Arabs in Israel are dated differently than those of the Jews. They are known not by licence of the car but by the date.

"Israel was very clever. It claimed democracy and freedom of speech, which never existed. The free speakers always suffered consequences. It's very hard to say anything. It's always the wrong thing. It's like giving a bird in a cage a lot of food. They cut our wings, dwarfed our personality, and tailored us to suit them. The standard of education even in camps is higher, because you are freer there. In Israel you have to fight for civil rights. In West Bank the fight is against occupation."

ASIZ SHEHADIH: "No one is allowed to form committees with political or national implications. PNF exists clandestinely. Two ways to solve the problem: 1) politically; 2) war. Those trying for political solution are going to fail. Israel will not withdraw from areas. Arabs will not accept settlement. America could pressure Israel to withdraw in near future. They have enough trouble worldwide politically. Unilateral annexation is void. Will of people could make it bilateral. They have a *de facto* situation economically. They are behaving as though they have annexed."

ARABI AWAD, a teacher: "Israeli officers would come to our school and check up on the books we used in the classroom and in the library. They didn't allow any of our national poetry or national democratic books. They don't allow student meetings. They don't encourage education. They want us only as labourers. That is why teachers are paid less than workers."

BASIL SAHAR, a principal: "We will not sacrifice Saladin for Herzl in our text books. For us it's a Palestine cause not an Israeli cause. They are changing maps. I used to get one quarter of my present salary but I was better off. School fees have gone up eight times."

* * *

Within the occupation, and especially in East Jerusalem (see also chapter 11) and the West Bank, the loss of land and homes is felt particularly acutely, because the people often witnessed the destruction of their homes, and the confiscation of their land. This method of collective punishment is widely employed in the Israeli occupation. The details vary, but the general pattern is usually the same. When certain occupants of the territories were arrested, the authorities decide arbitrarily that the house where the arrested person lived should be blown up (or otherwise made uninhabitable). All the persons living in that house are turned out of it, usually on short notice, without any provision for alternative housing. This punishment is inflicted on people who are completely innocent of any crime, even in the opinion of the authorities themselves, as shown by the fact that they are not charged. Many, in fact most, of those punished in this way are people who are incapable of the crime: children and even babies, the ill, the old, and the infirm. The punishment is often inflicted even when the person who is suspected by the authorities is already in custody. Since no justification for the destruction is given, the punishment is completely arbitrary. It is carried out on short notice in the most inclement weather, often causing intense physical suffering. The blown-up houses may have housed a great number of people. Cases are known in which twenty people were thrown into the street by the demolition of one house. The following statements reflect the Palestinians' experiences.

Foud Shehadi: "Between 1948 and 1967, 840 villages have been demolished and erased from the map."

Aref Al-Aref, historian and former Jerusalem mayor: "It is true, in the West Bank at the moment it is tranquil. But you can't say quiet and you can't say peaceful. Although the people in the West Bank are less troublesome than the Gaza people, this does not mean that the West Bankers are happy. We all hate occupation whether it is Israeli, British, French, or even Russian. How can we say that we in the West Bank are happy when we know that still more houses are being demolished? More people are being deported. More people are being arrested. Unfortunately the number of houses demolished by the Israelis is increasing from day to day. It was, in 1968, about five thousand houses; now it's increased to seven thousand.

"Beit Nuba, Yalu, and Geita, the three villages on the old Jordanian-Israeli border north-east of Jerusalem, were erased from the map immediately following the June War. These three Arab villages were occupied by the Israeli army on the sixth of June, 1967, without any resistance. It is not because they welcomed the occupation, but because they had no arms to fight or to resist. Our king did not fortify the front here, and he did not allow our people to get firearms. So the Israelis were able to occupy these three villages within half an hour without any resistance. Then they came to these three villages and demolished them. Had they demolished these villages during the fighting I would not have blamed the Israelis because war is war. I got the names of the owners of houses that were demolished, 1,464 houses – I got the names. You can copy them if you like; you can photostat them if you like and show them to the Israelis. Now the ten thousand people of these villages were kicked out from their places. About four-fifths of them went to Transjordan and one-fifth remained in the country. They said: 'Allow us to go back and we are prepared to live in tents.' They were not allowed to go. I shall not be surprised if somebody comes one day and tells me that about half of the ten thousand became terrorists."

MUNZEV, an engineer, who returned from Jordan for a visit: "My house had been demolished. Our family records go back seven hundred years. We lived in Old Jerusalem, in Mosque of Omar area. It overlooked the Wailing Wall. All our family (fifteen families – 105 persons) were born and lived there. A day after reaching Mosque of Omar in 1967, they locked the house and forbade us to use seven or eight rooms. Their behaviour was horrible. After a month they gave us two days' notice. They took all of us to houses in suburbs of Jerusalem. The house was not finished. The person who owned it was Arab. The house was labelled 'occupied by army.' They worked under our house to break foundations. I said I wouldn't leave. One Sunday at 9:00 A.M. they came, twenty soldiers, twenty porters. They hammered at the walls. Some packed. In two hours everything was packed. They took things outside of Jerusalem and said, 'Come and get them when you find a house.' Our great-grandparents were Muslim sheikhs who taught in the area and lived in the house. The Israelis offered compensation, but we refused on matter of principle. It was the family home for seven hundred years."

BASIL SAHAR: "Two old women. Bulldozers came. Saved their honour by signing land away."

ASIZ SHEHADIH: "Meanwhile they are applying the law of absenteeism. The Custodian of Abandoned Property, an Israeli government official, takes over state domains and lands of absentee people. Israel took over the Jordan valley. The advantage of annexation without announcing it means that facts are being created. They are masters in these tactics. My children are in Kuwait. If I die my property goes to the Custodian not to the children. The Custodian has power to sell."

ABBRA JABBOUD: "Arabs can have their rights in the courts, but not with respect to property. We have lived here for a hundred years. My brothers are in Amman. They left before 1948. So they were absent. The Custodian for Abandoned Property came. I had to pay 30,000 IL to buy back the house, which was ours for a hundred years. If the Israelis want the lands they make an excuse."

* * *

The loss of property and acreage has usually also meant the departure of the people from their homeland into exile. But not infrequently one meets individuals or groups of people who have stubbornly refused to leave. The people of the village of Surif, west of Hebron on the old Israeli-Jordanian border, who lost their best lands in 1948, are a good example of this stubbornness. Abu Wasef, the muktar of that village, briefly told us the story of his people.

ABU WASEF: "Our people have lived in Surif village not less than five hundred years. We have about five hundred families or four thousand people on about twenty thousand dunams of land. One dunam equals one thousand square metres. Twenty-eight thousand dunams was taken by Jews in 1948. They took the best agricultural land. If there was a price we wouldn't sell it to them. It was taken without compensation. After 1967 another hundred dunams were taken from the village. Main crops before 1948 were olive trees, also wheat and grains.

"Each family had its own land. Half the families had their land taken away from them. Most of the families had a part of good land. Nonetheless all our people determined to stay. After 1951, many worked in Jordan. Several times they have tried to occupy the village. The people have resisted with weapons. Ibrahim Abu Dayeh is one of the leaders who was killed in battle. Now a school is named after him. He was a young and clever fellow who loved his land.

"Would anyone just give in? We are occupied and can't do anything. We agree with those who fight for us. Palestine should have its own rulers. Someday there will be a Palestinian government. Our Palestinian people will keep on fighting. We have an enemy occupying us. If we have the chance to fight back we will fight back."

* * *

The loss of villages and houses produces bitterness. But bitterness also arises from the denial of the Palestinian Arab way of life and achievement, whether this be in agriculture or in other areas. The Palestinian Arabs have frequently been accused of being poor stewards of the land. Often overlooked are the huge citrus groves, which the Israelis took from them, and the magnificent olive orchards and vineyards established on steep and rocky hillsides throughout the land, all before the advent of modern agricultural technology. The Arab genius for making rocky hillsides bear abundant fruit is visible throughout the land. One of the most difficult experiences of the exile was that in addition to the loss of their land, the Palestinians were robbed of their culture and denied their heritage.

RAJA FARRAJ, a businessman in exile: "Qual Quilya lost all its fertile lands when they shifted the armistice line after 1948. They were left with a mountainous area, rocky, barren, unutilized. Well, they were expert farmers. They had their orange groves. They knew how to plant the trees. So they cleared the rocks from the mountains. They drilled wells, and they have one of the best orange groves in that district. They made up out of barren land a green and fertile valley. I think of the land that was developed in Gaza between 1948 and 1967 and the work that was created by the people and refugees in Gaza. If you take it and compare it to what happened in Israel, it is just as spectacular. Lands that were condemned as not fit for plantation by the British were planted. They were successful, and they had exports all over the world.

"The land of Palestine was not sorely neglected by the Arabs. Gaza used to export barley to Germany and it was one of the main sources of raw material for the beer industry in Germany. When the British came into the country, for some reason they forbade the export of barley. Many people suffered losses at that time and after that the whole thing was neglected. So the British Mandate, which was supposed to put the country in condition, discouraged Arabs from developing their own resources.

"Another thing is overlooked by many observers of Israel. Palestine was never known for its hill lands of Judea or for the activity of the Nablus area. It was known for its oranges. It was known for the rich coastal land taken over by Israel. This land was rich and very well exploited by the Arabs. Those weren't all malaria-infested swamps. Not at all, actually. The fact is that the orange groves brought in 122 million sterling every year. Arab orange groves, grown by Arabs."

GRANDMOTHER FARRAJ: "The orange groves were there before the Jews came, you see. Before I was born, my father had two orange groves, and they exported 23 million boxes from Jaffa in 1948. The tour conductor kept talking about these orange groves that the Israelis had planted since 1948. Fortunately, there was a little American lady on the bus. As the tour conductor talked about the great achievements of the Israelis in orange planting and all that, she exclaimed: 'Nonsense, that orange grove is certainly older than twenty years.'"

KHALED MOUAMMAR, a systems analyst: "One of the main Israeli exports right now is oranges. And these oranges are called Jaffa oranges. Jaffa is a twin city of Tel Aviv. How come these oranges are called Jaffa and not Tel Aviv? It is very simple. They are Arab groves and Arab oranges."

ALBERT HADAWI, a graduate student: "Long before the Jews ever came to the country, the Palestinian farmer was well known throughout the Middle East and most of Europe for his agricultural skill and acumen. He had developed his orchards, his vineyards, his fields to such an extent that they were self-supporting as far as all agricultural produce was concerned. They show you pictures of orchards and say, 'See, this is what we did.' They don't tell you that the Arabs planted them. We look at an apple tree and don't realize that it takes years and years for it to grow to that height and to start bearing fruit. It is completely erroneous to assume and to take for granted the Jewish argument that they came and made Palestine from a desert into a heaven."

AYSHEH, a needlework lady: "The real builders of any country are the agriculturists. We can still cultivate small plots using our hands. We don't need any machinery."

KHALIL ABDELHADI, a medical doctor: "And then, of course we have figs. You know, figs are mentioned in the Bible. We continue to subsist on figs. During the war when people didn't have sugar, they ate figs for the sake of sugar. And then we have, of course, wheat and barley, and all that. And we have millet. You know what millet is? It is small. We call it 'burra.' The same as corn but it's a smaller seed. People subsisted on that. Some of the fruit we have is called prickly pear. They are now canning it and sending it outside. This is all over the Arab world, and it is so nutritious and can give much energy and food. All the summer they eat it. I enjoy it. When I go to the villages they offer me some. But I eat a limited amount. If you eat a lot of it the seeds grow together and they may give you constipation. But if you take a small number it's all right.

"You remember the Aswan Dam? The whole world was worried about statues. They lifted them up, lifted them up on the hills so that they would not be lost to the world. And yet, people don't worry about the people of Palestine who have their culture, who have their whole life of the country from its beginning. It is in their songs, it's in their habits, it's their way of life. It's their goodness, their generosity."

FAIZEH SAKKIJHA, a volunteer in women's movement: "My father was a merchant. He owned about three orchards of citrus, lemon and oranges. Jaffa was all oranges and citrus fruits. It was all full of these orchards."

ISSAT AL-ATAWNEH, a Bedouin sheikh: "Another thing, they are appropriating our traditional dress and food. For instance, you have the humus, fallafel, and other dishes. These are all ours, but now they are Israeli. We have lovely embroidery. This embroidery has been there for years and years. Once I suggested to a friend of mine that probably Virgin Mary sewed and embroidered in the same manner. Now they say that it is theirs."

ABLA DAJANI, a news writer: "The Israelis claim that the embroidery is their national dress, not ours. They are trying to make the world believe that they had that history and culture and habits, which they did not have in their country. They claim that these Arab dishes are theirs. That is why we formed the folkloric troupe. We have a culture of which we are proud."

GAMAL EL-SOURANY, a diplomat: "What Hitler has done to the Jews in Europe, they are doing to us here, torturing us, exterminating our homes, our fields, our churches, our mosques. Nothing in our life was respected by the Zionists. They moved in a way that is not known by any nation in the world."

* * *

The experiences of Palestinians in occupied lands are not everywhere the same, as is illustrated by the accounts that follow from Gaza, Bethlehem, and Jericho, areas to the south and east of Jerusalem. Gaza is a narrow strip of land adjoining the Mediterranean coast, once administered by Egypt, where a crowded refugee situation gives rise to many commandos and where security measures are extremely tight. Bethlehem, relatively serene and peaceful, has since 1967 sacrificed its prosperity to Jerusalem not only because building projects draw workers away but also because of the peculiarities of tourism in the Bethlehem area. Jericho has in some ways become a ghost town because of the flight of so many people from the area in 1967 and because of its proximity to the tension-filled frontier.

First Gaza.

AHMAD FARIAH, a camp resident: "We Palestine people don't like to transfer to another country. We want to stay here. I don't know when we will finish our struggle. Maybe after three years, maybe six years, maybe a hundred years. But we Palestine people want our country. That's all we want. I want my country. I want my country because my grandfather lived here, and I have ever been here. I have trees, buildings and land in Palestine. Not too far from here. About five kilometres. I see my trees. I see my building.

"Let me remind you of something about the difficult circumstances which we live in. Someday it happens. The ruler of Gaza gathers all the men in a large area and they sit down. One of the soldiers, he has a gun, begins to shoot many unarmed persons. They didn't do anything and four of them are killed without any cause. This is very bad. It happened in the camps. And one day, one person in the Beach camp refused to go out from

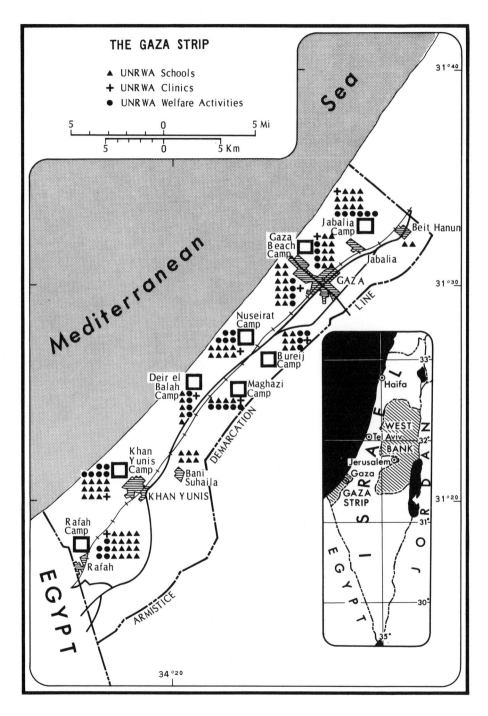

THE GAZA STRIP

▲ UNRWA Schools
+ UNRWA Clinics
● UNRWA Welfare Activities

his home because they were going to destroy it. He refused to go out. A large bulldozer removed his house, and he was killed, because he refused to leave, and his two sons also.

"We had an imposed curfew for thirty consecutive days. No one was allowed to go out of his dwelling except for three or four hours, which was not enough for the people to bring all of their supplies and to bring their foods in. And throughout this month there was much hitting of the people, shooting, and imprisonment. Why? Because of nothing. They don't treat us as human beings and this is very bad.

"There was a family at Beach camp. The father of the family refused to go from his house also. So the Jews, without any arguments, without asking him to leave, they just came and they destroyed his house with his children. You know a lot of families now are living with just a cover of leaves or with just a tent, and one of the worst cases that happened occurred with a woman in labour. They came to her house to destroy it. She refused to go. In a tent she had her labour, and she delivered in such very bad circumstances."

MUSA AYOUB, a camp chauffeur: "An Israeli soldier shot a man dead here this morning. Houses have been blown up here. I live with five children. I lived here ten years in a tent. There weren't any trees here then. All this was destroyed. The houses were destroyed. They're building roads. Every day there are incidents. Every day a brother or a father or a son is taken away. Some of the bulldozing had been done this week."

MAHER THABET, a camp resident: "Why are the houses being blown up? I don't know, but the government says that they want to make some streets. Maybe one thousand houses have been blown up in every camp."

CONSTANTINE DABBAGH, administrator of volunteer program: "They say for security reasons. They pull down houses to open roads to have more space for their equipment, for their tractors. I don't think it is the right excuse. They have the right to open roads here and there, but they should, before opening these roads, make available houses for those people to move in. But now what is going on? People being put in trucks and moved. They don't know where to go, they don't know what to wear, they don't know how to live, no schools, no doctors, no nothing. And I think this is not the aim of security. It's the aim to move people. Their policy from the beginning is to evacuate people from this strip. In the past they have encouraged them, persuaded them, but now they are forcing them. They come in the night, they mark the houses, pull them down the next day. People are obliged to go on the trucks. They put them in the houses of the Egyptians."

* * *

Next Bethlehem. At first glance it seems that nothing has changed. But the old-timers see the changes at Manger Square. They remember how often the police station has changed hands: first the Turks, then the British, then the Jordanians, now the Israelis. And the younger people know how the tourist business has been affected since 1967. Belonging to the generation in between is Elias Freij, an award-winning businessman. He and his son explain the present situation.

ELIAS FREIJ, businessman: "My family was in Bethlehem for nearly five hundred years. Bethlehem proper is built on hills and these hills are barren. So the Christian community of Bethlehem in the past centuries chose to develop some handicrafts to live on because they have little farming to do. And these handicrafts started with olive wood and with some seashells from the Red Sea. Then with the development of techniques, our people for the last fifty years have developed this business. They started to travel abroad, especially to Europe and America. They took samples of their products and sold them.

"During the Jordanian regime the mother-of-pearl business reached its peak. Lots of tourists were coming; people learned how to develop it, and they did a good job. After the occupation of our country, the Israelis also did their best to help, and they gave the exporters premiums or incentives to export. On the other hand, cost of living has almost doubled on the West Bank, even though we earn more money, the money doesn't buy as much as it should or as before the war. Now we are suffering from shortage of labour, because we are about five miles distant from Jerusalem. So a lot of our labour is now working in Jerusalem, and most of the factories in the Bethlehem area are short of skilled labour.

"It takes, for example, three years to train a craftsman to do mother-of-pearl carving. Then for any simple reason this craftsman will just leave me and go to work in Jerusalem. And we have complained about this matter. There should be found a solution to this because they drain skilled labour from this area into their own district. Bethlehem as a whole lives on cottage industry. There are over a thousand factories, small factories or home workshops in this area. And the main source of income is mother-of-pearl and olive wood. And unless we export our handicrafts abroad, a lot of our people do not find work.

"We employ about a hundred people. Most of the people who work for us do so in their own homes. They now are paid by the piece. And in this way people earn almost three times as much as they do working for me by the hour. Ninety per cent of my products are exported. The 10 per cent which we consider is just what we sell locally. We are the only exporters on the West Bank who are officially approved exporters. We were also selected as one of the ten best exporters in Israel. There is more money now circulating between the people than before, and there is full employment in the West Bank.

"Tourism in Bethlehem is flourishing as never before. Huge numbers of people are coming. But unfortunately the tourists are shepherded by the guides as sheep. They come to the buses, they brief them beside the church for a few moments, they explain to them the story of Bethlehem and the church, they take them back into the buses and out to Jerusalem. Some shops which are opened on the way between Bethlehem and Jerusalem are doing business, but the shops in the Manger Square are not doing much business. They just go inside the church, from the church back to the buses. We have complained about that. We have very beautiful shops, and we hope the tourist office in Jerusalem will arrange to let the tourists stay in Bethlehem at least for an hour. The tourists are entitled to the country at Bethlehem. I believe that the tourists would like to talk to the people of Bethlehem, to see the streets of Bethlehem, but not to go to a few selected shops on the street outside of Bethlehem. And besides, the guides who come with the tourists take 20 per cent commission of the gross gains. So every tourist, whenever he buys something, the guide takes 20 per cent of the commission, everything has commission for him."

GEORGE FREIJ, salesman: "Most of the tourists stay in Jerusalem. They eat in Jerusalem, sleep in Jerusalem, they have more time in Jerusalem than Bethlehem. They come here for just ten minutes to visit the church, then they are away to Jerusalem. We hope the government will do something to let the tourists stay here another thirty minutes or one hour to get an idea about the town, to get some pictures, talk to the people, to rest, to bring something from Bethlehem."

* * *

Finally Jericho. One of the saddest places on the West Bank, as some of the remaining residents report:

IBRAHIM FARBI, administrator of voluntary program: "Life in Jericho is very quiet. There is not much to say really about us because many people left after 1967. You can easily see most of the houses are empty. The camps are empty. Everything is getting quiet. No jobs like before. Many gardens are destroyed because their owners are not here anymore. They left, and they are dry. There is not much social life, like before. No activities really for young people in this area at all. In Jericho the distress and need is great because we're right close to the border, and we have had difficulties in transportation between Jericho and Jerusalem. I am actually from Jerusalem, but when I enter Jerusalem I have to have permission. Just recently, two or three months ago, we are permitted actually to go to Jerusalem without permission. At the same time Jericho and Jerusalem road are closed every morning up till seven o'clock now or six-thirty.

"Jericho used to have around 100,000 refugees, with the Jericho inhabitants, I mean. After 1967 War, I think 90 per cent of the people have been evacuated to the East Bank. Very many of the people left Jericho due to the fighting between the Arabs and Israelis."

HAZBUN, a refugee at Allenby: "It is hard for us to cross the customs here, at the Allenby bridge, emotionally hard."

FAIZ DAJANI, restaurant owner: "Restaurant? No, no work. No customers are coming to Jericho. Jericho is now nearby the ceasefire line and people are afraid to come here. This is why. And second, maybe I can say it, in summer it is too hot. Winter is shorter. Jericho's winter is shorter, you see. Before 1967 I had between forty and fifty labourers working here, but since last eighteen months I did close the restaurant."

LEILA NASSER: "You see I am the field supervisor. This Thursday I had a big problem with the women because they didn't want to take the money. There was 20 per cent devaluation of money, you know, so there were two pounds less than usual. And I had big difficulty with the women. The same thing yesterday and today in another village."

* * *

The resistance to the occupation, especially since 1973, has led to many arrests and imprisonments, with due process of law rarely granted. The number of people in prison is not known by anybody except the Israelis, but almost all the Palestinians we talked to knew someone who had been jailed. The following are typical reports.

ISSA KHADER, a teacher: "My nineteen-year-old brother Ayed was arrested in April and has now been in prison for four months. He was arrested along with 139 other 'active people.' The accusations were four: participation in the illegal Palestine National Front (PNF), helping the Front, recruiting three members into the Front, carrying a bomb from one person to another person.

"He did not sign a confession statement. Put in 'administrative detention' in different prisons. My brother was tortured fiercely for fifteen days. He was struck on his penis. Six men hit him on his legs and his feet. His breasts were irritated until blood oozed out. He was strung up by his hands for several days. Brought to court, he was asked to confess. He refused. The trial was postponed.

"He was picked up at 12:15 A.M. About a hundred troops were around the house. They knocked on the door. Mother answered door. They asked for Ayed. House was searched everywhere. They found nothing, but they took him and moved him through the streets till morning throughout Ramallah region to frighten him. They threatened to get his sister and mother. They threatened to send him to Amman. They asked him to sign that he was in army of PNF. He was fifteen days in isolation. They allow a one-hour family visit once a month. His spirit is good. They don't want us to speak politics. Everybody speaks politics, but we can't. You are free to speak, but afterwards the problems begin."

BASIL SAHAR, a principal: "Wife in prison four times. She's a rebel. Last time, she was pregnant. She said: 'Take me, but if I bear it will be at your expense.'"

FARAH AL-ARAJ, a mayor: "Five from my town are in jail. Ages sixteen to eighteen. There were fifteen. I pleaded for ten students with union offenses to go on to university. They wrote boyish slogans on the walls like: 'No for occupation.' 'We are not afraid from prisons.' 'Nobody likes occupation.'"

HANNA NASIR, college president: "Examples of resistance? There were slogans on the walls. We were told to paint over slogans. Painter went over exact letter with fresh and darker paint. He had followed the letter but aggravated the Israelis. Israeli soldiers forced him to repaint. Anti-occupation slogans include: 'Long live the free fedayeen,' 'Remember the 5th of June,' 'We shall not vote.'"

ANITA DAMIANI, college teacher: "Visit our offices sometime. There is a lot of literature, especially on prisoners under Israeli occupation and inhabitants whose property is destroyed. Part of our job is to collect information for the Human Rights Commission of the United Nations. They pass through here about once every year to collect data. And I think they haven't been allowed to go into Israel. So they get together clippings from newspapers, Arab newspapers, the *Jerusalem Post, Life, Time, Newsweek, the Times* and the *Observer.* We collect data and catalogue it as precisely as possible indicating dates, ages of prisoners, sentences passed, the charges, etc. We have big binders that are distributed in five chapters on these prisoners."

AREF AL-AREF: "Then in the prisons nowadays there are about 5,000 people. There were about 10,000, but some of them were sentenced, some of them were banished, some of them were acquitted. At the moment I believe there are in Israeli prisons some 5,000 people, 3,500 against whom sentences were passed by various courts and about 1,500 who are still retained under administrative order. Some of them are being detained, some of them since three years without being to the courts. I am not against arresting criminals. I am not against blowing up houses belonging to terrorists, to criminals. But I'm against blowing up houses without trial. It is a crime in my opinion. What I want the Israelis to do is to have a little patience, to try the man whom they suspect in court, to give him the chance of defending himself. If he is proven guilty then apply the law. If in the law it says his house should be demolished or he should be sentenced to life imprisonment, then we Arabs will have no reason to complain."

* * *

Among those interviewed was Isam Abedilhadi, the politically active leader of a women's organization, who had been separated from her family in Nablus, jailed, and then exiled.

Q. "How long have you been on the East Bank?"
A. "Two years."
Q. "You came from Jerusalem?"
A. "No, from Nablus, one hour to Jerusalem."
Q. "And you were forced to leave?"
A. "Yes, I was forced after imprisonment."
Q. "You were imprisoned?"
A. "Yes. For forty-five days."
Q. "Because you were a leader?"
A. "No. Because of some accusations like assisting the resistance. I was elected in 1965 to be the chairman of the women's union."
Q. "Forty-five days in jail in Nablus?"
A. "In Jerusalem prison first of all and afterwards in Nablus."
Q. "Are you a mother?"
A. "Yes, of four children."
Q. "Is your husband here, too?"
A. "No, he lives on the West Bank with one daughter. The others are with me here."
Q. "Have you seen your husband in these two years?"
A. "Sometimes they allow him to come and sometimes they do not allow him to come."
Q. "You can't go back?"
A. "Not now. I am trying."

* * *

Monsour Kardosh, a Nazareth businessman, is one of the few who has been exiled inside his own homeland.

MONSOUR KARDOSH: "I think hundreds of people were imprisoned for different reasons from 1948 to 1971, the last of which was for taking part in the memorial for Nasser. And there are still cases in the courts for this. I was jailed ten or twelve times. I don't remember exactly how long. Sometimes for three days, sometimes for one week, sometimes for a month, here in Nazareth and in the prisons around Nazareth. I was exiled to a place in the Negev between Beersheba and the Dead Sea, for three months in 1964-65.

"I have suffered. I have been put in jail on several occasions. I have been exiled. I have been under room arrest for a long period. I had to report daily to the police to declare my presence in Nazareth. I was forbidden to practise my work freely. One hour after sunset until dawn I was subject to home arrest, not entitled to go down to my workshop which is my shop in the same compound. We tried organization but the government did not allow it. We tried to publish a newspaper. The government was against it. We are not allowed to work, to have political activities, any political activities as members of anything, of any organization or party.

"We have published eleven issues of *El Ard.* Ard means the soil, the land. We consider that we are the owners of a land and somebody is intending to build up something on our acreage. Therefore we have to fight for our soil and for our land. In the eleven issues which had been published, *El Ard* gave a full detail of what were our intentions. We were against terrorism, against using arms, against illegal organizations. What we applied for was the legal right to defend our ideas and the people.

"I have never had a chance to defend myself in a court. All the decisions and the orders which put me in prison or in exile or in home arrest were based on the emergency resolutions. I am not allowed to visit Haifa, for example, except with a police permit, or Tiberius or Jerusalem. I am not allowed to enter the newly occupied areas. For what ideas was I jailed and exiled? Well, I am against the expropriation of Arab land. I'm for complete equality between Jews and Arabs. I'm for the idea that the Arabs must be organized in one way or the other to defend their houses. I'm for the partition, for the implementation, the exact implementation of the Palestine partition resolution. I am for the repatriation of the refugees."

* * *

Most of the people under occupation try to make the best of the situation, even though they may be resisting in their hearts, to the point of obeying and cooperating with the military authorities.

EMIL SAFIEH, an accountant: "An accountant should not under any circumstances betray the principles of integrity or the carrying out of his duties even under an occupation which exerts pressures."

BISHOP CUBA'IN: "It is difficult to serve a people under occupation. You see, occupation and war create new avenues of service, create new problems, create new needs, and it is the duty of the church to face this situation and face it on the basis of the principles of our Lord. And that is again peace and love. We certainly love our people, we love our country, we like to do our best for the interests of our people and for the interests of our country. But this can be done everywhere, again as I said, in a loving spirit and in a peaceful-mindedness."

AREF AL-AREF: "To say that I accept the judgements of Israeli law is not to say that I accept the occupation. What am I to do if the military government, if the army, occupies my country? First of all, I don't agree to any occupation, to the occupation of any part of my country. Secondly, if my country is occupied, I say it is up to the Arabs to negotiate and to find out some solutions. Until a solution is found, the Israeli occupying authority should govern in accordance with Red Cross conventions, United Nations resolution or Security Council resolution. If they don't do it, I'm against it. Now, for instance, the Security Council and the United Nations have several times decided that the Israelis should not change the situation in Jerusalem."

HANNA NASIR: "Here the fight is to be steady and faithful. Is it better for the community to be deported or to help the people? Anybody can be deported. It is harder not to be deported because when you are deported you are a somebody and you can shout against Israel over the radio. My duty is to help people live normal lives under circumstances . . . to prevent them from leaving. The more intellectuals are here, the more leadership is here. This is service in itself. People still want to enjoy life. So you promote folklore, dancing and intellectual activity so that people don't become only sheep."

* * *

The Israel occupation of all of Palestine is an accomplished fact, but the situation is complex. How the Palestinians experience the occupation depends on where they live. Haifa, Nazareth, Nablus, Ramallah, East Jerusalem, Bethlehem, Gaza, and Jericho all represent different situations. They have this in common, however. Everywhere Israel is making moves to strengthen its control ahead of the increase in Arab population by birth and also ahead of the increase in Arab hostility.

Eliya Khoury, an Anglican priest, tells of his imprisonment and deportation. Now he attends meetings of the Palestinian Liberation Organization – wearing a clerical collar.

"We don't need blankets . . . we need understanding," says Nimreh Tannous Es-Said, director of emergency refugee programs, Jordan.

Maha Al-Atawneh, a teacher of Bedouin background, reports on the educational problems of keeping a heritage alive.

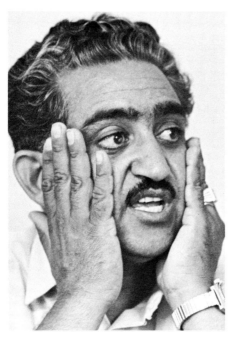

Leila Deeb, a refugee camp administrator in Jordan, reads from a poetry book. Many families fled Palestine, she says, to protect the "honour" of their daughters.

Nazri Zananiri clasps his cheeks as he describes napalm burnings of children and adults in the 1967 flight to Jordan.

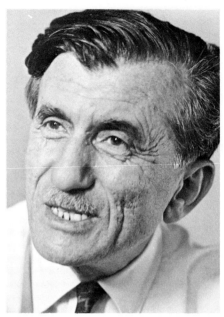

Above left: The renowned historian Aref Al-Aref reflects on his own past at his study in the West Bank town of Ramallah.

Above right: Rhoui El-Khatib still considers himself mayor of Arab Jerusalem. He was deported from the city March 7, 1968.

Issat Tannous, a medical doctor cum diplomat, recalls his negotiations with the British. "We tried our best," he said.

Above: Terraced olive groves still thrive a few miles south of Jersusalem and in other parts of the occupied West Bank. Once they were typical in all Palestine.

Left: A woman and child harvest beets in front of a new irrigation pump-house in the arid Jordan Valley near Karameh. Land is a central issue with Palestinians.

Children at Dera'a refugee camp in southern Syria stand at the entrance to their tent home where they have lived since 1967.

Below: Wearing donated smocks, kindergarten pupils play in their hilltop school yard in Marka camp near Amman, Jordan.

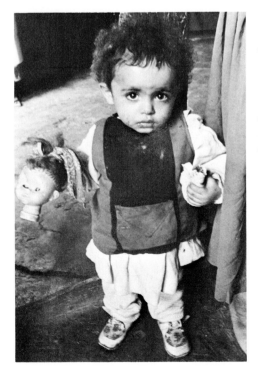

Opposite page: The main street of Marka camp, Jordan, never is empty of pedestrians.

Above: After a heavy rain, the streets of Baqa'a camp, located a few miles north of Amman, Jordan, turn to slippery mud.

Left: Clutching a sandwich in one hand, a broken doll in the other, a child stays close to her mother at Dekwaneh, Lebanon.

At Mar Elias camp in Beirut, Lebanon, a woman goes about her morning chores. Stones and bricks hold tin roofs on to crowded, brick and wooden shelters.

A resident of Baqa'a urges his donkey toward a central market where fruit and vegetables are sold. More than 50,000 refugees live here, the largest of 63 camps.

At the doorway of her tin shelter in Dekwaneh, Lebanon, a refugee prepares salad for her daughter and seven grandchildren.

A teenager in the Borj Albarajni camp in Lebanon looks out through the potted plants in front of her home.

Children play cards in the narrow passageways of a Beirut refugee camp.

Overleaf: Lining up at the school fence in Baqa'a, young Palestinians strike a symbolic pose.

Above: A resident of Khan Danoun, Syria, heads home with a supply of flour. Rice, sugar and cooking oil are also given to many refugees.

Left: An employee of the United Nations Relief and Works Agency (UNRWA) strikes a pose as he pauses in his work distributing flour.

Residents at Khan Danoun, a few miles south of Damascus, Syria, receive monthly rations at a UN distribution centre. About 60 per cent of registered refugees are eligible for basic rations.

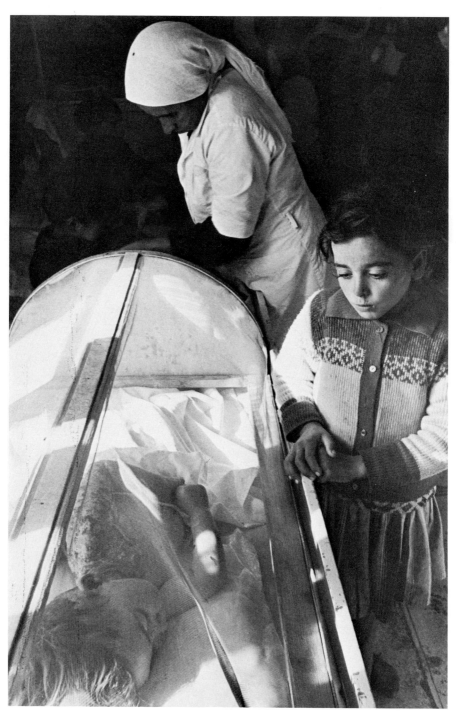

At an UNRWA health clinic at Baqa'a, Jordan, a girl watches her young brother
lie quietly under fly netting, as he patiently waits for his burned arm to
heal. The boy burned himself playing with a kerosene lamp.

Chapter 6

Emptying the Land of Arabs

"Is there a policy to empty the land of Arabs? He who sees deeply knows the answer. A Jewish family is always preferred before an Arab family."

— Issa Faris

The world knows about the first exodus of Palestinians in 1948 and about the second exodus in 1967. Little is known about the ongoing exodus, which leaves the Palestinians convinced that the Israelis have a long-term goal of emptying the land of all those Arabs not needed for the labour force, certainly of all those with some capacity for leadership.

The continuing exodus is due to direct and indirect pressure from the Israelis. The immediate circumstances surrounding the departure of individuals or groups vary. They include the desire to be reunited with their families, the sale of land at a profit to Israelis (particularly in the Jerusalem, Bethlehem, and Beit Jala areas), the bleak prospects for the future, the weariness that comes from continuous resistance and struggle, and, last but not least, forced deportations.

ASSAD, a commando in Lebanon*: "About 500 have been deported from the West Bank since the October War."

ISAM ABEDILHADI, in Jordan: "We have 135 men deportees from Nablus. Then we have more than twenty-five women deportees who were taken out from their children, out of their houses, and put over the bridge to the other side."

ELIAS FREIJ, in Occupied Palestine: "The Christians already are in the minority. We are on the West Bank only 5 per cent of the population, not more."

AREF AL-AREF, Occupied Palestine: "If I'm allowed to judge from what I see, from what is happening, I can say that the intention of the Israelis is to do away as much as they can with the Arab elements in the country and to make the Jewish element the majority so that they can rule the country with more success."

* In this chapter, place names indicate location at time of interview.

GEORGE GIACAMAN, Occupied Palestine: "There are various types of pressure, some direct and indirect. Immediately after the 1967 War, the direct was more evident in Bethlehem. Israeli loudspeakers told us we had two hours to evacuate before the town was destroyed. Some people left. We had learned the lesson of 1948. Our family decided to stay whatever happened. There are indirect pressures. Many families have been separated. Often the head of a family is not allowed to come back."

LEILA NASSER, Occupied Palestine: "We should be able to preserve the people of Palestine. Now what they are doing with us is like this: You have a jug of water, full of lovely water. Somebody comes and drops a stone. Some of the water flows out. That's what is happening to the Palestinians, that's what is happening to our own people. Are there still pebbles being dropped into the water, and are the Palestinian people still flowing out? Every day. They take us to the bridge and kick us out."

MARY NASRALLA, Lebanon: "Each American Jew who comes here displaces at least one Palestinian who has no other place to go."

SALAMA MAZEM, Jordan: "They are planning to throw out more Palestinians and to bring in more Jews."

ANTON ATALLA, now in Jordan: "I was banished from my homeland on the second day of Christmas in 1967. I was quite critical about Israeli behaviour in Jerusalem, especially with reference to annexation."

JABRA ABBASSI, Occupied Palestine: "Just last week I signed a paper for IL 80,000 – not to be political. I was deported in 1969 for twenty months. I was deported for reasons which I was never told. Came home for humanitarian reasons. Father very sick, lived only for six hours. I was permitted to stay forty days. Recently they agreed to my permanent stay in exchange for my promise. They came at 4:00 A.M. I thought they were patients. They asked me to dress. They took me to Allenby Bridge. My wife stayed thirteen months and then came to see me for eight months. They deported me together with a sheikh and a member of parliament. We went at the same time, but our return was different."

RHOUI EL-KHATIB, Jordan: "The Christians are disappearing from Jerusalem. Beginning 1948 before partition there were 28,000. Beginning 1967 before occupation there were 15,000. End of 1973 there were 10,500. Thirteen thousand left as a direct result of 1948 occupation. All left under pressure against Christians and Christian places."

SHAKIB A. OTAQUI, Occupied Palestine: "It is still happening, by the way. Oh yes, you should live in Birzait. Every day the planes came down and

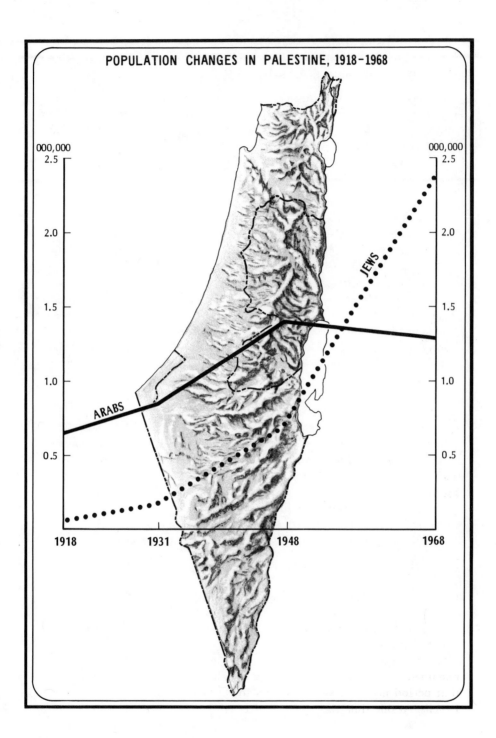

POPULATION CHANGES IN PALESTINE, 1918–1968

ARABS

JEWS

000,000
2.5
2.0
1.5
1.0
0.5

000,000
2.5
2.0
1.5
1.0
0.5

1918   1931   1948   1968

bang, bang. Ramallah's the same, not so much over Jerusalem, very seldom over Jerusalem, but over Birzait and Ramallah it's happening all the time. Patrols go around, firing in the air."

AMIN MAJIJ, Occupied Palestine: "No, I am not a fearful man. I was expelled from university in Beirut because of my politics. I was wounded in 1943 and attended all the fighting in 1948. They have not deported me, but I am not afraid. Whether they put me in jail or send me across the river – it is all part of the game. I won't be the first nor the last."

* * *

Palestinian intellectuals and community leaders living in the occupied territories are continually being arbitrarily expelled to Jordan. The expelled person is almost always the head of the family, and in consequence the family is destroyed. In many cases, even short visits are forbidden after such an expulsion.

The people to be expelled are usually arrested in the night. Only a short time is allowed for packing, and the family is prevented from contacting a lawyer or, indeed, anybody at all. Those to be expelled are then taken to a desert spot south of the Dead Sea and forced to cross the Jordanian border. If they remain near the border, shots are fired at them until they "move on." This punishment is usually inflicted on known community leaders.

The stories of those who have been deported are sad and deeply moving. I was particularly impressed by the experiences of three people: Rhoui El-Khatib, mayor of East Jerusalem at the time of the 1967 War; Eliya Khoury, an Anglican priest who was elected to the Executive Committee of the Palestine Liberation Organization following the October War, 1973, and who subsequently also received the electoral mandate of his people to become bishop (a mandate which the Archbishop of Canterbury could not or would not recognize); and Giries Kawas, a teacher, deported from the West Bank along with eight others in December of 1973. The first two were interviewed in Amman, the third in Beirut. First the mayor:

RHOUI EL-KHATIB: "I have a larger family and a smaller family. The larger family is the Palestinian family. The smaller one is actually the one I am looking after. It is composed of a wife, three sons, and one daughter. Two of the sons are graduated from American and British universities. The daughter has studied in England two years. The last one, still a kid of twelve, is with me.

"After my exile or deportation, my wife, my daughter, and my little son remained in our house at Jerusalem for almost eighteen months. During that period my wife was subjected to threats and to pressure from the Israelis. At one time she was also arrested, jailed, and sentenced without bail for a period of three months. She spent a few days in one of the prisons fifty kilometres from Jerusalem. After a protest made locally and from international sources, she was released. She was allowed to come and visit me three times. At the time of the last return, she was refused entrance and she has since then, for nearly two years, been living with me. Our house in Jerusalem is still closed. Our furniture is still there.

"Legally, I still consider myself mayor of Arab Jerusalem. I was deported by the Israelis from my hometown on March 7, 1968. Since then I have been living here in Amman in exile and trying as far as I can to serve my city and my people from the outside. I hope the day may come that I will be again in my hometown, my country, participating in the welfare of the city, my country, and my people.

"A number of Israeli armed soldiers dashed into my house after midnight on the morning of March 7, 1968, and instructed me to dress myself and to accompany them for interrogations at the headquarters in Jerusalem. I did and then, instead of taking me to such an office, they drove me directly to Jericho and kept me in an office until eight o'clock in the morning. By that time the assistant Israeli military governor of Jericho appeared and gave me the order of deportation, issued by the Minister of Defence of the Israeli forces. No trial, no accusations, and no self-defence. Immediately they put me into one of the cars, drove directly to the bridge, and told me to go to the east side of the Jordan and to Amman. It happened in five hours, from three o'clock in the morning till eight o'clock in the morning. My family was kept in the dark until mid-day, when they heard of my deportation on the radio.

"I discontinued my function as mayor on the date of the occupation of Jerusalem. On June 29, 1967, the Israeli occupying authorities illegally dissolved the elected Arab municipal council, dismissed me from my office and annexed the Arab side of Jerusalem, without the recognition of the UN and my people. Between June 29, 1967 and the date of my deportation on March 7, 1968, I remained in town, observing what was going on but not participating in any official duties. On the other hand, I was still considered by my people as the mayor. I was still considered and recognized by the international body and by the diplomats representing the several foreign governments in Jerusalem as mayor. I exchanged visits with their representatives in Jerusalem.

"Even after my deportation, I attended a meeting of the United Nations Security Council in May, 1968, in my capacity as mayor, and they gave a statement about Jerusalem and the changes taking place in Jerusalem. This was in New York. I appeared again in 1969, also defending the case of Jerusalem and the very many changes which were taking place illegally by the hand of the Israelis, who were trying to change the status and the character of Jerusalem to make it a Jewish city.

"My family had been living in Jerusalem continuously for the last eight hundred years. I was born, brought up, and served my whole life in Jerusalem. During the Mandate I served as a civil officer from 1931 up to 1945. And from 1945 to 1948 I served as a member of the Arab offices. After the Mandate I worked independently, started some small businesses in the field of electrification, feeling that the people of my divided city had been deprived of most of its means of living. Between 1949 and 1956 I was the chairman of three companies. One was the hotel company which built the first Arab hotel in Jerusalem, called the Ambassador Hotel. The second was a company to repair old houses and to build some stores to bring life to the city, and the third to generate electricity. In 1957 I was elected to the post of the mayor, and from 1957 until now I am mayor of the city of Jerusalem."

* * *

Second, the Anglican priest. Formerly of Ramallah, north of Jerusalem, Khoury was deported in 1969 and thereafter stationed in Amman, Jordan. In 1974 his leadership was recognized in two arenas. The National Palestinian Congress meeting in Cairo in June elected him to the Executive Committee. Soon thereafter his diocese, including Israel and the occupied territories, gave him the most votes as candidate for bishop. He had wanted to withdraw from the election, but the decision was taken by his pastoral committee that he accept the nomination. Eliya Khoury attributes the failure of the Archbishop of Canterbury to recognize the call of the people to the influence of Zionism on the hierarchy of the church. However, practical considerations were also part of the picture. A bishop unable to return to the West Bank would be handicapped in serving the people. Be that as it may, Eliya Khoury tells his own story best.

ELIYA KHOURY: "Yes, I am a Palestinian. My story is very long. I would like to speak about my story only after the Israeli occupation, if you don't mind. I was born in a certain village near to the Dotan area, the biblical area. I was educated in Jerusalem, and trained as a teacher in Jerusalem as well, and I had taught about thirteen years when I felt the call to the ministry. I had my theological training in London, England. After that I was ordained as a deacon in St. George's Cathedral in Jerusalem on St. Thomas Day, 1953, and to the priesthood in 1954.

"Since then I was working in the diocese of Jordan, Lebanon, and Syria as a priest. I worked in Nablus, in Ramallah, in Jerusalem, and now I am in Amman. Actually my coming to Amman was against my will, because I was deported by the Israeli authorities in 1969. You may be interested in why I was deported. I was the priest in charge of the Episcopalian congregation in Ramallah. It was the biggest parish on the western bank. I denounced occupation, and I refused to accept occupation for my country, my people, and my nation. I told this quite plainly and explicitly to the military governor of Ramallah. He knew where I stood.

"As a Christian I felt I ought to make a stand for truth and justice. I feel very sad about the occupation of my country and about the distress of my people. It is one of the very grim occupations known in history. Occupation is an aggressive act. The occupying of a country means the throwing of many people out of their homes and out of their own properties. This is something awful from the Christian point of view. And I told the military authorities that we used peaceful means to protest against occupation. I said that this was our right.

"What used to make me very sad was the sight of Israeli soldiers beating girls of eight, nine, ten, eleven, twelve years of age because these girls tried to protest against the occupation of their premises – not in the streets, but on their own premises – by not accepting to go into the classes. Sometimes they would stage a sit-down strike within the walls of the school. The Israelis used to beat these girls. As they sent them home they followed them on the street beating them with sticks, with the guns, with their fittings. I saw it myself, and I can testify before any commission on earth. I do not like to speak about things I have only heard about. I mention these facts that I have seen myself.

"My imprisonment? I can never forget the day. It was on the second of March, 1969, 1:30 early on a Sunday morning. Somebody knocked at the door of my house. I opened and the Israeli soldiers and officers were there by orders of the military governor to search the house. I was ordered to put on my clothes. My wife was ordered not to speak to me at all. They searched the house but found nothing. Then they searched the church building and the premises as well. They found nothing. Apparently they were looking for everything: weapons, explosives, and fedayeen – they call them terrorists. They didn't say what they were looking for. But they even searched my books. I have a library that contains about five hundred books. They even went through these books and searched every paper in my library and desk, and they never said what they were looking for.

"I asked them to let me go. I told them that I was a pastor and that I had to conduct three services on Sunday. I promised them I wouldn't contact anyone at all, and I would come back to them. They laughed. I told them that I was a sick man and that I had heart trouble a year before and if they had anything to investigate or ask, would they please put me under house arrest as a priest and do the investigation there. They said no. I was taken to Jerusalem to the headquarters and there they started their interrogation. During my interrogation and during my imprisonment, I was not subjected to any physical torture, though I felt the pains, sorrows, and sadness from within. I was subjected to very deep spiritual torture, which was far heavier than physical torture.

"But during my interrogation I had to observe a certain young man who was tortured. This young man I happened to know very well. His hands and his feet were tied with chains. His face, eyes, and nose were swollen. Blood was coming out of his mouth, nose, ears, and eyes also. His hands, both of which were tied by chains, were swollen. His feet were swollen. I thought that this man would not live longer than half an hour. I can never forget this young man.

"I was asked many questions: whether I was helping the fedayeen, whether I was carrying arms, whether I shared in planting any explosions that used to take place in Jerusalem or anywhere else, whether I was in contact with the Gaza people, whether I knew how to use arms. Believe me, they did not actually make an accusation against me. They just asked general questions. And I was interrogated about three weeks, not every day, but every other day, sometimes three times a week, sometimes once a week. I felt it was too bad to stay all this time in prison. I couldn't bear it, you see. I had never been in jail, and I felt that I was not the sort of man to be put in jail. Besides, I was sick. Honestly, I was sick. And I told them, 'Why don't you finish up your interrogation?'

"They never listened. They told me that compared to other prisoners I was living in a hotel. But I was treated as an ordinary prisoner. There were no special privileges for me at all, except that they did not subject me to any physical torture. I was not allowed to have a radio and listen to the news. I was even prevented from having a pen and paper to write. I could have written my best sermons inside the prison. But I had my Bible and my prayer book. I read my Bible all the time. You might be interested to know that I have read the Bible ten times through from cover to cover, a thing that I haven't done in my life before I was in prison. A layman from my church commented, 'Let us send all our priests to prison so that they would read their Bible ten times.' Some parts of the Bible gripped me more than others. I concentrated on the Book of Job and read about the suffering of man and the patience of man, about the love of man for God and the love of man for man. Each time I read through the Book of Job, I used to get a great message from it and I think it is a great, great book, this Book of Job.

"I was allowed to leave the prison on the fifth of April, 1969, after almost fifty days of solitary confinement. I saw my family only twice during this period and I saw my bishop twice also. During the first three weeks I was not allowed to see anybody, not even the bishop. My bishop tried to see me.

My wife tried. But both were prevented from seeing me. It wasn't until Dr. Eugene Carson Blake, the general executive secretary of the World Council of Churches, visited the holy land that I saw my bishop. He heard about my story, and I was told later that he contacted the Israeli authorities telling them that he would not leave Lydda airport before he got news that the bishop could see me. I shall never forget this man Blake for his courageous stand.

"I wish all our Christian people could take such stands because personally I differentiate between nominal Christians and active Christians. There is a great gap between the two, and this is the thing our people here, especially non-Christian people, can't understand. They believe that all the governments in the West are Christian governments – Britain, America, France, Italy. They see that these Christians have actually helped the Israelis to cause the tragedy to the Palestinian nation and, therefore, they doubt our sincerity. I try to tell them that there is a great difference between a nominal Christian and a worshipping Christian. A worshipping Christian always makes courageous stands for truth and justice. Real men of God make courageous stands, and one of these stands was the stand of Dr. Blake, and I shall never forget that.

"During my interrogation I asked them to allow me to cross over to live on the other side of the river because I didn't like staying in prison. Although it would pain me a great deal to leave my home and my country, I knew I was not a man for the prison. At first they said nothing, until finally they came and allowed me to cross over to Jordan. I crossed over on April 16, 1969, and came here to Amman. I was not allowed to see anybody except my wife and my only son. I was taken from prison directly to the bridge, down to Jericho and to the bridge. I crossed over to Jordan without seeing anybody, without telling anybody at all.

"I was elected to the PLO Executive Committee in June, 1974, having been a member of the Palestinian national parliament since 1969. I go to the PLO meetings in priestly garb. We are not a terrorist organization, but a government-in-exile."

* * *

The teacher and father of four children, Giries Kawas, from Gifna-Ramallah, was one of eight people deported simultaneously from the West Bank in December of 1973, two months after the October War. The deportees included Arabi Awad, 46, a teacher from Nablus, whose family of six stayed behind; he joined Kawas in telling the deportation story. The other six were: Walid Kam Hawy, 52, a medical doctor from Nablus with a family of five; Abd Algawad Saleh, 46, chairman of Beireh (near Ramallah) city council and father of six; Shaker Abu Heglah, 50, a Nablus teacher and father of seven children; Husain Al Jagkoob, 47, a Nablus judge also with six children; Abd Almohsen Abo Marzor, 44, a lawyer with three children, from Jerusalem, a member of the Higher Islamic Committee; and N. Dameen Odeh, 50, secretary of Bira Workers Union and member of General Union of Palestine Workers on the West Bank.

GIRIES KAWAS: "I was arrested and held without questioning. After eighteen days they let me go, and after one week they arrested me another time, for four days, also without any questions. The third time I was put in prison and a handkerchief put over my eyes. They put me in the car. Then after maybe three hours the car stopped. We heard some Jewish soldiers speaking. One of them told us to take the handkerchief off the eyes. They said to us, 'You are in the Sinai desert. To Aqaba is five kilometres.' We refused to leave. They took a paper and read it to us. This paper said that we had to leave this land. They were using a law of 1948 as a deportation order.

"They gave us a white flag. We walked two hours in the desert. We didn't know where we were going. We saw only sand. Every place we looked we saw sand. We didn't see anything moving or living. We sat down under an old tree to take rest. And then walked again for two hours. After that we saw a police car which came to us and took us to the police station. From there we were taken to Amman, nearly five hundred kilometres. We met with the prime minister and other responsible people. On the fourth day we asked King Hussein for permission to go back to the West Bank, and he allowed us. We went to the Allenby bridge in a peaceful demonstration in order to go again to our homes. There, the Jewish soldiers blocked the bridge. They pushed us back. They said we needed permission to go back. Then the Red Cross came and we told them our story. But it was no use. We came back again to Amman. Now we are all working here for the PLO in Beirut. We are working for the cause of our people.

"Why were we deported? They said for political reasons, because we refused their occupation all the time. Nothing more than that. Our protests against the occupation were public and not secret at all. They have deported from among our people about four hundred persons."

* * *

The deportations have continued to this day. Among those in exile is Hanna Nasir, the president of the only Arab college on the West Bank, Birzait College. The deportees can't come back and their family and friends are expected to follow them. The passing of time usually leaves them no alternative if family unity is important to them. But all are determined to go back.

Chapter 7

The Determination To Go Back

"We will go back. It may take a hundred years, maybe a thousand years. But we will return."

— *Omar, a farmer*

After the expulsion of the Palestinians from their land, the international community in general and Israel in particular hoped that the homeless Palestinians would behave as refugees have traditionally behaved and accept resettlement elsewhere. In this hope they were disappointed, as most of the Palestinians remained determined to go back. This determination became the strongest evidence that they had, indeed, left their homeland involuntarily. By establishing in 1949 the United Nations Relief and Works Agency, the international community had hoped that the emphasis would be resettlement and development. When resettlement was rejected by the Palestinians, Works were forgotten in all but the name as the accent was put on Relief.

The various Arab nations might be blamed for not absorbing the refugees in their midst, but the Palestinian people did not want to be absorbed. Everywhere they resisted efforts to make their habitation permanent. They remained determined that nobody and nothing would permanently separate them from their ancestral villages and from their fundamental human rights. To the outside observer, the possibility of the exiled Palestinians returning to their homeland seems remote. The older generations admit that for them time is running out, but they, too, hope for a return through their descendants. The chorus of voices symbolizing this hope is represented here.

Leila Bitar, Jaffa*: "The dream of everyone, of every Palestinian I have been with, was always to go back to Palestine and to their village."

Salama Thurayia, Hebron: "Any day. If they allow us, we will return."

* In this chapter, place names indicate place of origin in Palestine.

123

Shakib A. Otaqui, Jerusalem: "This is the first time in history that refugees have not accepted their refugee status and resettled when their homeland was no longer available."

Selim Rahab, Jerusalem: "Do I expect to go back myself? It is not important. I don't know. The important thing is that my daughter should go back, if I don't go myself. It is a long war, you know that. When we started our revolution, we knew that it was a long war. We are just at the beginning."

Albert Hadawi, Jerusalem: "I would like to go back but not under present conditions. I would like to go back to a Palestine that belongs to the Palestinians and the Jews who live there, but a Palestine, not an imposed Zionist state or a settler state. And I emphasize: it is a settler state and nothing else, based as it is on the rights of conquest and occupation. There is no legality, no morality to it."

Ahmed Ali, Acre: "Some day I hope I may be practising medicine in the democratic state of Palestine. I would love to do it. I would love to do it."

Nadejda Georgieff, Jerusalem: "Why shouldn't they go back? To their land, their homes, their work. They were born Palestinians. They should go back to Palestine, am I not right or no?"

Abla Dajani, Jaffa: "No Palestinian received any compensation. And we refuse to receive compensation, because we are returning. They took our homeland."

Fouad Yasin, Shagara: "Do I expect to go back to my village? Why not? But I can't say when, maybe a year, maybe five years, maybe after two years, maybe less, maybe more. But I can be sure that, if I don't go to my village, our new generations of Palestine people will see their land and will see their villages and have a chance to live. Ultimate victory is the important thing. Never mind that many of our comrades died before seeing the victory. They died to open the road in front of the coming generation. And we have a song on radio which goes something like this: 'We are fighting and ready to die in order that the coming generation can live in Palestine, plow and plant the fields and live in peace.'"

* * *

After 1948, the Palestinians remained relatively passive for a full twenty years, two long decades, waiting for the world to redress the wrongs that had been done to them. The subordinated, occupied, and exiled Palestinians believed that their case would be fully recognized by the United Nations, or by Arab governments, or by the big powers, or perhaps even by Israel. Since 1967, they have given up all of these hopes and determined to take their destiny into their own hands. Hence, the proliferation of commando movements under the umbrella of the Palestine Liberation Organization. Its members are called terrorists in the West, but they see themselves as freedom fighters similar to other liberation forces, like the French resistance against German occupation in the Second World War. Increasingly, they have begun to regard themselves as part of other "liberation" and "revolutionary" movements in the rest of the world.

Isam Abedilhadi, Nablus: "Revolution is a progressive worldwide movement that leads us to regain our rights."

Khaled Mouammar, Nazareth: "As a Palestinian, my struggle is a struggle for humanity. I support the Vietnamese people, who are fighting the Americans, the same way as I am supporting the Palestinians. Fighting for the Palestinians is fighting for humanity in the same way that in World War II fighting for the Jews was fighting for humanity."

Marwan Abdalla Azam, Safa: "We Palestinians are the vanguards of the Arab revolution and we are, every Palestinian, a part of the revolution. Any revolution that happens to any country, like Laos or Vietnam or Cuba, does affect us."

Abu-Jawad, Jerusalem: "We are part of the liberation movement of the Third World, against all sorts of occupations all over the world, whether it is in Canada or in Angola or anywhere else."

Nabeel A. Shaath, Safad: "Every revolution experiences setbacks because a revolution by definition is resistance of a small oppressed people, basically an unarmed people, against an oppressor who is much stronger. But a resistance movement or revolution acts as a detonator, as a vanguard of forces that are untapped. Our movement has attempted from the beginning to mobilize not only the Palestinians but also the Arab people around them, who are part of a larger entity threatened by Israel. We hope that our revolution will tap hearts and souls among the Jewish people in Israel and outside of it so that they will join us and end this oppression called Israel in order to create something better than a glorified ghetto. Needless to say we also hope to get support from all the world, from all the forces of people in the world who really feel strongly for the rights of people and for justice."

* * *

The active liberation movements among the Palestinians date back to 1965. They sprang up almost simultaneously in a number of places, a trend that accelerated after the 1967 War. Arising as they did in various regions, usually unaware of or out of touch with each other, they were generally

125

self-motivated and independent. Gradually, however, an umbrella organization emerged called the Palestine Liberation Organization, which has increasingly taken on the nature of a government in exile. Nabeel Shaath explains the intricacies of Palestinian organizations.

NABEEL A. SHAATH, Safad: "You can divide the various organizations into the following groups: there is Al Fatah, which is the Palestine National Liberation Movement, which is the largest by far and the most influential among the Palestinian organizations. It is really the organization that started the armed struggle in 1965 by making the first commando operations in the occupied territories in Israel on January 1, 1965 – preceding in fact by two and one-half years the 1967 War. The Fatah is probably the most independent organization, although it does take aid from several Arab countries and collects contributions from Palestinians in several Arab countries.

"Now you have the PFLP, which is the Popular Front for the Liberation of Palestine, which originally again was the military commando off-shoot of the old Arab nationalist movement. The Arab nationalist movement was a movement which believed in Arab unity and Arab nationalism. But having Palestinians as the most important element in its leadership ranks, it developed into the Popular Front for the Liberation of Palestine by 1967. That is Dr. George Habash's group. By 1969 it had split into four groups. One still is the PFLP, which is still led by Habash. Another is to the left of it, which is the Popular Democratic Front for the Liberation of Palestine. A third, which is a bit to the right of it, is the Popular Front for the Liberation of Palestine General Command, the PFLP General Command. And a fourth, which calls itself the Palestine Arab Organization, merged with Fatah. These four were off-shoots, basically, of an amalgamation of the Arab nationalist movement plus some smaller groups. The PFLP and the PDFLP identify themselves more and more now with the Marxist-Leninist leftist ideological orientation and depend for support mostly on Iraq and Syria. At one time, in fact, they were more or less tied in their relationship with these two countries. I think they are less so at this time. Their strategy has been different from Fatah.

"Fatah has believed from the very beginning in uniting people of different ideologies for the task of national liberation. Fatah also has from the very beginning identified its goal as the creation of a democratic state in Palestine. The two goals, liberation and democracy, identify basically with an ideological revolutionary leftist movement. The PDF considers its goal internationalist as well as pan-Arab and not just Palestinian. And the PFLP has resorted to tactics which are different from those of Fatah, like hijacking of planes, but in general has identified with Fatah on the goals of liberation.

"This brings us to SAIQA, or you can also write it SAYEKA, meaning Thunderbolt. This is the commando arm of the Syrian Ba'ath party. Then you have the Arab Liberation Front, which is the commando arm of the Iraqi Ba'ath party or of the Iraqis dominated by this party. And again, both contain Palestinians, believe in the liberation of Palestine, and use means very similar to those of Fatah, although they had been more or less tied in their relationship with these two countries.

"Then we have the Palestine Liberation Organization army, which is the Palestine Liberation Army and its commando branch, the Palestine Liberation Forces. These are the offshoots of the 1964 establishment of the Palestine Liberation Organization, at that time established by the Arab League.

"Since 1969, PLO has become the mother oganization for all the liberation movements, while it has continued to have a separate military arm. There are a few other less important ones. Most of them have merged now with Fatah. So what we really have now is the Palestine Liberation Organization, which contains all those represented in the Palestine Liberation Council or Congress, a 155-man council which includes both the fighting organization as well as some independents, some intellectuals, and so on. Out of these you have an executive committee of fourteen, which includes Fatah, PFLP, PDFLP, SAIQA and Arab Liberation Front. These are today the remaining strong or relatively strong forces in the unity.

"Where does Arafat fit in? Arafat is the commander of the forces of Fatah and the spokesman of Fatah originally, but since 1969 he also has been the leader of the Liberation Organization, the chairman of its executive committee, and at one time also the chairman of the central committee which now does not exist anymore."

A summary of the various movements and organizations is as follows:

A. Palestine Liberation Organization (PLO), the umbrella organization.
   1. Al Fatah, the largest of the groups and a new nationalist liberation movement.
   2. Popular Front for the Liberation of Palestine (PFLP), related to old nationalist movements. It has three offshoots:
      a. Popular Democratic Front for the Liberation of Palestine, to the left of PFLP.
      b. Popular Front for the Liberation of Palestine, General Command, to the right of PFLP.
      c. Palestine Arab Organization, merged with Al Fatah.
   3. National groups including:
      a. Syria: SAIQA (Thunderbolt).
      b. Iraq: Arab Liberation Front.

4. PLO Army and PLO commandos.
5. Small groups which have grown out of particular crises. (i.e. Black September).

* * *

In view of the many beginnings of Palestinian liberation movements, the oral histories are not the same everywhere. According to the PLO representative in Egypt, the real beginnings were at a meeting on the Mount of Olives in Jerusalem on May 28, 1964, of Palestinians who agreed then and there to found the Palestinian Liberation Organization. Gamal El-Sourany explains step by step how this nationalist feeling and determination emerged.

GAMAL EL-SOURANY, Gaza: "Israel erased the name of Palestine and the name of the Palestinian people, our most precious possession. But we were determined to retain it, and we began in Gaza to use the name Palestine in everything and in all our organizations: Palestinian Students, Palestinian Doctors, Palestinian Engineers, Palestinian Law, and Palestinian Police. We identified a Palestinian flag, we composed Palestinian national songs. We encouraged Palestinian authors, and we started a Palestinian army. The talks regarding a Palestinian entity began at the Arab League in 1958.

"By 1974 the organization had matured to a point where the Palestine National Council represented all or most of the military and non-military organizations of the Palestinians, the representation of the latter having exceeded the former to make a total of 167.

"This 'Parliament of the Palestinians' meets annually in Cairo for two weeks. The Council elects the Executive Committee of fourteen. This is really the Cabinet of Ministers of the National Council. Yasir Arafat is the president. There are now fifty-five 'embassies' or regional offices around the world and there is now worldwide recognition of the Palestine people."

* * *

Slowly but surely the PLO is developing into a government-in-exile with various ministries. One of the most developed is the ministry of the Palestine Research Centre, whose activities are explained by the Director, Ibrahim Al-Abed:

IBRAHIM AL-ABED, Saforia: "The Palestine Research Centre is part of the Palestine Liberation Organization, but it is an autonomous part; that is, it has independence in terms of its programs, its policies, and its publication plans. It was established in 1965. It aims at undertaking research on the Arab-Israeli conflict and on the Palestine problem in general. We have already published around three hundred books in several languages, mainly Arabic and English. We receive most Zionist publications and Zionist periodicals. We receive forty-six Hebrew papers. We have seven or eight people, experts in Hebrew, who have graduated from the Hebrew University in Jerusalem, who are now working with us.

"Our research program is divided into three main sections: one section is research on the Palestinian people – economic conditions, educational conditions, demographic situation, etc. Another section is on Israel. And the third section, the strategic section, is on the balance of power between the Arabs and Israel. On the other hand, we have a special section called archives that includes press clippings from around eighty papers. We also have a special documentation section that has all documents. We have a monthly journal in Arabic, called *Palestine Affairs*. We have published up to now thirty-six issues of that journal. It has a very wide circulation. And it is considered the best scientific journal on the Palestine problem in Arabic. We publish also, twice a year, a work called *Palestine Chronology* that includes day by day events and developments of the Palestine problem."

* * *

Integral to the liberation movements are the commandos. While the PLO does have an army, the burden of the so-called "armed struggle" is expected to be borne by small groups of armed men and women trained in the tradition of guerilla warfare. Large numbers of young Palestinians are currently in training. They are popularly known as commandos or "fedayeen," meaning "those who sacrifice themselves for a cause."

This sense of sacrifice is strengthened by Muslim theology which assigns a special status to martyrs. While only a minority train for the actual field operations, a majority of Palestinians refer to themselves as commandos. They all work for the restoration of their homeland, and this gives them a new hope and sense of purpose.

SANA FARAH, a student: "It is important for us to go back because it is our country."

NAJIB, Gaza: "We are all in the guerilla organization. We work lots of things. The condition to be a Palestinian is to fight. If any Palestinian says that he represents the Palestinian people, but does nothing for them, then he is an enemy and then we give ourselves the right to stop him where he stands, by hook or crook. I would do one thing against my father's will. When my father tells me to stop serving the revolution then I will stop serving him."

WADIE GUMRI, Jerusalem: "My age doesn't allow me to carry arms, a machine gun. What is wrong with fighting for my country? I am not doing anything wrong. Somebody took my home, my property, my house, my

129

furniture, my clothes, everything. I want it back. Is there anything wrong with that? No there isn't."

RHOUI EL-KHATIB, Jersualem: "Am I a commando? Well, in spirit, yes, but not with arms. I am trying my best since I have been deported to collect information of what changes are being made in Jerusalem. With this information I am trying to make the world aware of the violations of the Israelis with respect to Jerusalem and the people. I have issued two books, one in 1969 and one in 1970, both reporting measures undertaken by the Israelis to Judaise the city."

LEILA DEEB, Jerusalem: "General Moshe Dyan is supposed to have a daughter. And she is supposed to have said that if she was a Palestinian Arab she would be a commando."

FAOUD SAID, Jaffa: "Well, I support the resistance movement. For instance, they need lots of medical material at the Palestinian Red Crescent [Red Cross]. We subscribe to that. We give them all we can do in the way of material help to achieve their aim which is to liberate Palestine."

NIZAM NAZER, Hebron: "Why am I a doctor in the camp? Couldn't I have a more comfortable practice somewhere else? Being a Palestinian I am where I should be. Do you expect me to go to the moon in order to practise my work looking for a more comfortable work, or to work with those who are not my people?"

MAHMOUD AL-KHATEB, Zereau: "All of my six brothers joined the revolution. One was killed in an operation near Nablus in 1971. All of them and myself are willing to be sacrificed for the cause."

* * *

Our meetings with commandos took place in refugee camps and in unidentified apartment buildings in Beirut. Contact was gained only through the organizations and their representatives. Most commandos we met were in their early twenties, usually very conservative in the information they offered, but otherwise very determined and idealistic. Conversations with commandos like Haifa, Tarak, and others reveal the depth of their commitment to sacrifice and to be sacrificed. Even marriage becomes part of the revolution or must take second place to it.

HAIFA, from Gaza:
Q. "Is Haifa your real name?"
A. "It is my name here."
Q. "How old are you?"
A. "Twenty-two."
Q. "Your parents come from Gaza?"

A. "Yes."

Q. "How did it happen that they landed up in Lebanon?"

A. "Different Palestinians migrated to Syria, to Jordan, to Lebanon, and my parents came to Lebanon."

Q. "Why are you a commando?"

A. "Because it is the only way to liberate my country."

Q. "But you weren't born there?"

A. "But it is my country, whether I was born there or not."

Q. "During your twenty-two years, what has been your saddest experience?"

A. "There have been many sad experiences: the '67 War, the summer events, the recent clashes in Jordan. Life is full of them, one sad experience after another."

Q. "And the happiest?"

A. "When I joined Fatah, of course."

Q. "When?"

A. "A long time ago."

Q. "Where have you gone to school?"

A. "I finished my university."

Q. "AUB?"

A. "Not AUB, another university in Beirut."

Q. "Arab university?"

A. "No."

Q. "Fatah university?"

A. "Yes."

Q. "Free university, a liberated university?"

A. "Yes."

Q. "I didn't know that there was a Fatah university."

A. "I am a student in the Fatah university in one way or another."

Q. "What is your specialty?"

A. "Arabic literature."

Q. "Are any of you learning Hebrew?"

A. "Yes, of course. Many of us are."

Q. "Is it a must in the movement?"

A. "It depends on one's lessons and one's work. I began studying Hebrew."

Q. "What other languages are a must in the movement?"

A. "There is no must. Learning Hebrew is not a must as you understand it. I think it is essential for every Palestinian to learn Hebrew as many Israelis know Arabic."

Q. "Do you know some people who were killed in the Ajloun forests recently [the Ajloun forests east of the Jordan River near Jarash is where the commandos had their Jordanian hideout]?"

A. "I probably do, yes. I have many friends there. I assume that they have been killed. But many of my friends were killed in the September clashes and some before that and after that. Many of them were my best friends."

Q. "There have been many casualties and there will be many more. The price must be paid?"

A. "Of course."

Q. "Are you willing to die?"

A. "Yes. Otherwise I wouldn't have joined Fatah if I wasn't willing to die."

Q. "So you joined the movement . . . "

A. "Because I want to liberate my country whether that entails dying, being a prisoner, or working all day, night and day. I don't care. As long as I am working to liberate my country, I don't care what price I give."

Q. "And you do anything that you are told to do?"

A. "Of course."

Q. "Who gives you orders?"

A. "It is not orders. If I feel it is my duty to do this, I do it. We rarely have orders in this movement. We are one people, we just don't feel the need for orders much."

TARAK, Nablus:

Q. "Tarak, how old are you?"

A. "About twenty years."

Q. "You have a rifle, does that mean that you are a commando?"

A. "Yes, of course."

Q. "Tell me about your commando organization?"

A. "The Palestine problem and Palestine matter is not only a Palestinian matter. It is all Arabs matter, Syrian matter, Lebanon matter, Egyptian matter. All Arabs matter. I have offered myself to fight against the Israeli military force which has taken our land."

Q. "How long have you been training? What kind of training have you gone through? What kind of operations are you ready to do?"

A. "I have joined many courses. I have not done any operation, but I am working on the political plans to get education for the people. If the time comes I will be ready to fight."

Q. "You are not afraid to lay down your life in a commando operation?"

A. "If I am not ready to do so, I shouldn't have joined the storm organization as a commando."

Q. "Has the commando movement been crushed by King Hussein in Jordan?"

A. "It has been crushed partly, but not completely."

NAJIB, Gaza:
Q. "How many Palestinian commandos lost their lives in Ajloun and Jarash fighting recently?"
A. "Well, the casualties were around 5,000 killed, wounded and lost."
Q. "How many were killed?"
A. "About 2,000 or 2,500 were killed."
Q. "Where were they buried?"
A. "Some of them were buried in mass graves."
Q. "There must have been really quite a massacre there."
A. "Yes, it really was a massacre. Our people have never seen such a massacre in their lives. The forests were burned."
Q. "With napalm?"
A. "With napalm and phosphorous bombs. Some of our fighters were there for eighteen days without food and water and it was really a massacre."
Q. "Couldn't they see this coming?"
A. "Yes, but we had to stay and resist there."
Q. "Wouldn't it have been better to escape?"
A. "No. That is revolution. We resist and fight and stay in our places."
Q. "What is your job?"
A. "I have tried not to answer that question before."
Q. "Can't you describe it even in general terms?"
A. "General, but not specific. I deliver my convictions, my beliefs and what I practise according to my convictions to other people."
Q. "Which means that you are maybe a public relations man, maybe an agitator, maybe a propagandist, maybe an educator, maybe a journalist, maybe a preacher."
A. "A real revolutionary is in a sense a preacher, a man of religion, a man of police, a man of law, a man of politics, a man of economics. A real revolutionary would work any place with anyone to serve his cause."

MARWAN ABDALLA AZAM, Safa:
Q. "Married?"
A. "I am not married."
Q. "Why not?"
A. "She must be revolutionary too."
Q. "So if you go looking for a wife, you will be looking for a revolutionary one?"
A. "It is not a matter of going and looking for a wife. It is a matter of the moment, a woman who will live with me and accept this kind of life."
Q. "What about your salary?"

A. "It is only what is enough for us to live."

Q. "Is there anything else that you would like to say to me?"

A. "The Western part of the world and other parts of the world are under the influence of the Zionist propaganda."

SAMIR, Bel El-Shik:

Q. "Why is it that so many of you wait so long to get married?"

A. "We are waiting to get a better chance."

Q. "Do you have a girl friend?"

A. "Yes."

Q. "In Syria?"

A. "Not in Syria, that was in Saudi Arabia. When I was serving there, an Indian one."

Q. "You mean that the Palestine Liberation Army is also in Saudi Arabia?"

A. "No, but I was serving there as Minister of Health."

ABU-JAWAD, commando officer:

Q. "Are you married?"

A. "No."

Q. "Any plans?"

A. "That's not very important."

Q. "Or don't the revolutionaries have time for marriage?"

A. "No, most of our revolutionaries are married, and their wives are fighting together with their husbands."

HATIM, Jerusalem: "We are married to the revolution, and are not ready for anything else. We will marry later, after we liberate our country. The liberation comes first for our personal lives. The revolution is much more important than anything else to us. So we are married to the revolution."

REEMA, Haifa: "I am working in the revolution, and now I don't feel any need for having a boyfriend."

NAJIB, Gaza: "Get along without girls and get along without sex? No, no, no, no. When I want to get married, I won't get married, I won't get married to someone who isn't ready to sacrifice, because I might die any time or I might be imprisoned any time. If I get married I will get married to a revolutionary girl who is ready to face and fight and do anything for the revolution like me. And you see from that that our first ties are not to marriage. Our first tie is with the revolution. What if I get married and I have a nice comfortable suburban house with two cars standing in my garage and all of these things, and I have no land, no dignity? I am a Palestinian. I am proud of it, because it takes much to be a Palestinian. As long as I can't support myself, as long as I need the movement to support me, for example, then I won't get married, no.

"Even if I have to face, what is called in the West, sexual frustration. Personally, I am in love with a revolutionary Palestinian girl, and when I can afford it, I might get married to her. It is not that we are abnormal or something. We have our needs like eat, drink, and sleep. Maybe to you in the West sex is like that. We give priority to things. I don't feel frustrated. I am only frustrated for my country. I don't feel frustrated physically. Not that I or anyone of us doesn't get married in the sense of physical marriage when we feel the need . . . . Some things are secondary.

"Do all of us fellows abstain? Oh no. Abstain from sexual relations? Oh no, we are not homosexuals, for example. You misunderstand. This is again something that we don't think about all the time. So it is something secondary . . . ? We don't go around like other boys, seeking it. We have better things to do, much more fruitful. We have sex only if it happens. Arafat is not married, and as far as I know for at least seven years he has been without a woman. He is not married and he has been doing without sexual relations for such a long time. For seven years at least, because he stopped his social life. He is giving all his time to the revolution."

* * *

Palestinian women have always been on the forefront of participation in education, the professions, and community leadership. This is probably due to the fact that Palestine has for centuries been exposed to influence from Europe. The struggle of the Palestinian people has now brought the women even more into the forefront. Traditional mores and expectations concerning women have been deeply affected.

ANITA DAMIANI, Nablus: "Does the revolution mean a change also in the sexual mores of the Palestinian society? I don't think so right now, because we don't change tradition overnight. There are very strong traditions, and girls who go out and live in the field with the men are outcasts in a way. We do frown upon them a bit. But I think eventually, we will have to accept their going out and living in the fields without giving it connotations of sexual liberation or something."

NIMREH TANNOUS ES-SAID, Jerusalem: "Does the revolution then mean that the Palestinian women easily lose their virginity and chastity? Not as a rule, not as a rule. But if the enemy uses this as a weapon against the Palestinian people, I don't consider this as a loss of prestige for the women. On the contrary, I consider it a crown for her, and every man should be proud to marry that woman who has been assaulted as a result of her resistance.

"It is high time that we have to choose between the land or the personal

135

chastity. And I think we would choose that land as such, and God will forgive us for this sin if it is a sin, because it is an indirect sin, you see. It is not wilfully done. I don't want you to think under any circumstances that I was condoning this laxity in moral values. I was only referring to the challenge when the girls have to join the resistance and contribute in their own share. It is no longer a stigma, if a girl is raped by the Israeli authorities, who use this as one of the most pressing measures to get her or her men folk, brothers or fathers, to confess to crimes and to being in the resistance when they are not."

LEILA BITAR, Jaffa: "This I would like to illustrate with an example. I was talking to a young man of about thirty-five, I think, a well-educated man, a doctor, as a matter of fact. I don't know how it happened that we started talking about this subject, and he said, 'You know something, it is about time the revolution started making use of this sort of thing, making use of sex as such, using the women for certain purposes through sex.' I said this was a bit much to ask of most women, Arab women especially. And he said, 'I think for the greater good we should instil in the minds of people that this isn't such a bad thing ultimately. You know the end justifies the means, so to speak.' And I thought that was quite a great change from the usual attitude of our men. And this is a sign of revolution.

"If a girl loses her virginity or chastity through an assault brought about by an enemy then it is not a stigma. But that doesn't mean that Palestinian women make themselves free to all men. No. A man would not commit a crime of honour, as they say, against one of his women, wife, sister, daughters, etc., if she becomes 'unchaste' through the attack of an enemy."

* * *

The parents of the young commandos view the actions of their sons and daughters with mixed emotion. For instance, Najib Nassar, who was born in Jerusalem in 1911, wanted his son to complete his university education. William, however, felt the call of the revolution and ended up being sentenced by the Israelis to Ramleh prison for 150 years. The father tells the sad story, although not entirely without pride. We talked to him first in 1971 and again in 1974.

NAJIB NASSAR, Jerusalem: "My son was in early 1967 at the University of Spain, and I happened to be with him in Spain, in Madrid, in the late days of May, 1967. I left him there on the understanding that he would not leave the university if he heard anything about war breaking out in the area. My son William left and joined the resistance movement and went to Algiers. I went to Algiers, but they said he had gone to Damascus. I followed him back to Damascus, but by the time I arrived in Damascus, he was gone. Six months later I learned that he was in China. From there he went to Vietnam. I waited until he came about a year later. It was January 1968.

"I met him in Damascus on the understanding that he would finish his duty with the resistance movement and go back to the university. And he asked me to find a place in a university in England rather than Spain. So I went to England and managed to find him a place in the university. I couldn't find him in Damascus and the people there told me that he'd be back in a few days. And then I heard Israel broadcasting that he was arrested in Jerusalem. Three months later he was sentenced and given 150 years in jail.

"All of 1968 I couldn't see him. I managed to put world pressure on Israel to allow a father and a mother to see their imprisoned son, and I succeeded in getting the permit. Now a question is directed to me by some people. Why is it that these young chaps join the resistance movement? They want an answer. The answer I give is the same one I gave to that general who asked me that question in Israel. I said that in 1947, when I knew I was to leave Jerusalem and join the university, I had a nice home. And William was about seven months old, the boy who is now in prison. I was playing with him in the garden at my home and a couple passed by and asked me if I knew of a flat which they could rent. They looked to be decent people. I learned later that they were Polish and Jewish, driven out of Poland by the Nazis.

"They were looking for a flat. So I told them to look into my flat. I was leaving for Egypt and they could take my place. They went into the flat. The lady liked it very much, and I remember she said: 'This is too expensive a flat for us.' I said: 'Don't worry about the expenses, you just take that and the rent is one shilling per month. I want you to look after the furniture. That's all I want you to do, I don't want the rent.' And three days later I learned they were Jews, both of them.

"I accepted them, I accepted them gladly into my home, left everything there, and a week later I left for Egypt. As I said, this was in July 1947. And since then I never saw my home again. This is a story I related to my son. Naturally, this left a mark in his heart, and this applied to every Palestinian boy. It left an impression, a feeling. He had to do something to get back to his home. This is what forced him to go and join the resistance.

"He left Jerusalem when he was six years old. He doesn't know anything of Jerusalem. But it is there in his heart, especially after that story that his father was so kind to give to a couple of Jews his home to live in free of charge, and he was never allowed to see that home again with all its contents. I don't want to boast. This applies to all the young boys, the young Palestinian boys. When they grow up they have it in their heart to

137

get back to their Palestine, to get back to their homes, to get back to their family. Whether they knew Palestine or not, they know it in their heart.

"My son's morale is very high, very high. His condition is bad. And every time I see him, every time I enter the prison I carry it in my mind to ask him to be patient. Instead of doing that he asks me to be patient. Naturally a man in my age cannot carry arms and resist, but I have to do something for these Palestinians. And the only thing I can do to help the resistance movement is to be in charge of a house where we accommodate one hundred daughters of the martyrs. We give them full board and full education. It's here in Amman. Recently, after the events of June, we had to expand and build up a home for babies. This is all I can do at my age to help the resistance movement, to look after the daughters of the martyrs.

"We are allowed to correspond through the Red Cross. The Red Cross has special forms. We are allowed three lines on these forms. But I found out that out of forty-eight messages I sent to my son on these Red Cross forms since August 1970 until August 1971 – I made it a point to send a message every week – he received only two of these. I complained to the superintendent-general of the prison. By luck the representative of the Red Cross happened to step in and I complained to him in the presence of all. He said, 'Every letter received we deliver to the prison.' The general checked with the prison authorities around the prison, and they said: 'I will give you a list of the letters that were delivered to William since January 1971.' And they gave him this, and my son was correct, the list showed only two letters were delivered to him from the Red Cross.

"Now I wanted to have an answer regarding the remaining forty-six letters. But no one could give me an answer. The Red Cross delegate said: 'We deliver every letter we receive to the West Bank and to the delegate of the Red Cross on the West Bank.' My son and all other prisoners are allowed to receive letters from abroad. For example, he received six letters from his brother in America. He received three or four postcards from Moscow sent to him by my daughter-in-law.

"There is another story about William, and about his friends in Karemeh. I sat down with a crowd of people, and then one of these young boys with the gun on his back passed by.

"I said: 'What's your name?'

"He said: 'My movement name is William.'

"I said: 'William? Can't be William. Why do you carry this name?'

"He said: 'Do you happen to know William Nassar?'

"I said: 'Well, I happen to be his father.'

"He said: 'Are you really father of William who is arrested? I carry the name because he got arrested. Give him a kiss when you meet him in prison and tell him that I carry his name. The moment he is back I'll give him back his name.'

"Now I get a letter from William once every two or three months. He is in Ramleh prison with five hundred others. His work is to iron clothes. His physical health is improved and his spirit is high even though he has been in prison six years. He fasts from time to time, in one year 180 days. He is a fighting man and will remain a fighting man until his death."

LEILA GEORGE DEEB, Jerusalem: "May I add a few comments about William? I never met him, but I'm quite close to some of the men who were with him in Karameh, and they can talk about nothing but William all the time, and William's dedication. Apparently, he was a terrific teacher while he was in Karameh. He would do anything, you know, spend hours and hours instructing young men how to do certain things. If he had to do it twenty-four hours a day he did. As a matter of fact, one of them had his cap after William was arrested in Jerusalem. He'll keep on wearing the cap . . . . And going around saying: 'This is William's cap, I'm proud to wear William's cap.'"

* * *

The Arabs are known for their rhetoric, which sometimes appears to be a substitute for action. The use of words, as an alternative for deeds, is a human tendency, which can be accentuated by given cultures and in certain sets of circumstances. In the case of the Palestinians, the situation often leaves them little choice. They can do very little about going back, so they talk about going back. On the other hand, the actions of people like William indicate that more and more Palestinians are ready to translate their resolve into action.

This resolve has come gradually with the growing realization that if they didn't fight for their future, no one else would. For a long time they did look to the United Nations, the Big Powers, and Arab governments to do something about their case. When, however, they discovered that they could expect very little help from these sources and when they realized how much time they had lost, they resolved in their hearts to shape their own future. The result was a strong thrust in education and in training for guerilla warfare. At that point also the "armed struggle" became a more likely option.

Chapter 8

The People and the Revolution

"I don't know if the armed struggle is the only way, but so far there is no indication that anything else worked except force. No one will choose violence to arrive at something if he can arrive at it through other means."

— *Shafik Farah*

All the Palestinians desire is to return, or the right to return, to their homeland. They feel themselves a part of "the revolution" and of "the resistance" for their cause. They may even call themselves commandos. The commandos who prepare for, and are engaged in, armed struggle number in the tens of thousands.

Most of the Palestinian people still hope for a peaceful return to their homeland. But their patience is running out. For many years they have waited for Israel, the Arab states, the Big Powers, and the United Nations to arrange for their return in accordance with previous UN resolutions, but to no avail. Increasingly they have been persuaded that violence may be the only way. The debate regarding the best means is far from resolved, although non-violence remains the preferred way. But the question of the return itself is not debatable.

The degree to which "the revolution" has become a popular movement is reflected in the involvement of the artists, the women, the children and, of course, the men.

SAMI EL-KARAMI, statistician: "The non-violent methods are very beautiful and very easy, and we wish we could win with these methods. Our people don't carry machine guns and bombs because they enjoy killing. It is for us the last resort. For twenty-two years we waited for the United Nations and the United States, for liberty, freedom, and democracy. There was no result. So this is our last resort. This is the only way to get back to Palestine. It worked in China, it worked in Cuba, it worked in many other countries, and it is going to work in Palestine. For our part we are willing. And we can. It doesn't cost us much. We are not losing billions of dollars of effort, we are not losing the human manpower, we are not losing anything other than time. And time is on our side. The longer time it takes the easier it will be for us to defeat Israel as well as United States imperialism in that area. We have nothing to lose other than our tents. The only losers will be the ones who throw the atomic bombs because they have everything and we have nothing. That's their problem."

Samir, military camp leader: "I have hope and the will to go back. I am ready to die there. If there is not any hope we have to fight, and we are ready to fight. That is my personal belief. We can stand up to the Israeli military machine. Yes, of course. Why not? They are not more courageous than us. If there are some mistakes in 1967, they will not be repeated again. They have some better organization, some. But not equipment. We have got better than them."

Marwan Abdalla Azam, radio announcer: "Let's take the Zionist movement. That movement had an aim to establish a state by force. This movement and this state were established by force and it can't be met but by force. That we learned by our study of Zionism."

Nimreh Tannous Es-Said, refugee camp director: "In 1967 the Palestinians and especially the new generation realized that none but our own nails could scratch our back. This is an Arabic colloquial proverb. And they started taking the case into their hands, instead of resolving to defeat and despair.

"I don't know where I should start with the Palestine problem. Ever since I was born it has been in my blood. I have had the honour of contributing during the 1948 hostilities, when I thought that there was something to be done and we were really going to achieve something. I joined the resistance movement in 1948 in the hope of liberating the occupied areas which are known now as the state of Israel. But unfortunately I have discovered several loopholes and shortcomings partly due to our disorganization and mistrust and maybe miscalculation of the political arena and situation."

Raja Farraj, businessman: "I think for the first time in Israeli history they feel that people are up in arms and they're fighting. They haven't experienced anybody who fought them. For the first time in their history there are people who are motivated, dedicated, who feel that they have lost their homes."

Said Nasralla, businessman: "What is taken by force will be again taken by force."

Najib Nassar, father of imprisoned commando: "I tell you why they fear the resistance. Because they themselves have experienced it. They know that when they resorted to popular resistance themselves they succeeded in occupying the land, they succeeded in occupying Palestine. So they know how effective popular resistance is because they went through it themselves."

FUAD FARRAJ, engineer: "You must remember one thing, that we've waited almost twenty years for peaceful solutions to come from pacifist nations, the United Nations. What has come? Nothing but more destruction, more ruin, more talk, more helplessness. So the only result of all this is to fight for your rights."

FOUAD YASIN, radio director: "This is our victory and we are not searching for any other victory. Oh never mind, never mind how long it takes, how many souls it will cost. I think when we carry on our struggle we will, of course, lose some of our souls, but I don't think that what we lose through our armed struggle is much more than we lose in the camps. This is why I say never mind what time it will take – or what souls it will cost us. But this is the only way to restore the land and liberate the country.

"I confess that Phantoms and napalm and the huge arms of Israel and America are formidable, but at the same time I believe that they shouldn't frighten us. If any revolutionary power will be afraid in any time or place it will not be successful. You spoke about the jungles and the mountains in Vietnam and there are no jungles and mountains in Palestine now. I think that the first circle in the popular war is the man himself. I don't think that the mountain will fight, or the jungle. The man will fight. If you have mountains and jungles and men don't like fighting, can you make a revolution? Of course not."

AHMED ALI, medical doctor: "I don't think that the armed struggle is the only factor. I think it is one of the factors. Along with other factors it can contribute to a settlement, but by itself I don't think it can do much. It's not easy for the commando. He has to face the Jordanian army leaving. He has to face the Israeli army entering. He has to face the Israeli army going back and the Jordanian army coming in. Four check-points on the way."

NAJLA KANAZEH, homemaker: "The armed struggle is very necessary. There is no other way, I think."

* * *

Karameh is located on the east side of the Jordan to the north of the Allenby Bridge. It was just a small village before 1948, a centre for farmers in the area. When the refugees came from the West Bank, a camp was established, increasing the population considerably. Some say that by 1967 there were more than 60,000 persons at Karameh. The village had become a major agricultural centre, exporting fruits and vegetables directly to Kuwait and other Arab centres. Then came the Israeli attack in March 1968.

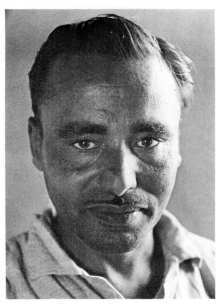

A Bedouin woman tells how
migration patterns of nomadic tribes
are interrupted by new boundaries.

The articulate eyes of a resident
at Baqa'a, Jordan, speak of sadness and hope.

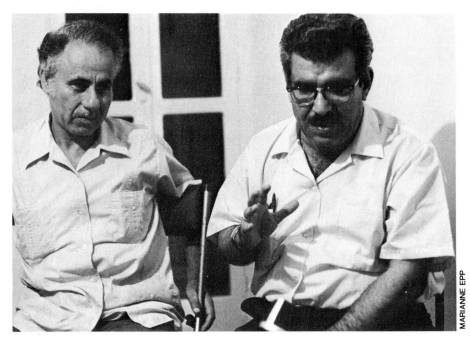

MARIANNE EPP

Giries Kawas and Arabi Awad, two of eight West Bank leaders deported in
1973.

how effective popular resistance is because they went through it themselves."

FUAD FARRAJ, engineer: "You must remember one thing, that we've waited almost twenty years for peaceful solutions to come from pacifist nations, the United Nations. What has come? Nothing but more destruction, more ruin, more talk, more helplessness. So the only result of all this is to fight for your rights."

FOUAD YASIN, radio director: "This is our victory and we are not searching for any other victory. Oh never mind, never mind how long it takes, how many souls it will cost. I think when we carry on our struggle we will, of course, lose some of our souls, but I don't think that what we lose through our armed struggle is much more than we lose in the camps. This is why I say never mind what time it will take – or what souls it will cost us. But this is the only way to restore the land and liberate the country.

"I confess that Phantoms and napalm and the huge arms of Israel and America are formidable, but at the same time I believe that they shouldn't frighten us. If any revolutionary power will be afraid in any time or place it will not be successful. You spoke about the jungles and the mountains in Vietnam and there are no jungles and mountains in Palestine now. I think that the first circle in the popular war is the man himself. I don't think that the mountain will fight, or the jungle. The man will fight. If you have mountains and jungles and men don't like fighting, can you make a revolution? Of course not."

AHMED ALI, medical doctor: "I don't think that the armed struggle is the only factor. I think it is one of the factors. Along with other factors it can contribute to a settlement, but by itself I don't think it can do much. It's not easy for the commando. He has to face the Jordanian army leaving. He has to face the Israeli army entering. He has to face the Israeli army going back and the Jordanian army coming in. Four check-points on the way."

NAJLA KANAZEH, homemaker: "The armed struggle is very necessary. There is no other way, I think."

* * *

Karameh is located on the east side of the Jordan to the north of the Allenby Bridge. It was just a small village before 1948, a centre for farmers in the area. When the refugees came from the West Bank, a camp was established, increasing the population considerably. Some say that by 1967 there were more than 60,000 persons at Karameh. The village had become a major agricultural centre, exporting fruits and vegetables directly to Kuwait and other Arab centres. Then came the Israeli attack in March 1968.

NABEEL A. SHAATH, professor and PLO organizer: "The really happiest moment of my life was definitely the day of Karameh, March 21, 1968, when the Palestinian revolution was truly born. It was the day the Palestinians beat off a twelve-thousand-man Israeli expedition to wipe out the Karameh camp of the Fatah. It was the day that these invaders were repulsed. For the first time liberation was possible, feasible. We were not doomed forever to exile. We were not doomed forever to a life of homelessness. And I think the resistance movement has been since then the greatest thing that has ever happened to my life."

RAJA FARRAJ, businessman: "I think the happiest moment was the birth of the resistance movement, and the manifestation of this birth in Karameh."

MUSA ABU TALEP, tourist guide: "Why do the fedayeen look upon Karameh as a victory? Every year they celebrate Karameh as a victory. Karameh, in Arabic, means dignity. That was the first battle face to face. Really the main battle was between the tanks and artillery. They crossed the river from three main points. But they reached Karameh from one point only and it was a big battle here. In that day the airplanes were useless. The fighting was face to face. You see, they ruined all the city."

AHMED MAZEN, refugee at Allenby Bridge: "I think there is a program to build a new Karameh. There are forty-four units already now. The people are coming back. Are they fearful about coming back? No, no. By the way, they cultivated their land under shelling."

* * *

Accompanying the growth of the resistance movement and often nurturing it has been the revolution in the role of Arab women. Palestinian women have been in the vanguard of this revolution and, having been touched also by the worldwide liberation, they have readily supported the men and occasionally even led them.

RAHAB SELIM, librarian: "The role of the Arab women throughout the Arab world has changed already. And it is changing. The Palestinian women are the vanguard of the women's revolution that is coming to the Arab world. It is true, the Arab woman was not so much in society. She stayed in the home, took care of the children and cooked the meals for her husband. But the Palestinian woman went out to work for her country since the Balfour Declaration. The first thing the women did was to demonstrate against the Declaration and send telegrams to the British government."

144

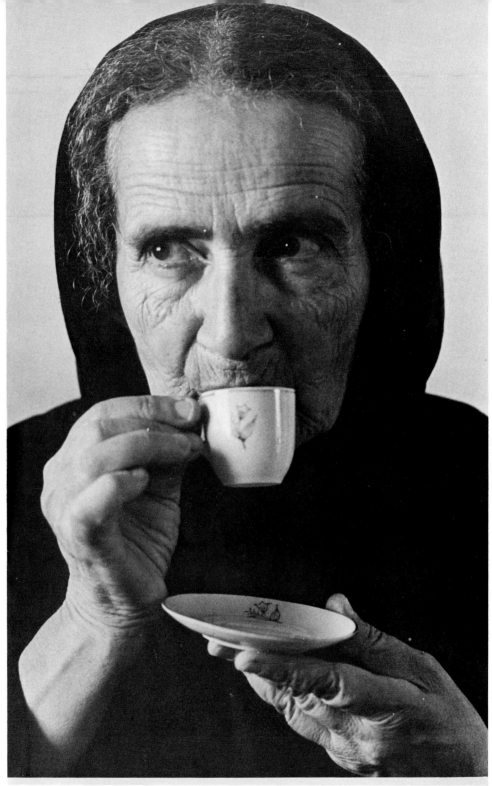

Hajja Amad reflectively sips Arabic coffee during an interview at her hospital in Nablus, West Bank.

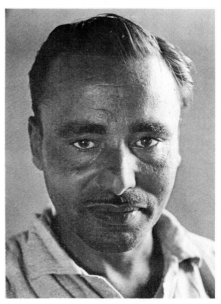

A Bedouin woman tells how
migration patterns of nomadic tribes
are interrupted by new boundaries.

The articulate eyes of a resident
at Baqa'a, Jordan, speak of sadness and hope.

Giries Kawas and Arabi Awad, two of eight West Bank leaders deported in
1973.

Ali Mohammed, now working as a cook in Amman, Jordan, tells of his 1948
flight from Palestine. "I am little man. Big man make decision."

MARIANNE EPP

"I am painting the future," says
Ismail Shamout, an artist in
Lebanon. "How it looks is not clear."

Abu Wasef, the muktar of Surif, a
borderline village on the West Bank,
has no thought of surrender.

An Israeli patrol moves through Rimal Beach refugee camp, Gaza. Of the two occupied territories, Gaza experiences the greater authoritarianism.

A resident at Beach camp, Gaza, gesticulates during a roadside interview. Bitterness and frustration dominate the emotional climate of the Strip.

Karameh, on Jordan River's East Bank, symbolizes Palestinian resistance.
On March 21, 1968, El Fatah commandoes repulsed the Israeli army.

"Life in Jericho is very quiet," says Ibrahim Farbi. During the 1967 June War,
tens of thousands of refugees fled – for the second time.

Left: Each day he visits his grandchildren, orphaned during fighting
in Black September, 1970, between
Palestinians and Jordanians.

"Children of the Palestinian martyrs," offspring of those who died during the
1970 Jordanian civil war, gather for lunch at the orphanage in Amman.

Above: Young Palestinians play ball tag in the narrow streets of Jerusalem's Old City. Ownership of the ancient enclave, surrounded by high stone walls, is still disputed.

Right: Counting the few coins she normally keeps wrapped in a handkerchief within her garments, an elderly woman makes her way through the marketplace of East Jerusalem.

A traditionally garbed woman sells grapes to other Arabs in modern apparel at one of numerous fruit and vegetable stalls found within the old walls of Jerusalem. Though such traditional scenes are still typical, the city is changing rapidly.

Housing for Jewish immigrants rises on the hills overlooking Jerusalem. Judaization of the city is proceeding in various ways.

An Israeli works next to the city walls. "In Jerusalem you should use a toothbrush, not a bulldozer," says Hazim Mamoud El-Khalidi.

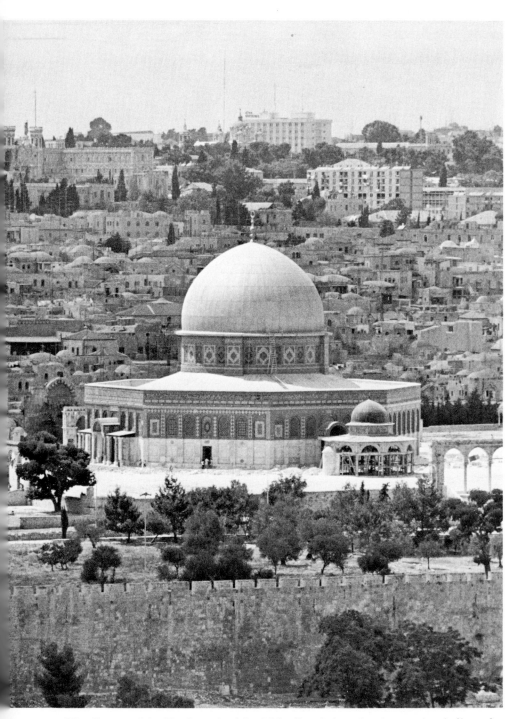

The Dome of the Rock, a cherished Muslim shrine, dominates the skyline of Jerusalem – a religious centre for Muslims, Christians, and Jews.

Left: Kindergarten children at Marka, Jordan, play and sing together during class.

Below: Interrupted from studies at Dekwaneh, Lebanon, a pupil musters a coy grin.

Their classes over and teacher gone, school girls at Baqa'a let loose giggles of excitement and curiousity.

Students at the Woman's Vocational Training Centre in Ramalla, West Bank, practise their craft on each other.

School boys jog during a mid-morning workout in their school yard at Sbeineh camp, a few miles south of Damascus, Syria.

Sewing is one of several home-making skills taught to young camp women in Marka, Jordan. Several other camps offer similar classes.

Despite the ever-present threat of Israeli shelling which flattened the nearby town of Karameh in 1968, farmers return to hoe tomatoes in the arid valley on the Jordan River's East Bank.

ANITA DAMIANI, college teacher: "I won't say that the Palestinian woman has achieved liberation, but she is struggling to be liberated from traditions. I think the role of the women in the Palestinian revolution is one of the most important factors of reform and advancement and improvement in the Arab world. Women form half of the population of any country. And if the woman is backward, she cannot help either her children or her husband in his work. She will be an ignorant mother. She won't have the benefit of education, of cleanliness, of sanitation: all the values that we need to produce a healthy society. And we are, of course, very concerned to build a healthy society. And we are very concerned to build a healthy nation. So what does the woman do? She has to carry on like a man. She lives in the mountains and caves as he does. She leaves home and even puts all thought of marriage aside. This is a very new concept. If she marries, she knows that her husband may die one day and that she will have to look after the family.

"At present I help in the Arab Women's Information Committee in summer, and I am a volunteer receptionist for the Fifth of June Society during the week. The society was founded in Lebanon as the Lebanese and Palestinian women's response to the 1967 June War. It has served mainly as a source of information for foreign journalists, academics, and students. [The Society has since merged with the Arab Women's Information Committee.]

"Every Monday I go there and I talk to many student groups. Lately the Arab Women's Information Committee has a very big campaign for the Gaza refugees. They sent packages of literature all over the world in tremendous quantities, and it was very successful. They got very positive results from Belgium, Sweden, France, U.S.A., South America, India, and Pakistan. The money is being sent to CARE, I think, for the people of Gaza who are suffering without shelter, without food, and without employment."

LEILA GEORGE DEEB, camp administrator: "The most important role for the woman is to bring up a proper generation, a good revolutionary generation. And, therefore, the woman has to be much better prepared mentally, spiritually, socially, and educationally than the man."

REEMA, commando: "The Palestinian woman is now working in factories. She is teaching, she is part of the Red Crescent [known in the West as the Red Cross]. She is a fighter. She has armed weapons. She is in jail also. She has led many demonstrations in Jerusalem and occupied Palestine. She has children."

ISAM ABEDILHADI, exiled women's movement president: "Concerning the women after 1967, they were the first to lead demonstrations asking for

161

withdrawal, rejecting occupation, asking for something. They were the first prisoners. They were the first to ask for strikes. Won't we all be put in jail or be deported? Well, it's all right. We have to endure, because we want back our homes and rights. We have to endure. I was in prison and there were more than five hundred women in all the prisons, inside the occupied territories, and twenty-five of them were deported. I tell you that really our women are taking a very courageous part in the resistance.

"The General Union of Palestine Women was announced as a result of a conference which was held in Jerusalem, June 15-21, 1965. The conference was attended by 140 ladies, representing four women's groups. As a result of that conference our union was announced to mobilize and organize the Palestinian women and prepare for their coming role in the liberation of Palestine. This union has twelve branches in Jordan and in every other host country, and in Europe, too. We have rehabilitation centres here in Jordan and in every other country where Palestinians have been relocated. Through these centres we reach the women inside their camps. We fight illiteracy. We conduct symposiums and seminars. We teach them weaving, knitting, embroidery, and sewing for their future. We teach them first aid and battle aid. We take them to militia training camps and train them in the use of arms."

NIMREH TANNOUS ES-SAID, refugee camp director: "There is no differentiation between a man and a woman. The woman is not a machine for raising children. She can replace the men if they are away. The women's role is becoming more vital than it was before, and this was brought about only through the revolution. When I read that the first commandos in the Israeli prisons were women, I became convinced and proud that there was a Palestine revolution. The woman is becoming an asset and a legend in the resistance for the liberation of the country."

SALWA KHURI OTAQUI, medical doctor: "The Palestinian women really rose to the occasion. In spite of having children, they took jobs and kept the family going for many years until their husbands were able to rehabilitate themselves. I think this story of Palestinian women is something really to be proud of.

"I have something to say about European and Western opinion concerning Arab women. Wherever I've gone they've told me as a woman: you can't be both a doctor and an Arab. You're either a doctor or an Arab. This is the idea. What is the background of this Western idea that Arab women are either riding on a donkey or walking behind her husband who rides the donkey? You know the joke about the difference between the Arab women before and after the world wars. The story goes that she used to walk behind her husband when he rode the donkey. After the war she walked in front of her husband, in front of the donkey, with her husband on the donkey."

ABLA DAJANI, radio announcer: "What are we as Palestinian women doing for the revolution? I am working in the Voice of Palestine radio as a news editor. I am a member of the Palestinian Red Crescent Society and also a member of the Palestinian Women's Union, and through these I serve the revolution. We don't cry in self-pity. There is a woman who lost all of her children, her boys in the Al Fatah. We went to see her and found her crying. She said, 'I am crying because I don't have ten children to give them to the revolution.'"

* * *

The social revolution that is changing the roles of Arab women through elimination of seclusion and illiteracy is strongly stimulated by such educational and vocational training schools as the UNRWA Centre at Ramallah on the occupied West Bank. There, over six hundred teen-age girls, mainly selected from refugee camps, receive education in teaching, various aspects of home-making, business, and medical care. There are nine similar UNRWA centres in other areas serving some thirty thousand refugee boys and girls.

Many children have also been drawn into the movement by their parents or older brothers and sisters, but most of all by the socialization of the camp way of life. Some, but not all, of the elders are supportive of the militarization of the young.

The children have, of course, been born in the camps. (It must be remembered that some families have been in the camps for twenty-eight years – since 1948 – others for nine years – since 1967.) They generally have a happy life. They attend school – not necessarily a well-equipped or well-built school – and play games and laugh like other children.

Both home and school are strong influences. The curriculum is Palestinian, and the families speak constantly of the homeland. So, although the young have never seen it with their own eyes, the idea of Palestine has become fixed in their minds and hearts.

ISAAT G. TANNOUS, diplomat and doctor: "If my grandsons could come to me and say, 'Grandpa, what do you want us to do?' what would I tell them? Just follow my footsteps. Just go and fight for your country. Be good doctors and engineers. Be as good as possible, but always have Palestine as your aim, never give it up."

SAMI SALIM KHOURY, chest surgeon: "It is wonderful to feel that my children, who have hardly seen Palestine, are more Palestinians than myself."

SALEH ABDEL-JEHIL, teenager in orphanage: "My father told me to study, to be nice, and good. After a while, he told me, he will die, and then I must

163

care for my family and work, and give my family some money to live and something like that."

HALDA DAJANI, student: "In a way I am a commando. When they call me to fight, I am going to fight. I am taking training. Most teen-age Palestinian girls feel that way."

GHANEM DAJANI, radio producer: "How do I feel about my daughter going off to fight with the commandos? If she feels so, why not? I don't impose it on her. I don't ask her to do that, but if she feels it, it is her right."

RAHAB SELIM, librarian: "It is my daughter's right to go to her homeland. Our daughters now are politically trained, and we hope that maybe this summer they will get military training. Where? I don't know yet. It depends on where they will send us. We just have to enter her name, and then she waits for her order at any time. She will get her training, wherever they will send her."

ISAM ABEDILHADI, exiled women's movement president: "If it's the only way to regain our rights, it's all right. We have to endure. We have to sacrifice, and we have to offer not only ourselves but our sons and a new generation."

LEILA GEORGE DEEB, camp administrator: "I am proud to see that our children are able to do that. I am only sorry that it is necessary that they should do it. Our children don't have much of a childhood. They don't have toys and things, and even when they play games, they are mostly war games. It is a pity that a child should lose the best years of his childhood on this, but it is necessary. I believe that this is a very good sign for the moment. As one of our songs says, 'I am fighting so that the future generations will reap the wheat.' I think it is very important. And if you come to talk to the children about it you will find that they feel the same."

OTHMAN MAROUF, camp resident: "How many children are on this playground? About a hundred or more. They are playing football, a match about two cups. All are from our Karameh camp. These are the hope of the Palestinian refugees. These will be the people who will reach the sea. The grandfathers and the fathers will die, and the children will reach the sea."

MOHAMMED DARRAJ, camp teenager: "All the Palestinian people are workers. The employees, the children, the women, all the people. They want to fight everywhere, in the mountains, in the cities, and every place, to reach their aim of returning to their homeland which is Palestine, which was abducted by the Israelis."

NAZRI ZANANIRI, administrator: "No, no, no. We don't teach our children like this. Myself, we don't teach it. We don't tell them to fight. We don't show them trouble. We don't try to show them this kind of business. One of my children asked me why we were in Jericho and why we couldn't pass back and forth from that bridge, Arabs here and Arabs there. And I didn't have any answer for him. I said it was not our home right now. He tried to ask me why, and also who are the Jews? I said they are people living in this country. Our neighbours. I don't teach them to fight, no. I don't want them to fight."

HALDA DAJANI, student: "Do I think that age twelve and thirteen is a little too soon to learn the use of weapons? Some of them can handle weapons, some of them can't, physically and emotionally."

KHOUDER ABU TAWFIC, camp resident: "When a child sees his father or mother killed he decides to be a commando."

DALIE SAMI KHOURY, student: "If all of us are killed and only one pregnant woman remains, the resistance will continue."

* * *

The artists, writers and poets are not many. But all seem to have become champions of the resistance and of Palestinian nationalism.

Our meeting with Ismail Shamout in his Beirut apartment, which also serves as his studio, confirmed this. Shamout is one of the foremost artists among the Palestinians. Once a commercial artist, whose prospects of high income were considerable, he offered his talents to become an artist of the revolution after 1967. His paintings illustrate the tragic departure from Palestine, the loss of life by gunfire, thirst, hunger and disease, and the optimism and self-confidence of the resistance movement.

There was a sad but determined look in his eye:

ISMAIL SHAMOUT, artist: "I come from Lydda in Palestine. I was born in 1930. I am from a simple family. My father was a vegetable seller. We used to live a normal life. My father had to work all his life just to build a small home for his sons and daughters to live in. We were seven daughters and sons. In 1948 I was 18 years old. When Lydda was occupied by the Israelis or Zionists, I remember we were at home and we couldn't go out to buy food. The second day they came and took my elder son to work with them. The Israelis assigned him to putting sand in the sacks.

"After three days we were forced to leave the home. At first we thought that an event of the British Mandate was being repeated. I remember 1936-39 when, during the Palestinian revolution, they used to make masses of people to go to one place, a wide place like a big square. Then the British would go through the home and look for weapons. We thought the Israelis were doing the same. That is why we left our home without anything.

"There was a big square in Lydda and thousands of people were crowded together. Then we were surrounded by soldiers and asked to walk in a certain direction. We passed Lydda town in the central part of Lydda. The shops were open. Dead bodies here and there. A very bad smell. Little by little we found that we were leaving town. Nobody could turn back, under threat of being shot. And many were shot. It was July, 1948. When we left, I mean when we found ourselves out of town, it was a very hot, very hot day. I had four brothers and three sisters, one older, and others all younger. They were very thirsty. I found some water. At that moment many people came when they saw the water. Then a jeep with an Israeli officer and two soldiers came. They put a pistol to my head and said to put the water down on the ground.

"Then we went on because soldiers were here and there, until there were no roads. There were just very rough mountains, no trees, nothing, and no water. The people became very tired, especially the old people. Old mothers and fathers were left. Many children were lost. People died of thirst. Then there were some natural wells near Ne'elin where you can find some water but very dirty. Hundreds of people come to that well and they tried to take some of that water. I could drink some. I took it to my mother. My mother was dying of thirst and so were my brothers and sisters. Then I noted the very astonishing thing that my mother didn't care about her sons and her daughters. She was caring just about herself. I mean it was a very bad situation. I saw hundreds of bodies dead from thirst. This was a very horrible day. I remember a man who was responsible for water in Lydda for maybe twenty or twenty-five years. He was the person who had to open the fountains. I remember him lying on the ground and screaming for water. 'I was giving you water for twenty-five years, please drop just enough to wet my lips.' The next morning there were cars and trucks to take us from that place to Ramallah. We were put in a school. We were about sixty persons in one room. We stayed there for two or three weeks.

"I became known as an artist in Gaza strip. Then I decided to go to Cairo to continue studies. I went to Cairo to study art. I used to work and study at the same time until I had an exhibition. My first exhibition was in 1953. Next year I had another exhibition in Cairo. Then I went to Rome and I finished my studies in Rome in 1956 and I came to Lebanon. I worked two years with UNRWA as an artist designer. Then I left UNRWA and I worked on my own exhibitions which I did every year. I have done many exhibitions all over the world. I have done exhibitions in the U.S., England, Soviet Union, Sweden, France, in all the Arab countries. Since 1956 I have been working with PLO as chief of art in the cultural section. My wife also went to Cairo to study art. And we met each other there in 1954 when we had one exhibition. That exhibition was under the patronage of President

Nasser. He opened it himself. And then we married in 1959. We have three nice children.

"Do I consider myself a revolutionary artist? I consider myself a human-being artist, because I don't know what you mean by a revolutionary artist. An artist himself should be a revolutionary. Once you call a man an artist he is a revolutionary. His nature is revolutionary. The artist creates something for his own people. He can see things which not everyone can see. The artist can see things nobody can see. For example, that painting there, I call it *The Way.* I did it in 1964. It shows the determined faces of Palestinians, and hands touching guns. I anticipated the fedayeen movement.

"*The Way* refers to the armed struggle. I believe there is no other way. This I did in 1954. I call it *We Shall Return.* It is, as you see, people who have gone out. It is the story of the Lydda people when they were forced to leave. As you see, there were no young men on that day, only many, many children and old people. The child is asking his grandfather, where are we going? And the grandfather is wondering and just looking back.

"This is a 1953 painting. I call it *Two.* I wanted to express my feelings towards the first stage of tragedy, people being lost in 1948. And I felt that Palestinians were walking in a desert. Even the tree has no roots, no life. The grandfather has to carry his grandson. And they are asking him, where to?

"I call this painting *A Drop of Water.* It is the story of the thirsty on the way from Lydda to Ramallah. In this painting the young man represents myself and this women is my mother and this is my brother and sister here. I brought some dirty water in this little tin. Hundreds of people were running after me.

"Would I lay down my painting brush and pick up the gun? No, because I believe paintings are as strong as the gun. I am painting the future. How it looks is not clear. The only thing that I believe is that there will be no peace in the Middle East unless we Palestinians have back our rights. Looking back in history fifty years, the Palestinians were all the time fighting, suffering, and sacrificing. They don't give up, and I believe they will never give up. Maybe for the time being our situation is not so good, but this doesn't mean that they will give up."

* * *

Arab poets and artists within Israel share Shamout's sentiments. One we met in Haifa remembered Ain Hod, his village near Haifa. It was an Arab village, but in the 1948 War the inhabitants had to abandon their homes, and become refugees scattered all over the neighbouring Arab countries and the surrounding villages. Ain Hod has become a centre of Jewish

painters. Its mosque has been turned into a bar. Isam Abbasi, the Arab
poet, speaks to a Jewish painter living there:

Isam Abbasi, poet:
   "You who supply paints to the canvas,
     Shades that are drunk with secrets
     Inhaled from the shape of a breast, of a thigh
     From the howl of a drunk drenched with wine –

   "Tear, rend your canvas, rip it off the easel;
     Hurl away your colours, smash your brushes to pieces;
     Look beyond your painting; you will see it is the shadows
     Of betrayal and of my shed blood which stain your painting.

   "You think that Ain Hod has inspired you?
     Listen to what you find in the dead of night –
     Whispered echoes in every lane . . . in the dead dust;
     Listen to the voice of your own conscience – you will shiver.

   "What you feel quaking beneath the foundations of your house
     Is the ghosts, is the souls that sloughed their flesh
     And left their bodies beyond the barred borders,
     While you are drinking from the heart, from the spring of Hod.

   "You say, 'my hope.' Ah! this house was built
     With the blood of those now scattered – and for them.
     Can you feel at ease, does your painting come to you easy
     While they are seared with longing for their home?

   "Have the walls not told you the pure truth,
     Have the flowers not exhaled their innate smell,
     Can you happily dwell in the refugee's home,
     While his bread is nothing but memories?

   "Getting drunk on the prayer mat in the mosque,
     In front of the pulpit, where the man used to preach,
     Were you suddenly startled by the holiness
     Or did you just pass out because you were drunk?

   "I wish you the ability to put on your canvas
     A creation that would tell anyone who sees it the truth;
     A creation that would put the deceiver to shame,
     A creation that would win your honour."

* * *

The peaceful, non-violent way of return remains the preferred one. But
because the UN, while in a position to assist their return, has not acted,

Palestinians are becoming impatient and reluctantly reaching for the gun. Even so, they say with Yasir Arafat the closing lines he used before the UN General Assembly in 1974: "I come, bearing both a freedom fighter's gun and an olive branch. Do not let the olive branch fall from my hand." Among those who are still resisting the gun is a West Bank mayor, who believes that the non-violent way can succeed:

FARAH AL-ARAJ, mayor: "The young people now say that those who attended the Jericho [annexation] convention of 1949 did not represent the Palestinians. In that time and in those circumstances it didn't seem so. There had to be an authority and an army to keep law and order. A lot of Palestinians were crossing as refugees. Most difficult time was in 1948. I was in favour of accepting the partition, but the extremists overpowered moderates by the gun. If we had accepted partition, we wouldn't have suffered and lost the land. We [Jews and Arabs] were all Palestinians, bearing the same British passport.

"Yes, I feel that I am having success. There are hundreds of thousands of workers who work in Israel. I haven't heard of a single accident or bomb. This proves that if the people are treated in their work by the same standards the Arabs will not turn to violence. The majority of workers want adequate work for adequate pay and they don't think about political problems.

"Some people don't like my policy of openness and candour. We have tried to solve the problem the old way. We need a new and advanced way. We have tried negativism and violence. My way is positive. I try the peaceful method and peaceful ways. The Jews in the last two thousand years, because of persecution and pogroms, have become very suspicious of all gentiles. Any little word makes them more suspicious. We should prove that we have a right and that we don't want to kill them or throw them to the fish in the sea. The peaceful way may be the better way. Violence brings violence. Bloodshed brings bloodshed."

ABU-JAWAD, commando officer:
Q. "You know it is hard for me to imagine you Palestinians as fighters?"
A. "Why?"
Q. "Because when we look into your eyes, into your homes, and into your villages we see kindness, gentleness, humanity, hospitality and . . . "
A. "We of course don't like war. What we like is to keep the peace. But we are forced to fight. We were thrown out of our country. We have been scattered for more than twenty-three years. We are forced to fight. Of course, the characteristics that you mention are simply the way we were brought up. Our people were living there in peace. They welcomed all sorts of immigrants and refugees from all parts of the world. Armenian

169

refugees that fled from the Turkish fight came to Palestine looking for refuge there. Even Jews from all parts of the world came to Palestine to live together with us in Palestine. And we Arabs are famous for our hospitality. The price we had to pay for all this hospitality was being kicked from our land, from our villages. We have to fight, and we even have to train our little kids to take arms when they grow up and to take the responsibility of continuing our fight."

Q. "I was in Karameh camp last year. The children were all in their uniforms. This afternoon we were there for about fifteen minutes and they were playing football. It seemed much nicer for children to play football than for children to play at war."

A. "That is in the case of peace. We are now in the case of war and everybody has to fight. We mobilize all our people, children, women, men, and even old folks. Of course, our children now have to go to school, to continue their education, and altogether they have started themselves to continue our fighting and to continue our war of liberation."

SAMI SALIM KHOURY, chest surgeon: "I don't want to hate the Jews or the Zionists as much as they want me to hate them. I don't like to, I am a Christian. I am quite convinced of my Christian background, of my spiritual calling. I always believed that we Christians, we Arabs, are witnesses to Christ. I always wanted to live up to that spiritual teaching but I just can't understand. I just can't see so much inhumanity. I have seen so much of it. I worked in the Augusta Victoria hospital in Jerusalem for eight years. I have seen what is the meaning of suffering. I have seen what is the meaning of malnutrition among refugees.

"I attended a good bit of the fighting as a doctor in 1946 when it started between Zionists and the British forces who were trying to keep peace between both Arabs and Jews. I have seen a good bit of it during my lifetime. I used to treat the Jewish terrorists. I treated terrorists also in Haifa, Jewish terrorists. Actually Mayor Feinstein was one of the terrorists who threw a bomb in the Jerusalem railway station. He was brought into the government hospital where I was working, and had I closed my eyes five minutes he would have died. He was very upset because I did not call a Jewish doctor for him. He did not want me to take care of him. He threw the bomb at the railway station which killed forty-five Arabs. I must say I look back now with great happiness that I have done my bit for the Jews, the Zionists. In my profession we do not discriminate at all. I told you before, I saved the life of a Jewish terrorist. I would save the life of anybody. We treated army soldiers. We treated commandos. We treat anybody who comes to us."

SAMIR, military camp leader: "Yes, God said we should love our enemies.

And we should pray for those who persecute, turn the cheek to those who hit, and walk a second mile for those who compel. It's when you are in your land you do it. But we are not in our land. You have been in our land and you know how we are treated. Our boys are in prisons. Shall we give them more boys to put in prison? Shall we give them more land and more of us live in refugee camps?"

GEORGES KHODR, church bishop: "The Palestinians need a Martin Luther King. A bishop can be Martin Luther King of the Arabs, only after he has preached the love of Palestine. I think that maybe the emergence of this superior approach is just around the corner. The Palestinians will discover it themselves. After they are defeated by the other Arabs, after they are persecuted by the Arabs, they will have to choose their own way, which will be different."

NAZRI ZANANIRI, administrator: "My idea is that everybody should go walk down the bridge, and sit there without food and without water and wait for the bridge to open. And the people would all go back to their homes without any trouble. And this is my feeling. We should do it. All Palestinians. We should go down and wait until we have the chance and then maybe somebody could feel with us. But as long as we are sitting here in camps, getting flour from here, getting bundles of clothing from there, getting self-help from there, it is not going to help us."

SHAFIK FARAH, education director: "I am not a pacifist. I don't like war, but I have not made up my mind whether war is justified or not."

NAJIB, commando: "We are still a very peaceful people, and believe me when we kill we kill with a lot of misery, hating ourselves for killing. We are peaceful. We have been living with the Jews for two thousand years in peace and we are determined to live with them for four thousand years more in peace if they choose to."

GEFFHAH NIGA, needlework lady: "I hope we can go back easy without war."

GAMIL SAYEGH, chauffeur: "We hate to see bloodshed. We want to have an abiding peace. It is safer for the Jews to share the land with its inhabitants."

EMIL SAFIEH, accountant: "Peace will come when we will have left and only the Jews are here. Then they will fight among each other."

BISHOP CUBA'IN, church bishop: "You see, my conception of peace may differ to the common understanding of it. In my opinion, peace emerges from the heart. Unless you have peace in your heart, peace of conviction, peace of thinking, and peace of mind, then you are a disturbed human being. This is the first thing we should work for is to create this peace in the heart of the individual. Now if you are referring to the Arab states, I wouldn't say there is no peace. I would say there is no deep understanding and there is no deep confidence between the authorities and the people. There is in the Middle East, as there is all over the world, a sort of revolution in their thinking, in their aspiration, and what they are doing now is to help their country internally and locally to be organized."

HIKMAT, needlework lady: "One has to look calmly at the situation and smile."

* * *

Since 1973 the question has often been asked in the West: Does the PLO represent the majority of the people? These pages contain the answer.

Chapter 9

About Enemies and Friends

"First we blame the British, then the United Nations and the Americans, and lastly we blame the Jews and also the Arabs, including ourselves."

— *Abbra Jabboud*

During their time of trouble from 1948 on, the Palestinians have had more enemies than friends. Only recently, and more particularly since the October War of 1973, has the world community given them a hearing. Their admission to the United Nations General Assembly debate on the Palestine question in the fall of 1974 was a high-water mark of recognition, friendship, and a decent hearing. More often than not, however, their tribulation has been increased by the scheming of the big powers, by the failure of the United Nations to implement its resolutions, and by the effects of rivalries and power plays among Arab nations on the fragmented world of the Palestinians.

The Palestinians tend to feel that all the states involved in the Middle East have been against them at one time or another. Rightly or wrongly, they believe that governments *per se* are against them. This feeling arises, first of all, from the way the Middle East conflict is delineated. For them it is defined too often in terms of power rivalries rather than of human rights. The interests of governments rather than the needs of the people are constantly pushed into the foreground of international thinking by the mass media and by the states themselves. Thus, peace is seen coming to the Middle East if and when the super powers reach an understanding on spheres of influence, or if and when the Suez Canal is reopened (as it now has been), or if and when Israel and the Arab states agree on the boundaries between them, or if and when the future of Jerusalem is internationally decided.

Obviously, all of these factors are ingredients in a permanent peace, but to the Palestinians they are not its fundamental requirements, because they overlook the basic cause of the conflict. Underneath the conflicts between the super powers, and between Israel and the Arab states is the struggle of two peoples, the Israeli Jews and the Palestinian Arabs, for the same parcel of land. All who fail to acknowledge this fundamental fact are enemies of the Palestinians. All who remember it are their friends – be they

Russians, Chinese, Americans, or Egyptian, Syrian, Lebanese, Jordanian or Libyan Arabs. Or Jews. At least some Palestinians believe that a democratic coexistence of Arabs and Jews in a secular state remains an option.

As quick as they may be to blame the rest of the world for their plight, the Palestinians recognize that they themselves have occasionally played into the hands of their enemies. Naïveté, lack of political maturity, inadequate organization, weak leadership, and disunity have been major handicaps, all of which they can justify from history, but not all of which they can easily excuse.

ALBERT HADAWI, Canada*: "No, we weren't asleep when the British and the UN gave our land away. But the Arabs unfortunately have one very, very, very detrimental characteristic, and that is that they are extremely religious. They believe in their holy book and they also believed in the goodness of man. They put their faith and trust in humanity that nobody could do what was done to them. And I think we were duped several times into believing that Israel wasn't going to be created, because many commissions came over and reiterated and stipulated time and time again that the intention was not to create a Jewish state in Palestine but merely a home for refugees."

AHMED ALI, Lebanon: "The Arabs have made mistakes. They have played into Israeli hands all these years. Repeatedly, repeatedly. And I believe they are still doing that, unfortunately. The Arab mind is simple. I think the major factor in the problem of Palestine is the Arabs' simple mentality facing the sophisticated technically minded European mentality which is Zionism. We are not up to their methods. We can be taken by a good word, by a smile, and they are different. They have been planning and thinking for such a long time, and I am sorry to say, though we have improved, we are not up to the standard that we can face them or use their own methods.

"The Arabs tend to oversell themselves to the world. This in my humble belief is one reason why the commando movement has failed. They lost control over themselves."

SAID NASRALLA, Lebanon: "The Arabs made a lot of mistakes; yes they did. They were not organized, and before the British Mandate we had the Turkish rule here for four hundred years. They were ignorant during the Turkish rule."

ANITA DAMIANI, Lebanon: "We were deceived by ignorance, naïveté. We were under the British Mandate. We didn't have our own army in Palestine. We didn't have our own newspaper. We were politically immature."

* In this chapter, place names indicate location at time of interview.

LILY GUMRI, Lebanon: "I think we are a very stupid people, and, as you see, we argue about everything."

LEILA BITAR, Jordan: "The Arabs became dependent on others; they should have depended on themselves right from the beginning."

LEILA GEORGE DEEB, Jordan: "Well, I wouldn't say we're stupid. I think we're naïve or just good-hearted, too good, as a matter of fact."

FUAD FARRAJ, Jordan: "Maybe the Palestinians have been too much orientalists and sentimentalists and not very pragmatic in dealing with their own problems. Now, after twenty-nine years, the Palestinians are becoming more pragmatic, and they believe now that if power is the only language that the Western world understands, they will have to use it."

GEORGE GIACAMAN, Occupied Palestine: "The Palestinians and Arabs before 1967 did not give enough attention to public opinion."

SHAKIB A. OTAQUI, Occupied Palestine: "I was saying to a friend of mine the other day: the Russians are the wrong thing in the Middle East. They shouldn't send all these weapons. (We were talking humorously, of course.) They should really send us a hundred million pieces of sticky tape to cover the Arabs' mouths."

ISSAT G. TANNOUS, Lebanon: "The mistakes the Arabs made? I don't know whether they are mistakes or not. We were not up to it yet to do the right thing. When England came in 1918, the country had been under Ottoman rule for four hundred years. So we wanted people to come and civilize us. That is why, when the British came, we welcomed them. But, we found that they were not really interested so much in the people as in making a national home for the Jews there. So our mistake was a lack of foresight. We never thought that the West would go so much with the Zionists. Why did they have mandates? They had the mandates so that better, more educated countries could come and teach people who are not up to that mark."

* * *

The Palestinian incriminations against themselves extend to other Arabs and to Arab governments, although a feeling of partnership and unity has come to replace the old enmity. Again, the October War of 1973 and the Arab summit conference which followed in Morocco a year later symbolize the changing situation. But it remains true that more Palestinians have lost their lives in clashes with Jordan in 1970-71, and in the Lebanese Civil War in 1975, than in the armed struggle against Israel. The experience of the bitter and bloody clashes in Jordan is partly reflected in the following comments:

ANITA DAMIANI, Lebanon: "The Arab governments let us down. Definitely."

DALIE SAMI KHOURY, Jordan: "People are always better than their governments. The people are not usually the government. People are people and the government is the government. Most people don't know anything about what is happening."

WADIE GUMRI, Lebanon: "And why our stupid Arab governments don't demolish all their equipment here, I don't know."

ALBERT HADAWI, Canada: "All I can say is that if I were in charge of those countries that do have the oil, I would use it, use its whole force. Our governments, as far as I am concerned, are feudal semi-dictatorships."

HAZIM MAHMOUD EL-KHALIDI, Occupied Palestine: "Well, the oil is in the Middle East. Someone had to find it, and market it, and consume it. It so happened that the people who most required it and were able to consume it were in the West. And this being business, like any other business, the stronger party exploited the weaker party, until the weaker party was more aware of its rights. In the past few years the Arab countries have been getting a far better bargain, commercially at least, than they were getting fifteen years ago."

KHALED MOUAMMAR, Canada: "The Palestinians do not intend to occupy Jordan. Their land is Palestine. Their enemy is Israel. They have been forced into this conflict with the Jordanian regime."

SAMI EL-KARAMI, Canada: "Arab capitalists are our enemies as much as the Zionist organization. They are all enemies. We don't rank them one by one other than in terms of who is killing more than others. Sadat can be classified as an enemy in the long run, but he is an ally now rather than an enemy. All these regimes are living for the interest of the classes which they represent. I would like to see all that oil nationalized and run by the people themselves in their interest: to fight hunger, to fight disease, and to build more universities and industry and to bring the whole economy up."

ABU-JAWAD, Lebanon: "We now consider the Jordanian regime to be our enemy as much as the Israeli army. We have to fight on both fronts, because Jordan is one of our basic places, and 70 per cent of our people live there. This does not mean that we want to form a Palestinian state in Jordan. We simply want to have a national Jordanian government support our revolution."

NABEEL A. SHAATH, Lebanon: "You find that most of the bachelor's degrees are earned in Egypt, because Egypt has from the very beginning offered the

Palestinians free education, and that amounts to a large percentage of university graduates. Egypt has, politically at least, been a little aloof, but in all fairness, the Egyptians have made many contributions towards the education of the Palestinians. Most graduate work has been in America and in three countries of Europe: England, Germany, and Austria."

FAIZEH SAKKIJHA, Jordan: "We don't want Jordan. We want our Palestine back. We don't want Jordan, it's not our country. We don't care for him or for his throne or anything. We are here as visitors, that's all. We are here as refugees."

NAJIB, Lebanon: "If the Hashemite Kingdom chooses to stand in the way of the will of our people, then it has to go. It chooses to go. We have no plans, no plans whatsoever to rule one single inch of Jordan. Our aim is to liberate Palestine and to found a democratic non-sectarian state. I repeat, we have no aims in Jordan except to defend our backs, and we leave that to the Jordanian vanguard.

"A government that chooses to be the enemy of the Palestinians will be like Israel to us sooner or later. And as a Palestinian, aside from being a Fatah member, I advise every Arab government to reconsider and recalculate everything he is trying to do anew for we have patience, great patience. We were taught patience by the Zionists themselves, and we know how they work. We can be patient, but not with the Arabs. We can be patient with the Zionists but not with the Arabs because they should be in our own trench fighting against the same enemy."

* * *

The proverbial disunity in the Arab world can be understood in its historical perspective. Tribalism and clan wars go back to ancient times; frequent conquest by imperial powers was usually based on dividing the local peoples, and maintaining control by keeping them divided. Four hundred years of Turkish rule sapped Arab energies, and discouraged Arab initiative. The new Arab nations became independent only after the Second World War, and when one considers the problems – like war and population pressures – that beset them the disunity is not too surprising. Indeed, that they achieved as much unity as they did in the 1973-75 period is something of a miracle. In the comments that follow, the Palestinians reflect on both the persistence of disunity and the signs that it is being overcome by a feeling of oneness in the Arab nation:

KHALED MOUAMMAR, Canada: "It is true, that the Arab world in general and the Palestinians in particular are divided, but we should not always despair of these things. This situation exists in every underdeveloped country. Underdeveloped countries are like that. It is hard for them to have the organizational structure and the disciplines that exist in the West because of the status under which they have lived for the last four hundred years. The Arab masses are united in feeling, and I think the Palestinians have dominated the politics of the Arab countries since 1948. The Palestinians have been the leading intellectuals and driving force behind all the Arab parties which appeared on the scene, asking for Arab unity, Arab progress, and socialism."

ABU-JAWAD, Lebanon: "Today we have complete unity in the military fields. Of course, there are some differences concerning ideologies. Ideologically speaking, Fatah is a national liberation movement that believes in national unity of all the people and all the masses, while other organizations have various different ideologies."

NABEEL A. SHAATH, Lebanon: "Not just the formal education but also the process of socialization in exile brings about differences in mentalities. The Palestinians have been in exile for twenty-three years and the new generation has come. It identified itself at one time with the exile area in which the people were living. This in a way accounts for some of the reasons why Palestinians have not been able to unite their ranks as easily as one would have wished. But I am optimistic about Palestinian unity. I have worked a lot through my participation in the Palestine planning centre and the Palestine National Congress. In helping out with the unity plans, I have seen it develop and gradually progress, so I am confident."

MARWAN ABDALLA AZAM, Lebanon: "The time will come for unity between the governments of the Arabs. We ask God to keep them and to group them into one government."

NIMREH TANNOUS ES-SAID, Jordan: "The people in the Arab world are united. Their aspirations, their hopes, their problems are all alike."

MUNZEV, Occupied Palestine: "We Arabs are famous for our differences, but their [the Israeli] contradictions exceed ours."

HAZIM MAHMOUD EL-KHALIDI, Occupied Palestine: "The source of disunity amongst the Arabs can be traced back to the long colonial rule of the Ottomans followed by European colonial rule. They can be traced back to avariciousness in certain persons and self-interest in the richer countries or certain Arab states. Some of the states were manufactured for former colonial powers to hold to as their offices. Perhaps it is similar to certain vested interests in the history of the United States when new states were reluctant to join the federal government. This happened in Texas. It happened in California at the beginning. But later on when they were convinced that unity makes a stronger nation and that unity would be more beneficial for the average persons, federation came. My people are not going to be always poor and ignorant and governed by others. It may take time, but ultimately I believe the Arab people will unite."

AHMED ALI, Lebanon: "I think the Palestinians should now have a lesson. They should gather the educated leaders among them to take more active part in the whole problem. So far the educated élite have not been taking active part in the whole problem. Some of them have tried. I hope now that the commando leadership has learned a lesson and that they can get together with the educated leaders. To me, throwing Israel into the sea is nonsense."

ABU ALWALID, Lebanon: "We have suffered much from disunity, but we are finding our unity."

FARAH AL-ARAJ, Occupied Palestine: "We are looking forward to the unity of the whole Arab world. It is important that the Palestinian feels free. First step of unity comes with Jordan with whom we have open bridges. Any future status should be on an equal basis, without regard to clan, family, or religion."

* * *

Leadership in the Arab world is assessed in terms of Arab unity and in terms of a united opposition to Israel. The late President Nasser of Egypt in many ways symbolized the greatness and aspirations of all the Arab peoples. But depending too much on a single individual has its drawbacks, and for this reason the Palestinians want diffuse leadership, with everybody assuming responsibility.

GAMAL EL-SOURANY, Egypt: "Arabs are proud that they are Arabs. They have an old civilization. They are part of the world heritage and part of the world history, and Abdel Nasser came to materialize their ambitions. The problem was that Abdel Nasser was far more ambitious than his possibilities. This is the problem of Nasser. He was always not looking from an Egyptian point of view. He was always looking from an Arab point of view. Nasser was the symbol of the Arab future. The symbol of Arab pride. The symbol of Arab inventiveness; the symbol for Arab freedom. The symbol for Arab unity. This is Abdel Nasser."

KHALED MOUAMMAR, Canada: "He was an Arab, he was a nationalist, he was a liberal. He was looking for the welfare of the Arab people. And that's why the Arab people everywhere looked to him as their hero. Even in Africa they call him the father of Africa. He was one of those who implemented the non-aligned bloc in the world. He was for the African Unity Organization.

"No, we have no single leader. We never want that to happen. The moment that we have a person who becomes indispensable, we have really lost our ability to mobilize our people, to make them participate each and individually. We don't want Yasir Arafat to be indispensable the same way that Nasser was indispensable to the Egyptian people. We want every Palestinian to carry the banner for this struggle against Zionism."

SAMIR, Syria: "Nasser was the hero for the whole Arab nation. Sadat, even if he is very clever, will not take the place of President Nasser. He is doing his best just to fill the vacuum left by Nasser. But I don't think that he will fill it. He is trying and we hope that he will be as Mr. Nasser was before."

SAMI SALIM KHOURY, Jordan: "I think Sadat is a little bit wiser. Sadat – and this is what probably is upsetting Israel – is playing their game. He is telling them, now I want peace. Now they are trying to create all the pretexts to try to avoid what Sadat is offering."

YOUNES ZIGADEH, Jordan: "The Arab world is not necessarily waiting for another Nasser, but a new leader who can replace that big personality of Nasser. It is not easy for anyone to occupy the place that he left behind him. To the Arabs as a whole he was the only personality who could achieve."

ISSAT AL-ATAWNEH, Occupied Palestine: "I believe that late Gamal Abdel Nasser was working for peace, and I wish the Jewish authorities were wise enough and human enough to cooperate with Gamal Abdel Nasser."

* * *

The Palestinians speak freely of the role of the super powers in the Middle East. What comes through is a clear differentiation between the people of America, for instance, and the American government. American people, values, and social institutions are generally appreciated, but there is a great dislike for the policies of the American government. Most include Canada in "America," but some Palestinians recognize a clear difference:

AN ARAB IN ISRAEL, Israel: "America? – A country you feel obliged to respect and obliged to pity. Who wants Russia and who wants communism? How can one believe that the world of Jefferson, Washington, and Lincoln is committing such funny mistakes?"

ELIAS FREIJ, Occupied Palestine: "I'm sorry to say that America has never had any successful policy for any place. They blundered in Korea, North Vietnam, Japan, Europe, everywhere. What has America gained in Vietnam? We Arabs have never done anything wrong to America."

JABRA ABBASSI, Occupied Palestine: "If the American government told

Israel: Go away from Gaza, he would go now. But Americans give him Phantom, give him Sky Hawk, give him everything. American people are all right. American government is no good because American government give guns, give airplanes, give everything to Israel."

SAID NASRALLA, Lebanon: "I think the Americans could put more pressure on Israel and this matter would be solved. They could if they wanted to."

NE'MEH SIMA'AN, Jordan: "The whole regime in the U.S. is a problem. Every four years the whole world is worried about the new elections because now America is the leader of the Western powers. But if this leader is a good leader the whole Western power will benefit and if not, the whole Western world will suffer."

HIKMAT, Occupied Palestine: "No peace except you change ideas of Western world."

SAMI SAYEGH, Jordan: "Russia, America, France, they like the fight and they like the war. All countries, they like this. If no fighting in Vietnam, if no fighting in Palestine, they have no factories."

MONSOUR KARDOSH, Israel: "Not the Christians. It's the class which rules. The white-Anglo-Protestant Americans. The banks, the heavy industry, the whole machine, the Pentagon establishment is composed of WASPS."

WADIE GUMRI, Lebanon: "I don't want to smoke American cigarettes. Yet we are buying everything from them, they have such big markets. And they are working against us to ruin us."

ABU-JAWAD, Lebanon: "There are large numbers of Americans who support us, and we consider them to be our friends; same thing applies to the Russians."

RHOUI EL-KHATIB, Jordan: "I have been observing that Canada is trying its best to be a neutral element, helping the refugees through its contributions and also Arab countries through the selling of wheat. Canada has also not recognized the annexation of Jerusalem. In addition Canada has embraced thousands of the Arabs in its country, offering them free opportunities to live and to serve their own country without any interruption."

KHALED MOUAMMAR, Canada: "Discrimination is something that I think a Palestinian cannot escape from, if you mean by discrimination a slanderous attack on the character of a Palestinian or Arab. The first thing that I noticed here in Canada is the barrage of lies, of prefabrication, of character assassination. According to the cartoons, you know, Arabs are barbarians. We are organized in Canada, but not if you mean a Zionist-type organization. We'll never match that. We have our local groups in cities.

No, we have nothing to match the Jewish Defence League. First of all, we never thought that we should use this approach in Canada. We cannot resort to any activity which can be used as a pretext by the Zionists to clobber us, because we cannot go to court and defend our people. We don't have financial resources or lawyers who will come to our help, or newspapers who will come to our help. So we are very careful to be law-abiding in Canada."

SAMI EL-KARAMI, Canada: "I already applied to be a Canadian citizen and was refused. The reasons are not supposed to be publicized according to the official letter from the minister. I believe I was rejected as a citizen because of my ideas and activity, because of my outspoken criticism of Israel, of Zionist and American policies in the Middle East. It is as simple as that. I never participated in any violent demonstrations or in any stone-throwing at the American Embassy or anything which could be classified under the Criminal Code. So I cannot see any reason whatsoever why I should be rejected."

ELIAS BANDEK, Occupied Palestine: "I feel all respect for Mr. Trudeau. He understands not only Canadian problems but the universal problems."

FAOUD SAID, Lebanon: "The wealthy businessman in North America owes quite a bit of his wealth to this part of the world. He has tremendous interest in this part of the world and those material interests he should not jeopardize. The Arabs have been very good customers and have nothing special against the Americans. The average good American is admired by the Arabs. Our impression of the good American is the impression that we have developed over a hundred years ago. They came to establish the American University of Beirut in the face of all risks, dangers, and deprivations. They came out all the way for no ulterior motive whatsoever except to serve the cause of Christ and to serve humanity. They did a brilliant job and everybody in the Arab world is so indebted to that institution. It is a pity that politics have changed that aspect now and people don't feel that way about the missionaries who were dedicated and fine people, who had no ulterior motives except to serve the cause of Christ."

* * *

With respect to the U.S.S.R. the reverse is true. The Soviet people are less known and so are their institutions, but Soviet policies vis-á-vis the Middle East are viewed with favour. The basic conflicts between Arab religion and communist ideology are recognized, but so desperate have the Arabs been for international friends that a marriage of convenience was not ruled incompatible because of ideological differences. Within Israel, Palestinians have found their most satisfactory political expression and their happiest association with Israelis in the context of the Communist Party. That was about the only place where the we/they relationship disappeared and where both Arabs and Jews recognized each other as human beings.

AHMED ALI, Lebanon: "I think the feelings toward the Russians are feelings of friendship by necessity. We have no choice. By the nature of our religion, we are antagonistic to communism. We are basically pro-American and anti-communist, but our friendship with communist Russia and with China is beneficial."

WADIE GUMRI, Lebanon: "But please don't misunderstand. We are not pro-Russian. If you come all over the Middle East you don't see anybody who speaks Russian. We are not pro-Russian. But the Americans are pushing us. They are pushing us to the Russians. We have no other alternatives."

SAMI SALIM KHOURY, Jordan: "Russia is much cleverer than America. Russia is getting into the country in a very sure way, among the people and among the refugees, of course. Russia is not naïve. In Russia they are playing the game exactly as the Zionists are playing it. What I am afraid of is that the time might come when only Zionists and Russians will laugh, not Americans or the Arabs. They will laugh in the end."

MUHAMMAD ALAZEH, Jordan: "Churchill has said that you have to make friends even with the devil if you think he will help you out or stand and back you."

NE'MEH SIMA'AN, Jordan: "We can never be for communism. We never can stand for the communists. Injustice is throwing the population into the hands of communism."

KHALIL ABDELHADI, Occupied Palestine: "Russians are rushing in now with their ideas of communism. In spite of our need for help, we are not taking to communism. We are not for communism because we are believers. We believe in God, we believe in the prophets. We believe in all these things."

ELIAS FREIJ, Occupied Palestine: "The Arabs are one of the most religious people there are. If they can look to Russia or to China, it is out of desperation. They are always looking to the West for help. Now the West is not extending any help to the Arabs. When we are in such a situation, where will we go?"

AHMED FARIAH, Occupied Palestine: "We like communists. Not, not because I am communist. No. Because communists help me to fight my enemy."

NAJLA KANAZEH, Lebanon: "Am I a communist myself? No. But I'm for socialism. I think socialism solves the problem of the Middle East, if it does not solve the problems of the whole world. The only party which is not a Zionist party in Israel is the Communist Party."

IBRAHIM SAMA'AN, Israel: "I went to a Baptist school in Nazareth. Then I was in the communist movement, not in the party itself because I was too young for that. Then a collision took place in my personality. When I had a meeting of the Communist Party I had to go, and then one time there was a meeting and I wanted to go to church, not because I was too religious but because it was a feast. When I went back to the communist meeting they told me, 'Listen this is your church. We have a meeting here.' I said, 'Then I will make up my mind and decide where my church is.'

"After about a year of questioning and arguments with the Baptist personnel in Nazareth, I reached the conclusion that I did not like the Greek Orthodox Church of my father. If I wanted to take religion, for sure I wouldn't take that, bowing before pictures of saints and doing all kinds of things which are not biblical according to my present ideology. So I decided to change. And in the East it's not so easy to change really because changing your religious ideas sounds more or less as if you are a traitor, or as if you are changing your nationality. You are born into your own religion and you cannot choose it for yourself. It wasn't quite easy for me to decide but I did it. It was in 1956 that I became a Baptist.

"It appears to me sometimes that Christianity and communism have many things in common, because the first commune was the commune of the disciples. And to me it sounds sometimes that communism is a kind of Christianity without Christ. That's how it is in my books. So, the choice of the church did not necessarily mean the complete rejection of the other ideas. I joined another political party in which I'm still a member and that's the Mapam Party. It's Marxist, socialist. But in this party I feel more freedom to be a Christian and more freedom to be a politician because they, in Mapam, deserted the struggle between religion and politics long time ago. So in my political activities, I'm an individual like anybody else and I don't try to mix religion with it. In my church work I don't try to mix it up with my political ideas. That helps me to take from both sides, politics and religion, the positive human approach, the improvement of Arab-Jewish relations in the country."

EMILE TOUMA, Haifa: "I got my Ph.D. in the Soviet Union in 1967. I wrote a thesis on Arab unity, which I hope will be published. To tell you the truth, I joined the Communist Party intellectually. Economically speaking or financially speaking I was well off. My father could afford to send me to Cambridge. That is to say, I did not feel the pressure of class motivation. I came to the party intellectually. You see the Communist Party is the only party capable of leading this country, Israel, towards its independence. It was the only party you see which actually had a democratic platform. All the parties in Israel or before in Palestine were national parties, whether among the Arabs or among the Jews. I mean all, all the parties in the Jewish sector were Jewish parties, specifically Jewish. And the Communist Party was the only party you see which in fact organized Jews and Arabs together, although it was illegal and persecuted. Nevertheless they were able to work. Their influence was not great among the Jewish population, neither was it great among the Arab population.

"In 1942, for the first time, the communists were able to work legally. In fact our paper *Lit Had* was published during this period. It was not then the organ of the Communist Party, neither was it the organ officially of the communist movement; it was really the Arab organ of the communists. During the crucial year 1947, when the United Nations was discussing the problem of Palestine, I felt that the best solution was the establishment of a Palestine democratic state. In fact during that period we met the Arab leadership, and we insisted that they be willing to establish a Palestine democratic state.

"But this leadership was corrupt; the British had great influence and the Americans also had their men. The Arab leaders called for an Arab Palestine, which would give rights only to those Jews who were in this country in 1917. It was a most stupid and foolish approach, you see, to suggest this in the twentieth century after the Second World War, after Hitler, after the holocaust. At any rate, unfortunately, there was no way out except the partition scheme. We knew that partition would be implemented and we knew that this would bring disaster, but naturally the party supported it as the only solution. We supported it because it meant first of all the liquidation of the British Mandate and the evacuation of the British forces. It meant the recognition of the Jewish right to self-determination, and it also recognized the right of self-determination for the Arabs of Palestine."

* * *

As might be expected, the attitude of the Palestinians changes with the attitudes directed toward them. The King of Jordan, for instance, is once again becoming their friend. This could also be true of the West if only ignorance and indifference were replaced by understanding and empathy.

Chapter 10

The Religions: Judaism, Christianity, and Islam

"Our religion? My name says it. Muhammed Issa Musa. Muhammed Jesus Moses. We believe in all three."

— *Muhammed Issa Musa*

There are three major religions in the Middle East: Judaism, Christianity, and Islam. Judaism is the oldest of the three; its name derives from Judah, one of the two tribes of the southern kingdom formed by the division of King Solomon's empire in 926 B.C. Judah outlasted Israel, the northern kingdom, though both were conquered by eastern invaders who sent most of the citizens into exile. The ten tribes of Israel were lost among the nations, but the people of Judah, or Jews, continued their traditional religious practices.

Judaism, the first major monotheistic religion of the Middle East, began with Abraham, and some of its most important symbols date back to the exodus from Egypt under Moses and to the wanderings in the wilderness. The model of the portable temple used for forty years in the Sinai desert later became fixed as a permanent structure in Jerusalem, built and destroyed several times. One of the remaining walls of the last temple, known as the "Wailing" or "Western Wall," is now Judaism's holiest shrine. The Old Testament and the Talmud, which interprets and enlarges on the Old Testament, are Judaism's most sacred literature. The land, which Abraham claimed, which Joshua partially conquered, and which David and Solomon ruled, is their holy land. "Eretz Yisrael" it is called by the faithful.

That same land gave birth to a new religion, today called Christianity. Its founder, Jesus of Nazareth, was a Jew who taught about the kingdom of God as he wandered about Galilee, Samaria, and Judea for about three years. He was crucified under Roman authority and with the complicity of certain Jewish leaders *c.* 30 A.D. His first apostles, who spread the religion far and wide, were all Jews who accepted the writings of the Old Testament, but who also provided a new literature, today called the New Testament. In due course, Bethlehem, the place of Jesus' birth, Nazareth, his parental home, and Jerusalem, the site of his crucifixion and resurrection, became Christian holy places.

Christianity was partially responsible for the claims of the Catholic crusaders from Western Europe, of the Orthodox pilgrims from as far away as Russia, and of British and American Protestants who tended to see the Middle East involvement of their respective states as the fulfilment of prophecy.

Islam is the third monotheistic religion originating in the area (c. 700 A.D.). The founder, who accepted both Judaism and Christianity and who expanded on both, was Muhammed, after whom his followers are sometimes known as Muhammedans. Their more official name, however, is Muslim (or Moslem), meaning one who submits himself to God, Islam being the religion of submission.

The prophet Muhammed lived and preached in two Saudi Arabian cities, Mecca and Medina which are therefore holy cities. But Jerusalem also became holy for Muslims, both because of Jewish and Christian traditions and because it is believed that Muhammed himself ascended into heaven on a horse at the very place where Abraham sacrificed. Today, a magnificent Muslim mosque marks the site, which is just above the Jewish "Wailing Wall."

These three religions and the energies they generate are related to the Middle East conflict. We can observe a connection in at least three different ways. The first is the historic competition between and among the three religions. All three are interrelated and the latter two claim to include what came before. All are monotheistic. All have concepts of a chosen people, a holy land, and holy wars. All claim Jerusalem as their holy city. Although there have been periods of tolerance and cooperation among the religions, the opposite has also been true. Today, the claims of Judaism and Islam stand in opposition to each other. Christianity is divided. Western Christians for the most part stand with Israel. The eastern Orthodox communities tend to hold with the Arabs.

Secondly, all three religions have distorted some of their noblest concepts. The idea of a chosen people has often been translated into racism, nationalism, imperialism, or denominationalism. The concept of the promised land has been used to justify stealing land rather than sharing it. The kingdom of God has, more often than not, been reduced to the kingdoms of man. Holy wars have expressed themselves not as contests against moral evil but as Christian crusades, Muslim jihads, and Zionist wars.

A third problem is that religious energy has appeared in new modern forms. Israeli nationalism and political Zionism are new expressions of Judaism for most Israeli Jews. It has been said that so many "non-religious" Jews have migrated to Israel because there they can be Jewish, according to acceptable standards, without being religious in the sense of traditional Judaism. Palestinian so-called terrorists go about their assigned tasks with religious dedication. When they die they are looked upon as martyrs of Islam. Pan-Arabism, on the one hand, and Arab nationalism, on the other hand, have the support of religion, and so do the various capitalist and socialist imperialisms imposed upon the region from the outside.

The majority of Palestinians are Muslims, dating back to the time of Arabic and Islamic movements out of Saudi Arabia in the seventh and eighth centuries. Most Muslims, however, do not see their religion as excluding Judaism and Christianity. On the contrary, they consider that Islam embraces them both, however general this religion, and however nominal for individual Muslims this embrace may be. How the Palestinians identify themselves as Muslims and how they see themselves in relation to other religions is revealed by their own words.

AHMED ALI, Acre*: "I don't practise Islam really. I am only Muslim by birth. The last time I went to the mosque was about ten years ago. I don't read the Koran. Religion is what you practise, not whether you pray or read the Koran. It's being good to your neighbour. It is being a good medical doctor and a good man."

NAJIB, Gaza: "I am a Muslim. Islam is a religion. It is not an easy religion. For me it means that I believe in one God. This God is the God of my people, not my people only."

BASAL EANAB, Jaffa: "Muslim. No, I am not very religious. I am not fanatical. But the holy places in Palestine are important to me."

HAZIM MAHMOUD EL-KHALIDI, Jerusalem: "Secularism is coming to the Islamic world. It is coming because there are certain things that cannot be explained to people religiously. A person who is scientifically minded cannot find for himself the given interpretation of Islam. Basically Islam is a universal religion. Perhaps it has not adapted itself well and fast enough for the present time and therefore in certain countries of the Middle East it is suffering, perhaps the same way as Christianity is suffering in the West. In other countries that are less materially advanced and less developed there is still that element of belief, and Islam is integrated into society and, hence, workable. In principle Islam is not in conflict with the times because it is an immortal religion, but in various more advanced countries, some of its interpretations are not alive to present problems."

IBRAHIM SAMA'AN, Haifa: "God promised that Abraham would prosper and that his descendants would be as much as the sand of the sea and the stars of the skies, and twelve princes, twelve kings, would come out of him and so on. If the Arabs consider themselves, and they do, to be the descendants of

* In this chapter, place names indicate origin in Palestine.

189

Ishmael, then they have the same promise given to the descendants of Abraham through Isaac."

FAOUD SAID, Jaffa: "I am not a religious man but happy to belong to a religion. I am a Muslim. I don't practise it unfortunately, because nowadays religion becomes nothing more than good morals, good conduct, and good behaviour. As such, all religions are the same because they all aspire to good conduct and a faith in the right and the wrong. Islam is one of the religions that tries to achieve that."

RHOUI EL-KHATIB, Jerusalem: "As a Muslim who has respect for and recognizes all the prophets, I do feel that if the three, Moses, Jesus, and Muhammed, happened to be on earth together, they would comply with the orders of the Almighty and call upon the humans to treat each other in the way that everyone expects to be treated, that is peacefully, justly and to live together as one family. I do believe the three leaders would embrace each other because they are chosen as prophets by the Almighty. They were students of one teacher following the commands of the Father. The Father is the Almighty."

ISA AKEL, Jerusalem: "The whole world is suffering from spiritual starvation and the Middle East along with it."

MARY NASRALLA, Nazareth: "Muslim Arabs and Christian Arabs get along very well."

ASAD, Bethany: "No difference between Muslims and Anglicans."

AREF AL-AREF, Jerusalem: "There was a day when both of us were fanatic; Muslims killed Christians and Christians killed Muslims. There was a day, but fortunately since the Mandate and since the British occupation and because of the joint opposition to the Zionists, we Muslims and Christians decided to work together and we succeeded. From 1917 till now, you have never heard about the Muslims killing Christians or the Christians killing Muslims."

RAHAB SELIM, Jerusalem: "The Muslim mother teaches her child about religion. First of all she teaches her children the Koran and other things of our Prophet. In the Koran there is much about the Jewish people. The prophets, all the prophets were Jews, and we believe in all the prophets, you see. They were sent by God, the same God."

ABLA DAJANI, Jaffa: "We believe in Judaism. If we don't believe in Judaism or Christianity we can't be Muslims. I am a Muslim, as I am a believer, I believe in true religion, because we believe in our Koran and our Koran speaks to all religions and of their prophets."

190

ISSAT AL-ATAWNEH, Hebron: "Some Israelis say that we are the descendants of Ishmael, son of Abraham and that Ishmael has his land in Arabia. And they are the sons of Isaac and this is the land of Isaac and his descendants. Actually, we were here, the Bedou of Beersheba, before Abraham. When Abraham came to Hebron and to Beersheba he came as our guest and the story known amongst every Bedouin is that we killed him a kid when he came as a guest. Because he was a generous man and a nice man and a fine man we paid him forty visits and he killed forty small goats in lieu of that one. We have entertained him. So really we have roots in this country."

* * *

The Christian communities in the Middle East are four in number: the Oriental Orthodox, the Catholics, the Eastern Orthodox, and the Protestants. They arise from important schisms occurring roughly every five hundred years since the birth of Jesus. A major division in the Apostolic Church occurred in 451, the date of the Council of Chalcedon, after which the Oriental Orthodox church declared itself independent of the establishment. Various regional expressions of the Oriental Orthodox include, among others, the Orthodox Copts of Egypt, the Armenian Orthodox, and the Syrian Orthodox (see Table 8). The Christian establishment became known as the Catholic Church, in which there was a major schism in 1054, resulting in the Eastern (Greek) Orthodox and Roman Catholic Communions. The latter in turn, was divided by the Protestant Reformation in 1517.

The Protestants entered the Middle East via the colonization process and the missionary movement. The Anglicans became most prominent in Jordan and Palestine, the Presbyterians in Egypt, Lebanon, and Syria. Other Protestant fellowships in Palestine included Baptists, Quakers, and Lutherans.

Yet Palestinian Catholics and Protestants tend to side with the Eastern church and the Muslims when it comes to the Palestinian question, and are extremely critical of Western Christianity and its position on the Middle East.

ABU-JAWAD, Jerusalem:
Q. "Are you Muslim, Christian, Jew, or atheist?"
A. "I am a Palestinian."
Q. "What about religion?"
A. "I am a Christian."
Q. "What is your background?"
A. "It doesn't matter much anymore."
Q. "Greek Orthodox, Catholic?"
A. "Protestant."

TABLE 8

POPULATION OF MIDDLE EAST
(By Region and Religion*)

	Arab and Non-Arab Mideast	Egypt	Iraq	Israel	Jordan	Lebanon	Syria
Total population	120,324,000	26,080,000	7,160,000	2,153,850	1,729,926	1,636,800	4,561,000
Christian:							
Greek Orthodox	2,688,774	89,062	100,000	18,000	10,000	149,000	172,873
Oriental orthodox		1,186,353	—	—	—	69,000	164,396
Catholics:							
Uniate & Latin	1,709,000	169,915	211,745	39,189	46,437	683,761	257,988
Protestants	334,921	153,914	1,164	1,933	9,124	20,149	44,648
Jews	2,045,950	13,500	6,000	1,880,000	—	7,000	5,000
Muslims	87,384,336	17,397,946	4,508,779	159,000	1,700,000	536,000	3,286,243

*Statistics based on 1962, most recent date for religious membership figures for the region.

ALBERT HADAWI, Jerusalem: "I was born an Anglican Christian. I don't have very strong feelings toward religion. And in a way I feel resentful towards the Christian religion, because I have come to realize that it is the church in many instances that perpetuates the idea that Palestine belongs to the Jews because of a promise made by somebody a few thousand years ago."

KHALED MOUAMMAR, Nazareth: "I am of Greek Orthodox parents in Nazareth. I have really lost faith in Western religion or religion in general because it has been used, misused, abused to justify crimes committed against human beings. The Christian religion has been used in that sense. The man who was born in Nazareth after whom the Christian religion was named had a vision. The Western world has distorted his religion. It has become a tool to justify white racism and exploitation of underdeveloped countries. Western Christian religion can only be a detriment to our cause."

SAMI EL-KARAMI, Ain-Karem: "I am of Roman Catholic background, but I hate to bring religion into it. I am not interested in discussing religion."

SOUAD ZANANIRI, Jerusalem: "I belong to the Orthodox church. Some of my family are Anglican. They belong to the Anglican church and some other churches but we are all Christians. None of them are Muslims. I cannot be a Muslim if my family is Christian. There cannot be any Muslims in the same family."

BISHOP CUBA'IN, Salt (East Bank): "Every Christian should call himself a Palestinian, if we believe this is the country of the Lord. So, in a special sense, all Christians should belong to Palestine. And the same thing with the Jews. The same thing with the Muslims. This is a sacred country for three major religions. There are other people who are concerned more directly with politics. We are concerned about how we can serve our people spiritually, mentally, and these days socially and on the basis of belief. All my activities are restricted within this framework."

NAJIB KHOURY, Occupied Palestine: "When it comes to injustice the minister should be outspoken and declare that the early church had to suffer many times because they had to tell the truth and declare it to the public."

LEILA BANDEK, Jerusalem: "Being a Christian doesn't make me less of an Arab. We Christian Arabs have to make up for harm from the West. We are disturbed by all these Christian groups who write and don't know what they are talking about. Let them write in the name of themselves, not in the name of Christianity."

HANNA NASIR, Bir Zait: "The Arab Christian has a special message for the whole world. The fundamentalists come to us and say to us: 'You have to quit. This land is for Israel.' I found it harder to speak to these rigid, rocky Christians than to Jews. God is not a land contractor. The Bible is not a real estate registry. I'd like to see delegations of Christians going out to the West to explain."

NE'MEH SIMA'AN, Nazareth: "There are governments who are ruling Christian populations, but they themselves are not Christians. I don't believe in Christian government in the world. Most of the people are mis-led by Zionist propaganda."

ISSAT G.TANNOUS, Nablus: "I believe that everything that has happened in Palestine, all the lives and all the blood that was shed in Palestine in vain, whether it was Jewish, Christian, or Muslim blood, is due to the Christian West. The Christian West was responsible for it. And the end of it will not be good, if they continue the same course. I think that the Christian West has done more harm to the Middle East. They have done more harm to Christianity because the Christians never were Christians in the West."

SHAFIK FARAH, Shafa A'mr: "The Christian church ought to play its role as the conscience of the state anywhere it is and should say its opinion about things and inform people if they are not informed and correct their views if they are twisted."

GEORGES KHODR, Syria: "If Western Christians could understand that the Christianity of this land has its own mind and tradition, they would completely change their minds about us. They would come to us as educators, technicians in the mass media, all kinds of Christian technicians, if you like, counsellors in all matters and professors of Old Testament, Hebrew and Greek, but not as missionaries. Yes, and they would then abide by the limits which were assigned to them. Now we have enough people who feed us spiritually, but we don't have enough people for education or administration."

SAMI SALIM KHOURY, Nablus: "I have become anti-church. Where is the Christian world? Where are they? The other time a bishop came from England and said he wanted to study something about the refugees. I just almost kicked him out of the house. I said, 'Where have you been all these years? Our Lord ran after the one lost sheep. He never stayed in palaces, call them Lambeths, call them forts, call them whatever you like. But it takes you twenty-three years to come and see these people. Where are you, where is the church?

" "Take the people who are in the Christian church, who say Israel is a fulfilment of prophecy. Do you mean to tell me that Christ must build his kingdom on the ruins of the Palestinian people, on their suffering? Is this the only way God works to build his kingdom? I don't want such a God, nor such a Christ. If you believe in the chosen people, aren't you dishonest if you don't become one of them, a Jew?'

"The Christian world has not stood up for humanity. If Archbishop Ramsey visited the refugees once in twenty-three years, he has not done well. If the Pope visited the refugees once only in twenty-three years, he has not done well. That is why I feel I am shaken in my faith in Christianity, in people who are calling themselves Christians. Please don't understand from me that I am against Christianity. I am against Christians. I am against hierarchy. I am against the Pope. I am against the Archbishop of Canterbury. As an Anglican I dare to say that. Of course I dare to say that. I listened once to Archbishop Ramsey when he came to Jerusalem and gave a most diplomatic sermon. Is that how we live the Christian life? For God's sake, if he believes it is wrong then let him say it is wrong. If he believes it is right, let him say it is right. Let the Prime Minister give such a diplomatic speech but not the Archbishop of Canterbury. It is these people who are ruining the world. They are not saying enough. They are not fighting enough. It is these people who should become Christ's and go after the one stray sheep."

IBRAHIM SAMA'AN, Haifa:
Q. "Do you feel that Baptists or North American Christianity in general is approaching this whole question with helpfulness?"
A. "No. No. I think that most of them are one-sided. And some of them are more Catholic than the Pope."
Q. "Some Baptists? In what way? Explain."
A. "Including Billy Graham. I don't trust him to deal with this problem."
Q. "Have you seen his film?"*
A. "It's horrible. He only thinks of Arabs as being Bedouins and trying to pull big loads with camels and donkeys. It's really terrible to hear what he is doing with such a film. I respect him as a preacher, and I hope he stays only as a preacher. He would make a pretty bad politician."

SALWA KHURI OTAQUI, Jerusalem: "I don't know if you go to church and how your service is, but ours, being Anglican, is like all Christian services. They pray for Zion and Israel all the time."

* * *

* The reference is to *His Land*, a one-hour colour motion picture on the State of Israel and biblical prophecy, released by the Billy Graham organization in 1970.

Palestinians, be they Christians or Muslims, take great pains to differentiate between religious Jews, whom they say they love, and Zionists or political Jews, whom they say they dislike. For them Zionism has taken on a particular meaning, which includes racism and imperialism. By racism they mean Zionism's goal to achieve a Jewish state – as Jewish as England is English. This, of course, cannot happen without the expulsion or subordination of the Arabs, on the one hand, and without giving a privileged status to newly-arrived Jewish immigrants, on the other hand. The Palestinians consider this discrimination racist. The expansionist policies of the state of Israel are considered imperialistic.

The more positive religious and emotional meanings of Zionism, namely the Jewish desire for a homeland, not to be confused with nationhood, are for the Palestinians overshadowed by those Zionist facts which affect them adversely. To them the political state of Israel is the incarnation of Zionist philosophy, as they understand it. The state must, therefore, be dismantled to get rid of the racist and imperialist tendencies. But this does not mean the elimination of Jews, as a people, whose legitimate aspirations can be respected in a state in which Jews, Christians, and Muslims are all equal. It is only in this context that the remarks of men like Sami Salim Khoury, a chest surgeon, a Christian Palestinian in exile, can be understood.

SAMI SALIM KHOURY, from Nablus: "A Zionist is a man, a Jew, who belongs to a political party. Zionists aspire to have Palestine all to themselves, to expand in the Middle East, to use the Christian world for their own ultimate aims. Zionists are absolutely ruthless. They don't care what they do, provided they attain their goals, the ultimate aims. The end justifies the means for them. I have met very, very fine Jews, and I don't know whether I am right in saying it in that way, but I feel that they have been brainwashed since the establishment of Israel. Those who were not Zionists at the time have been brainwashed.

"What piece of land do I think they want next? They want whatever they can get. I am sure they want Jordan. They are ruthless even to their friends. I am sure they don't care what happens to America. I think they are playing it very wisely in a way but ruthlessly in so many other ways. Take for example the Middle East. What brought Russia into the Middle East? It was the Israeli horse that brought them in. Israel wanted to create an East-West situation. And now they are stalling for time. I don't think they want to arrive at a peaceful conclusion to the whole problem. They are just digesting the occupied territories. And mark my words, they will never get out of one inch of land. They will digest it acre by acre, and they will go on creating problems in the Arab world through their agents. I just wonder how the Americans even are not afraid of Israel, because Zionists are really able to do it.

"Zionists know exactly what they want to do and their master plan is quite something. Of necessity they keep the rifle at the back of both the Arab and the Jew. I always put it this way. For the past twenty years, for example, Arabs have been shouting their heads off that they want war and the Israelis have been shouting their heads off that they want peace. And we have seen in 1967 that both were liars. The Israelis never wanted peace, and the Arabs never wanted war. Obviously their plan is to expand, but they are making good use of the foolishness of the Arabs and they are doing it with great psychological precision. They are really brains. I envy them. Much of the Middle East conflict is due to the cleverness of the Zionists and the foolishness of the Arabs.

"Look what is happening in the Arab world now. If the Arabs are not careful the Israelis will even occupy Mecca. Look what is happening. They have expanded more and more, so many times more than their own area. Now they are sticking to Jerusalem. They are not giving up an inch of it. After all, they want it because it will bring in quite a few million dollars at the end of the year, and they will never give up because of these millions of dollars. They will de-Christianize the city. There is no question about it. They know exactly what they want, and they are doing it with very great brains."

GEORGE GIACAMAN, Bethlehem: "Zionism is a movement which aims at acquiring land – a political state."

SAMIR, Bel El-Shik: "We do not hate the Jews as Jews, never. But we hate the way in which they are behaving."

IBRAHIM FARBI, Jericho: "I don't think that Arabs are becoming haters of Jews. But when you are in a state of war, you are frustrated. Basically the Arabs are against the creation of a state called Israel. I think the Arabs would welcome a Palestine as a democratic state where there would be Jews."

GEORGES KHODR, Syria: "I have no quarrel with the Jews being in that land. My quarrel is with the state of Israel, the philosophy of the state of Israel. It is somehow different because it is based on race. It is not strictly speaking, a racist or a Nazi state, but it is an ugly mixture of ethnic, racial, religious features. Our whole problem in the Arab world is the aristocratic view of the state. In this sense, the decay of Arabic states is good."

ISSA FARIS, Tiberias: "No, we don't hate the Jews. They are human beings. I have many Jewish friends. But I hate their political outlook and actions. I hate Zionism. The Jews should rid themselves of Zionism for their own sake. They should live as Jews and share the life with the inhabitants."

Khalil Abdelhadi, Shobeth: "The Jews taught the world the ten commandments, good deeds and all about God, and produced prophets! They know what it means to be persecuted and to live in hardship. How can they accept living in the homes of people who built them and lived in them and were born in them, and take the orchards which they sowed and tended, and their vineyards? How can such a people accept to live in the homes of others?"

Massih Abdul, Acre: "Judaism has been used, has been exploited deeply by the Zionist movement."

Muhammad H. El-Farra, Gaza Strip: "We believe in the oneness of religion. To be a Muslim you have to accept Judaism and Christianity. It is their belief which makes us want to have a place for three religions. Why can't we coexist? This tolerance should express itself more in the holy land. The seed of Abraham was promised to both Isaac and Ishmael. We are descendants of Ishmael."

* * *

Although the Middle East conflict is often defined in religious terms, not all accept that assumption. They see religion being used as an easy escape from the real issues, or as a pat justification of certain policies, as their responses to the question, "Is the Middle East conflict a religious problem?" indicate:

Samir, Bel El-Shik: "There are no religious leaders to whom the Palestinians look up. No Muslims, no Christians. It is not a matter of religion. I am Muslim but I am not religious. I believe in God, but I don't pray. I just work."

Margaret Khoury, Acre: "I believe that the Jews are preying on its being a religious problem, but it isn't really. They are covering up with a sort of religious covering. But the Jews, a lot of them, are not at all religious, the Zionists especially."

Sami Salim Khoury, Nablus: "I think it is a political problem, not a religious one. The Zionists have been trying to get into Palestine, by means fair or foul."

Ne'meh Sima'an, Nazareth: "This is the real problem. They try to have, not a religious centre, but a national home. The national home became a national state. And what is not mentioned, a national empire. The whole problem of Palestine is not a religious problem. From the very beginning it was a Zionist movement. It was a political movement. The Zionist movement in Palestine is 85 per cent atheist. So, you have them not observing, not believing even in the Holy Bible, not even Golda Meir. So the whole history is more a dirty policy and has nothing to do with religion."

AHMED ALI, Acre: "I think on the Israeli side religion is probably one of the major problems, because in Israel Judaism and nationalism seem to be the same and want the Zionist Jewist state. They are combining nationalism with religion."

GEORGES KHODR, Syria: "I disagree with Islamic theocracy, with the kingdom of Jerusalem of the crusaders, and with the Catholic empire, with America being the kingdom of God, with Russia being the kingdom of God, and with Israel being the kingdom of God."

NAJIB KHOURY, Occupied Palestine: "I think ministers better keep away from politics, because politics are not very clean and problems should be left to those politicians and statesmen and men who deal with politics. I would say it is a political more than religious problem. If you take Israel today, you find you have 10 per cent of the population who are austere Jews, and they say about 15 per cent are liberal Jews, the rest they don't have much place in the heart for a religion. So the problem is more political than religious."

NAJLA KANAZEH, Haifa: "Probably you are looking at religion in a broad sense, and in this case I say the Palestinians are fighting for a humanism which can be defined as religion. There are religious human values that we are fighting for. We are fighting for the good of the whole Middle East area, which in the end would really be fighting for the good of all mankind."

* * *

The Middle East conflict may not basically be a religious war in the usual sense, but certainly the distortions and rivalries of religions have contributed to the hostilities. Religious identities, preferences, and prejudices have cut deeply into the communities and nations of the area. Although the wounds thus inflicted may never be completely healed, religion itself may be able to play a part in the healing process. But it is unlikely that this will happen as long as the concepts of a chosen people, promised land, holy wars, and God's kingdom are defined by any one group in such a way as to deliberately exclude another people on the basis of race, nationality, class or culture.

If, for instance, "chosen people" were defined in terms of servanthood rather than super-race and mastery, in terms of respecting and loving one's neighbour rather than subduing and enslaving him, the whole psychology of the Middle East could change. A new religious self-definition could lead to the egalitarianism about which the prophets spoke. Palestinians could be giving to their "secular state" a meaning that surpasses in concept the present propagandistic usage, and Israelis could find that they were championing in their own state the kind of democratic society for which they struggled as the "underdog" in many nations of Europe.

Similarly, "promised land" need not carry the connotation of a reserve or a state defended by strategic weapons for the exclusive use of a privileged people, but rather that of a land area in which all the resources were maximized for the benefit of all the people within and immediately surrounding. Stealing could give way to sharing, and exploitation to stewardship.

A society's "holy wars" need no longer be fought against other people but rather against those elements in the universe, those principalities and powers, operating within people and nation-states, which tended to destroy them as well as every friend and foe. The kingdom of God could come to mean something other than modern nationalisms, nineteenth-century imperialisms, the Holy Roman Empire, and the Crusader Kingdom of Jerusalem. Instead, there could emerge a kingdom in which all men were chosen people and in which holy wars would come to an end; a kingdom in which the holiest city really meant the healthiest society, a kingdom in which "holy land" no longer meant a limited acreage, but reached out to the entire planet and its people.

Chapter 11

Jerusalem and the Bible

"Jerusalem is the holiest shrine in Islam. It's the most venerable religious city for the Muslims. I would say that Islam is incomplete without Jerusalem."

— Hazim Mahmoud El-Khalidi

The Palestinian people are ambivalent about their country being identified with holy places, chosen people, and infallible books. They appreciate, at least as much as the rest of humanity, significant religious symbolism, identity, and authority. They love Jerusalem and other holy places. They accept the Bible and/or the Koran. And they revere the prophets, Moses, Jesus, and Muhammed most of all. However, they also find themselves repelled by the excessive emphasis on holiness and chosenness where these noble religious concepts have been distorted and the Palestinians have become victims of this distortion.

Both Christian and Muslim Palestinians feel intensely about Jerusalem. Why, can be somewhat of a mystery to the outsider. The first impressions of Jerusalem, like the first sight of the Jordan River, are something of a culture shock. For people taught in several decades of Sunday school that "the river is deep and the river is wide," it is indeed disillusioning to discover that the Jordan is, at least during the summer dry spell, little more than a creek. Its shores are overgrown by brush and weeds, and the flowing water itself is hardly visible, and murky enough to discourage even the most pious from wanting like John to be baptized in its waters.

Whether one approaches Jerusalem from Jericho and the east or from Tel Aviv and the west, it is uphill all the way – about 2,500 feet above sea-level to the mountains of Judea among which Jerusalem is nestled. Unless alerted by a guide, one is likely to miss the first possible glimpse of the city. The buildings are low and grey like the surrounding hills from which the building materials have been extracted. Only some of the older towers and steeples and some of the new office and apartment buildings hint at the characteristic cityscapes so familiar in the West.

Actually, there are several Jerusalems, in spite of the administrative "unification" which took place after the 1967 War. There is the New City or West Jerusalem, dating back a hundred years, but for the most part built up since the state of Israel was established in 1948. This city has a

European and North American character, and the national government and its chief agencies are located there. Most of the 250,000 people of the Jerusalem metropolitan area, most of whom are Jews, live there.

About one-fifth of the people of Jerusalem live in East Jerusalem, which includes the Old (Walled) City and the area immediately around it. Most are Arabs, though their number is on the decrease. The Old City walls give it the appearance of a fortress. Inside and outside the walls are over thirty shrines and holy places of significance either to Jews, Christians, or Muslims. But the character of East Jerusalem is rapidly changing. To the north, northeast, and east, the hills have a new skyline of hundreds of apartment buildings erected for Jewish immigrants. The Israeli military, government, commercial, and cultural symbols are also becoming more prominent.

Palestinians like all Muslims are greatly disturbed by the changing character of Jerusalem. Their great concern is the implications of the population shift. Arab population, both Christian and Muslim, is declining, whereas Jewish population is increasing. As a result there has been a rapid expansion of housing and development projects for Jews, which means a continued erosion of the Arab quarters and traditional Jerusalem. All of this spells the Judaization of the city. Most offensive of all are the changing values reflected in the Old City, which to the Arabs spell moral corruption.

The Muslim Mufti of Jerusalem, Saladin Al-Alami, spoke from his position as the highest interpreter of Muslim law.

SALADIN AL-ALAMI, Mufti of Jerusalem:
Q. "How long has your family lived in Jerusalem?"
A. "About eight hundred years."
Q. "How important is Jerusalem for Islam?"
A. "We believe in our Koran. Our Koran is the word of God and our Koran said that God blessed the Al-Aksa mosque and the places which are around it. This means our Jerusalem. Jerusalem is blessed by God in our Koran and it means that we must bless it also. We believe that our prophet came at night from Mecca to Jerusalem. We have three important places in Islam, more important and more high than every other place in the world, Mecca, Medina, and Jerusalem. All the Muslims of the world believe that Jerusalem is a high place for them and that they must come to visit the mosque. Before 1967 in the month of Rammadan there were always every Friday more than 250,000 praying in the Al-Aksa mosque. But after 1967 none of the Muslims can come to Jerusalem to pray in the Al-Aksa mosque because of Israeli occupation."
Q. "They can't come?"
A. "They don't want to ask permission from the Israelis."
Q. "But if they would ask, then permission would be granted?"

A.   "I don't know, but they can't tell you to pray in a place under the occupation of Israel."

Q.   "If the prophet were living today what do you think he would say?"

A.   "Our prophet says everything from God."

Q.   "What would he say about the problem between the Jews and the Arabs?"

A.   "Why shall we ask this question? He didn't say. He will not. He died."

Q.   "What does the Koran say about this question?"

A.   "The Koran, I told you, the Koran only said that God blessed the Al-Aksa mosque and the places around it. That's what the Koran said."

Q.   "You are working for peace in the Middle East and in Palestine, are you not?"

A.   "Sure, I want peace, but I want justice before peace. If there is justice there is peace."

Q.   "What are the requirements of justice?"

A.   "Justice means give each one his land. Let him live free as he wants."

Q.   "Meaning for all the Palestinians?"

A.   "For everybody. The Palestinians and the Jews. The Jews must be free. Their party must be free also."

Q.   "What has been the saddest moment in your life since 1948?"

A.   "1948 and 1967. The saddest time in my life."

Q.   "And the happiest time?"

A.   "There is not any happy time. From 1948 till now there is no happy time for me."

Q.   "Have you ever felt in danger of being deported?"

A.   "I didn't feel yet. I don't know what they will do. I am living in my home."

Q.   "How old are you?"

A.   "Sixty, sixty or so."

Q.   "Do you think Jews and Muslims and Christians can live together?"

A.   "Surely they can, if there is justice and peace. They can live together if Israel will leave the West Bank and east of Jerusalem. I am sure they can live friendly. They are good neighbours. You will see many of them are friends."

Q.   "Someone told me today that Arab guerillas were killing Arabs in the Gaza strip. What do you know about that?"

A.   "Maybe they are working for Israel. I don't know. You may ask who killed them. I don't know. I didn't kill them."

Q.   "Isn't there someone that should make a protest?"

A.   "We make many protests, but they didn't hear us."

Q.   "Tell me about God."

A.   "About God?"

Q. "What's he like?"

A. "Surely he likes peace. God likes peace. As I told you, I want peace and I like peace, but if you want peace we must have justice."

Q. "In the West it is sometimes said the Arabs are turning toward communism."

A. "The Arabs are going to communism. The West is obliging the Arabs to go to communism. They don't want to be a communism but the West is obliging."

Q. "Can Islam and communism live together?"

A. "Surely can't. I believe that no."

* * *

Other Palestinian Muslims reinforced the view that Islam is quite incomplete without Jerusalem, that all the Muslims of the world would rise up in anger if the permanence of Jerusalem as a Muslim symbol were threatened, and that the Judaization of Jerusalem has already gone too far in offending both Islam and Christianity.

HAZIM MAHMOUD EL-KHALIDI, former tourist director: "My first Muslim ancestor besieged Jerusalem in the year 637 A.D. And after a siege of six months, Jerusalem surrendered to the Caliph. Jerusalem was not conquered. It surrendered after negotiations. And it was accorded the highest privilege that the Muslim could bestow on a city. The Caliph travelled all the way from Medina to Jerusalem to officiate over the surrender of the city. At that time the leading Byzantine personality was Bishop Saphronius, and he declined to surrender the city to any other person but the highest authority amongst the Muslims. My family has lived in the city ever since. I'm the thirty-seventh generation in Jerusalem."

ABU-JAWAD, commando officer: "Jerusalem is as important as all our cities and villages in Palestine. Of course, it is our capital. It is the capital of Palestine, but is not more important than the smallest village in the north of Palestine or in the south of Palestine."

NAJIB KHOURY, administrator: "Jerusalem is really nicer than Amman. It is the holy city in Palestine. You find different people, American, European, Russian, Muslim, Christians and Jews."

ABLA DAJANI, news writer: "Jerusalem is the holiest shrine in Islam. It's the most venerable religious city for the Muslims. I would say that Islam is incomplete without Jerusalem."

HAZIM MAHMOUD EL-KHALIDI: "For 1,300 years the Muslims tried very hard to keep the city open to the three monotheist religions. There were times when an unbalanced ruler for a period closed it to one denomination

204

or the other. But all in all, they've honoured that people have the right to worship God in the way they want and they desire. And so long as they have holy shrines which they honour in their hearts, these shrines should be open for them."

KHALIL ABDELHADI, medical doctor: "People should share in this country and not use force to dislodge the important people of this country. They are just as important as the relics. They are just as important as the holy sepulchre or the mosque of Omar or even the walls. In my opinion, they are more important."

* * *

The traditional rivalries and jealousies between Christians and Muslims with respect to Jerusalem have been overshadowed by the common competition with Judaism, but they are not entirely hidden. Some Christians feel keenly that Muslims should not make so much of Jerusalem because they also have Mecca. Muslims, on the other hand, take pride in the fact that harmony among the various Christian communions regarding the Church of the Holy Sepulchre could be maintained only if Muslim families were custodians of the keys. As far as desecrations by the various religions of each other's holy places are concerned it is recognized that some of this has been done in ignorance and because of different cultural values. There has, however, also been intolerance and fanaticism.

NE'MEH SIMA'AN, church bishop: "If you respect the historical place of redemption, you have to say that Jerusalem is very important for the Christian religion, much more than for the Muslim and much more than for the Jews. The Jews have the temple, they have the sacrifices. As you know from the gospels, since the crucifixion of our Lord, since the destruction of Jerusalem, in the year 70, there is no more sacrifice. The sacrifices of the Old Temple were only a symbol for the holy sacrifice of the cross. This is the Christian theology."

SHAFIK FARAH, education director: "Jerusalem and Nazareth are not important as monuments. They are important as places where the Christian presence will continue to be, and they are very meaningful to us. They are not only historical sites, but also important for us as places of pilgrimage. They are places of worship. They are centres of hope for the Christian. I don't know about the Wailing Wall. I will let the Jews answer whether they are overdoing it or not, but as far as the Christian and Muslim holy places are concerned, there is something very real about their meaning to us."

HAZIM MAHMOUD EL-KHALIDI, former tourist director: "As long as they have holy shrines in their hearts the physical shrines should be open to them. Two Muslim families have the key to the church of the Sepulchre. The key and guardianship. They're two functions. One is the key and the other one is the guardianship.

"The Israelis have accused the Arabs of desecrating particularly Jewish holy places, Jewish cemeteries, etc? Well, I think this is a most unfair accusation. There was no desecration intended. How could there be? What may have happened is that through neglect certain holy places, perhaps former synagogues, were not recognized after ten years as such and some desperate refugee, requiring an abode, a place to live in, moved in and adapted the place to their requirements. As far as cemeteries are concerned, well, the cemeteries are still there. Perhaps on the fringes, because graves were not recognized as such, someone added a plot of land to one he was cultivating. Then there is a difference in concept. Perhaps even government officials were not wise to the Jewish religious laws.

"We are accused of having driven a road from the main Jerusalem-Jericho road to the inter-continental hotels through a Jewish cemetery. With us Muslims, if a cemetery has been abandoned for over thirty-five years, it can be reused for other purposes. I don't know exactly what Jewish religious law is about this subject. They may have other laws than we have. But nobody drove that road with the intent to desecrate a Jewish cemetery. Neither do I believe that the Jews intended to do the same in another cemetery in Mammilla. They've converted the cemetery. They knew it was there. They knew its bounds because it had a wall around it. They made a park of it, and I think a road is not much different from a park. All I can say is that there has been no intention to desecrate. Desecration doesn't pay. You desecrate my shrine today, I will desecrate your shrine tomorrow."

HIKMAT, needlework lady: "The Holy Land certainly was considered holy by quite a number of people. Even the people from Europe, when they used to come to the Holy Sepulchre, they would creep on their knees to the Holy Sepulchre giving vows because the land was holy to them. And now what are we doing at the Holy Sepulchre? They are all wearing bikinis and trying to get into the Holy Sepulchre with cigarettes. High time to reserve some holy land for holiness before it is tastelessly and brutally wiped out.

"During the Mandate no night club was allowed to be open in Jerusalem. Why? The Britishers still respected it. What is the meaning of the Holy City if you have clubs, and prostitutes walking on the streets as we have it now? Not much holiness is left now. The first thing they did in 1967 was to open night clubs. You know that they have agents in the bazaar, Jewish agents walking from shop to shop offering women and bargaining how many pounds or how many dollars a night."

206

* * *

The Judaization of Jerusalem is proceeding, according to the Palestinians, in various ways. First is the application of Israeli laws and regulations. Next is the de-emphasis or even negation of the Arab and Islamic heritage and the giving of prominence to the Jewish heritage. This is accompanied by the alienation of Arabs from their own culture and thought through education and the mass media. Judaization is accomplished also by reducing the Arab and increasing the Jewish population, which happens through the expropriation of Arab lands and the setting up of new quarters for Jewish immigrants. The Judaizing of the Arab economy happens in many ways, not least of all through the non-licensing of Arab buses and taxis and the non-booking of Arab hotels previously serving the tourist industry. What follows is the testimony of those who know Jerusalem well, including, first of all, the Arab mayor-in-exile.

RHOUI EL-KHATIB: "The following changes have taken place in Jerusalem since 1973: The Israelis have continued to set up more Jewish quarters around Arab Jerusalem – apartment blocks like fortresses – so far thirteen have been completed. The Arabs in Jerusalem are being besieged from the north, northeast, south, southeast, leaving a small gap toward the east, but plans are to bridge it with two residential quarters – one mid-way between Jerusalem and Jericho. Into those quarters they have accommodated nearly 60,000 Jewish settlers, bringing total to 250,000. About 80,000 Arabs remain. They have continued illegal excavation under and around Al-Harem Sharif [the mosque area] very dear to the Muslim world as ascension site for Prophet Muhammed. Through these excavations they have cracked and endangered the buildings around the mosque and started to warn inhabitants to leave. Bulldozing of houses in Mughrabi Quarter, original home of Muslim settlers from Morocco since its building nearly twelve centuries ago, has continued. These excavations have reached under the mosque in four tunnels – now threatening the mosque to collapse.

"There are plans for more evacuations. Two campaigns have been lately noticed against residents of four more quarters inside the walls of Jerusalem. Warnings were directed by municipal authorities to Kirami Quarter to restore premises which were partly damaged during last work season. The people concerned applied for licences to enable them to start restoration. The licences were rejected. People of these houses – about three hundred – are facing a new season of troubles. The same thing happened to settlers in one side of the Arab quarters near Sharaf Quarter inside the city last year. They were warned to leave and houses were bulldozed. They found shelter in neighbouring quarters and villages. A second wave is now being directed at these three quarters: Hutta, Elwad, and Sadiyeh inside city walls. The municipality of Jerusalem is planning to move out of these quarters 1,000 Arab families and transfer them to a new quarter east of Bethany."

Issa Khader, teacher: "In 1968 Israelis expropriated properties in five quarters inside city wall. They announced at that time that new houses would be set up for 6,000 Arabs in new quarters. Since then 5,000 have been forced out. They built only 100 units, small units, for four to five persons each. They then published propaganda that they had accommodated the transferred people. But 4,500 had to find their own way. The same thing now will apply to the others. Majority of them remain in the city."

Wadie Tleel, oil company representative: "Jerusalem throughout history was always great, but never big. What they are doing now in Jerusalem through this big housing project is changing the whole sacred character of this city. At the same time they are trying to Judaize and monopolize Jerusalem which is a universal city."

Hazim Mahmoud El-Khalidi, former Jordanian tourist director: "In Jerusalem you should use a toothbrush, not a bulldozer. Jerusalem should be treated with sensitivity."

Najib Khoury, administrator: "I always loved Jerusalem because it had its old oriental form with its tradition. After 1967, with these new buildings, the shape of Jerusalem, the atmosphere, and the environment in Jerusalem have changed. We don't want to see Jerusalem like New York or Washington or Toronto or any other European city."

Bishop Cuba'in, church bishop: "The Jordan government and the Jerusalem municipality were against new buildings even on the Mount of Olives. Many were unhappy when the Continental Hotel was built. I know that the government has given a resolution to prevent any buildings on the Mount of Olives. This keeping the historicity of the city and keeping the nature of the city as it is, is an old idea. Now they see these new buildings and they think that the nature of the city is being changed."

Fatima, school teacher and welfare worker: "What's happening to Jerusalem? You have to see for yourself. They are building up the area in many ways, creating a *de facto* condition – changing the face of Jerusalem in any ugly way; tall apartment houses are going up where once there were two-storey villas. There were laws to prevent tall buildings. We used to stop on our way from school just to get a view of the whole east."

Shakib A. Otaqui, graduate student: "I am studying urban planning, which incidentally makes those buildings on the top of the hill here even more disgusting. Politically they are unacceptable. Secondly, the land that

was taken was expropriated with very inadequate compensation. In fa<
the word 'inadequate' doesn't begin to describe it. Third, is the aesthet_
objections. Fourth, is the planning aspect which is beyond the aesthetic.
Very, very bad planning."

* * *

In the same way that the Palestinians' experience of oppression and homelessness has affected their views of holy places, so also has their reading of
holy books, especially the Bible, been affected. Sometimes they feel that the
Bible is thrown at them by the West as a justification for the status quo.
Yet, it is as difficult for Coptic Christians to read certain Old Testament
passages, which cast Egypt in a negative light, as it is for Jews to hear
certain expository sections of the New Testament, which reflect adversely
on them and which suggest that Judaism has been superseded.

A more general but deeper problem with respect to the Bible is experienced by Arab Christians when they are confronted by Western interpretations which claim that the establishment and expansion of the state of
Israel is a fulfilment of biblical prophecies. These arguments cite as support the "covenant promises" of God with reference to Abraham (Genesis
12:1-3, 17:4-10, 19), with reference to David (2 Samuel 7:12-16, 24-26; 1
Chronicles 17:11-14), and with reference to Israel and Judah (Jeremiah
31:31-34, 38-40; 33:7-26), and certain Songs of Ascent to Jerusalem are
also cited in this connection (Psalms 120-136, 147). Of great significance in
this interpretation are the Old Testament prophecies of return to the land
(Jeremiah 33:7-13; 23:3; Ezekiel 28:5-6; 34:11-31, 36-37, 40-48; Joel 3;
Amos 9:11-15; Zechariah 2:6-12; 8:2-8, 22-23; 10:8-12; 14). Closely corre-
lated with these prophecies is a millennial view of the end times which in
turn is associated with the salvation of Israel (Matthew 24, Mark 13, Luke
21, Romans 9-11, Revelation 20-22).

Arabic Christians see great weakness in such interpretations, arguing
that they ignore the conditional nature of the covenant promises which tie
the promises to obedience (Exodus 19:5-6; 1 Kings 9:4-9; 2 Chronicles
7:19-22). They also insist on reading the passages most often cited in their
historical and New Testament contexts. By this they mean that the promises of return have already been fulfilled. Ezekiel 37, for instance, could
refer to Israel's return from Babylonian exile in 538 B.C. Other Old Testament texts they say are fulfilled in the coming of Jesus (compare Amos
9:11-15 and Acts 15:16-18; Jeremiah 31:31-34 and Hebrews 8:8-13).

The Arabs say that if the descendants of Abraham are to be identified
in the flesh, they must include the descendants through Ishmael, and exclude those Jews who have no geneological connection with Abraham, but
are descended from European converts to Judaism. If the children of Abraham are to be linked to him by faith, all true believers must be so linked. If

"Israel" as a concept and a language is to be insisted upon, the various biblical meanings must be considered. Israel is a symbol of the Christian church, and other things as well:

SHAFIK FARAH, education director: "The promised land is only a symbol for the kingdom of God. God is interested in people wherever they are; it doesn't matter really whether you are in Canada, or Israel, or in Japan. Any chosen people which does not go by the precepts of God, doing God's will, will cease to be chosen. So chosenness is a responsibility put by God on people. Everyone is chosen in a general sense, and in a strict sense the church is the chosen people.

"Historically speaking, the promises have been fulfilled, if you want to take them literally. But I don't take them literally. My interpretation of prophecy and the scriptures is much richer than the literal acceptance of what was given. I hope you follow my line of thinking. I am not saying that this was unreal, but I am saying that after Christ that has become the background. It had its time, but I am now sure that God does not want certain people to occupy land at the expense and at the cost of suffering for other people."

ELIYA KHOURY, deported priest: "Is modern Israel the fulfilment of biblical prophecy? I would never hesitate to say no, and quite bluntly, courageously, and freely. I am a priest who believes that the establishment of Israel is not, and can never be, a fulfilment of Old Testament prophecy at all, for historical reasons and for theological reasons. Historical reasons? Well, the period of exile in the sixth century B.C. They rebuilt the temple and lived there until 70 A.D. when Titus destroyed Jerusalem and they were dispersed, you see. From a theological point of view, I believe that all Christians who do not feel satisfied by the one oblation, by the one sacrifice of our Lord Jesus Christ himself on the Cross for the redemption of man, cannot understand the message of our Lord Jesus Christ. Those who believe that the establishment of Israel is fulfilled in Old Testament prophecy are people who like to get us back to sacrifices of bullocks. I can never go back to Judaism. We are living in the new creation of which our Lord Jesus Christ was the cornerstone. Therefore I can't accept this theory that the establishment of Israel is the fulfilment of Old Testament prophecy."

NE'MEH SIMA'AN, church bishop: "All prophecies of the Old Testament were for redemption and for the coming of Christ."

NAJIB KHOURY, administrator: "Some say that old prophecies have been fulfilled with the New Testament, with the coming of Christ. The ingathering of the Jews, this has been fulfilled long ago. We don't think that the Jews have the right, from a biblical point of view."

IBRAHIM SAMA'AN, journalist: "Well, the principles of peace are found through all the New Testament, and I don't think that we should ignore the prophecies in the Old Testament. Even the New Testament talks about the return of the Jews to their own land. At the same time, looking at the Old Testament, I don't think that the Jews ever occupied that part of the world by themselves only. They always had nations in and about Palestine. So I don't see any contradiction in my claim that the Arabs should have the right of this land and at the same time I also claim that the Jews should have the right. It's a kind of struggle between two rights, both parts have right over this country. At the same time we shouldn't ignore God's promise to Hagar and Ishmael."*

GEORGES KHODR, church bishop: "The prophecies about the return to the land were made in exile, and they returned from exile. There are some conditions of their return: the first it is led by God and the Messiah. Ben Gurion is not the Messiah. He maybe pretends that he is, but he isn't. Christ alone is the fulfilment of world prophecy. If they accept this basic position, the Christian axiom, that everything is already fulfilled, we don't have to expect anything after Christ, any fulfilment."

ALBERT HADAWI, graduate student: "The argument from the Bible? Well, I discount that totally. I don't think anybody can justify that a people's claim to a land exists because some 4,000 years ago somebody said, 'I promise you this land.' Even when you go back to the Bible, what was the Jewish claim to Palestine biblically? It was based on nothing else than conquest and a short duration of occupation."

BISHOP CUBA'IN, church bishop: "We read the Old Testament every Sunday, but we have to choose the lesson lest we create a spiritual difficulty to one of the worshippers. We have a real problem ahead of us vis-à-vis the Old Testament. Many of our people lost belief in the Old Testament and this is the duty of the church to explain to them the Old Testament is the beginning of the New Testament and that we should search deep for the spiritual teachings of the Old Testament."

HIKMAT, needlework lady: "We want the theologians to reinterpret the Bible."

* * *

The greatest difficulty on the question of prophecy is encountered by those Christian leaders whose training, orientation, and affiliation is Western, but who cannot reconcile Western theology with their Arab emotions. One

* The reference is to Genesis 21:13 in which Abraham is promised not only through Isaac (his son by Sarah), but also through Ishmael (his older son by Hagar), "a nation . . . because he is your offspring." See also Genesis 25:16.

such person is the Baptist pastor of Nazareth, Fuad Sahknini. He is caught not only between loyalty to his state, which is Israel, and to his people, the Arabs, but also between Western and Eastern Christian theologizing. A crucial point for him was the massive Prophecy Conference, staged in Jerusalem in 1971 by American Christians, to which he also was invited. He attempted to reconcile the two positions, on the one hand, by accepting the "fulfilment-of-prophecy" view but, on the other hand, by emphasizing the judgements rather than the triumphs, that accompany "fulfilment."

FUAD SAHKNINI, pastor: "I believe everything is working, even the division among the Arab peoples in the Arab countries, for the interest of the Jews, and it will work until the time when the great tribulation will take place. The anti-Christ is going to be a universal dictator. He will turn from a friend to an enemy and that includes the Jews. This means that the public opinion of the world will some day turn against the Jews. I don't know how, of course. This is not nice to say, lest you think I'm inspiring people to be against Israel, but it is my personal understanding of the things which will take place yet in future.

"Now is the time of the gathering and then there will be a time of chastisement. They come with their unbelief now and many are even atheists, and they live in sin and immorality. God is a holy God, and if he wants to treat the Arabs, deal with them according to their iniquities, I think he will deal with the Jews the same. But, God is no respector of persons, I believe. I believe it is now the time of the gathering of the Jews and this will not end the whole story. I believe there will be a great suffering. I myself believe the Jews are going to suffer a great deal in the future.

"As the believers in the Lord Jesus, we believe that the return of the Jews is according to the prophecy. God promised and God keeps his promise, but, as I said at the Biblical Prophecy Conference, I believe in prophecy with justice. If things are going to be fulfilled, I believe we should have this human side also and remember those who are suffering and those who have lost their homes and land. Those who live in camps, they are human beings like we are, I don't care whether they are Arabs or Jews."

* * *

The views of the Palestinians concerning Jesus are likewise colored by their knowledge, which is often quite scanty, by their experience, and by their political positions.

ISMAIL SHAMOUT, artist: "Well, the only thing that I can say is that Christianity is the biggest religion now all over the world. Christ was born in Palestine. He carried his message of peace to the whole world. The people

212

who have the power now are the Christians all over the world in America and in Europe especially. And what are they doing about Palestine from where Christ came? They are controlled mainly by Zionist organizations."

WADIE TLEEL, oil company representative: "I know his preachings at that time, but I don't know what he would preach now. He would try to get us together. He was preaching peace all the time for everybody from different nationalities. There were Romans there. There were Greeks. There were Jews. There were Syrians. Some of them believed in him, some of them did not believe."

EMILE TOUMA, editor: "Jesus Christ is a myth. I did not discover this thing. I discovered those scientists, thinkers, and philosophers who discovered this before me, but I accepted their conclusions. There are no historical facts to prove that Jesus Christ, as he appeared in the New Testament, ever lived in Palestine. It is true you see that there is a certain Jesus Ben Zera, who was actually an Essene. He lived and he fought against the Romans, and he was actually crucified upside down. But Jesus Christ as such, there is no historical explanation of him. Muhammed was born under the sun of history and historians know him. They mention him. He wrote letters. His letters have been kept. Persians you see have his story in their documents and manuscripts. Of Christ you find nothing. The only thing which you find is in Josephus, and it has been added, because if you read it well you see that it doesn't fit."

HATIM, commando: "He said that we should love and we respect duty. This is something we took from the Greeks. To love and to respect justice is something from the Romans. To love and respect humanity this is something we have taken from Christ. I like to see a dynamic church. Our Lord was most dynamic. When he was told not to go to Jerusalem, that there was danger to his life, he was the first man who was a commando and went to Jerusalem. And we want people to come over and go to Jerusalem."

NAJIB, commando: "Do I have anything in common with the revolutionary Jesus of Nazareth who lived in our land? If he was against Zionist oppression, yes."

ANITA DAMIANI, college teacher: "The land of Palestine gave birth to an important religious leader, Jesus of Nazareth, and does he have anything to say to this present conflict? As far as the teachings of Jesus are concerned, he became a Gentile. This is the whole point. He became a gentile, and so we cannot go back to the Talmud, the tooth-for-tooth, and eye-for-eye morality."

213

NAZRI ZANANIRI, administrator: "I have an idea that Jesus would spoil all the factories which make planes and bombs. That is the first. And then no more troubles. Jesus wants his followers to get rid of all of these things."

* * *

The words of the Palestinians on Jerusalem, the Bible, and Jesus confirm what has been noted in the earlier chapter on religion, namely the significance of distortion and abuse with respect to noble and holy concepts. In their minds, however, the main problem is distortion in the West, where notions of holy places, people, and books have been modified by the self-interest and imperial ambition of nation-states (*i.e.*, Britain and the United States) and the identification of Christian people with those interests.

Chapter 12

Moving with the Course of History

"I expect to see a liberated Palestine. We are moving with the course of history. The Zionist movement is against the course of history, against the ideas for which humanity fought millions of years: justice, humanity, non-discrimination, equality."

— *Massih Abdul*

"Something, I would call it a bud, has opened up. This flower is going to mature and fully flourish, and the Palestinians will regain their identity. Nobody and nothing can stop the process."

— *Fouad Bahnan*

The Palestinians have suffered many defeats, but in spite of all the losses and the bitterness they nurture, they have never given up hope. Although they have suffered at the hands of Israel, their leaders, the Arab nations, the big powers, and the United Nations, they have also continued to believe that the very agents who betrayed them would some day help to make things right. And they have also believed that a new generation of Jews will, someday, recognize them as equals.

Most of all, and especially of late, they have believed in themselves and that they will continue their struggle until their goal is achieved. In this struggle they see the October War of 1973 as a turning point. It was a turning point in their own hearts, in the Arab world, in the Western nations, in the United Nations, and not least of all also in Israel.

New recognition for the Palestinian people, their land, and their organization (the PLO) within the Arab world came with the seventh Arab summit conference at Rabat, Morocco, in October 1974. The right of the Palestinian people to return to their homeland and to exercise self-determination was reaffirmed, as well as the right of the Palestinian people to set up an independent authority, under the leadership of the PLO in its capacity as the sole legitimate representative of the Palestinian people on any Palestinian land that is liberated. In the same month the United Nations General Assembly invited the PLO to participate in the UN debate on the

215

Palestine question and granted to the PLO observer status. Previous to these events, the Palestinians had themselves broadened and de-militarized the leadership of the PLO Executive in the National Congress held in June 1974. Other affirmations of the Palestinians came at various summit conferences in that same year: the Non-Aligned and Arab countries meeting in Algiers, the Organization of African Unity meeting in Mogadishio, and the Islamic Conference in Lahore.

GAMAL EL-SOURANY, Egypt*: "The October War of 1973 brought many changes: 1) the Arabs worked together for the first time after centuries; 2) petrol was used as a weapon, maybe not 100 per cent but 35 per cent, next time maybe 50 or 60 per cent; 3) the Arabs were courageous, progressive, with a great deal of self-respect and trust for their leaders; 4) on the Israeli side the doctrine of superiority and closeness was shaken, the myth of the land without people was destroyed, and even the new boundaries of 1967 turned out not to provide security; 5) Arabs abroad were treated differently, as nation after nation realized that 'the gate to the Arab world is not through Tel Aviv.'"

RHOUI EL-KHATIB, Jordan: "The October War has shaken Israel and proved to U.S.A. that the Arabs will not yield and will not accept occupation forever. There is a definite rise in the morale of people under occupation. The unity of the Arab world has been accelerated. The petrol fight has shocked Europe. The Muslim world has been encouraged to back the Arabs on a larger scale than before. African peoples have broken relations with Israel. If Israel doesn't respond, it has to face another war. The Arabs are giving the whole world a new chance for a peaceful settlement. Nobody will blame them if they seek liberation of their lands."

ADLA ISSA, Occupied Palestine: "We feel better now after October. We have more hope of getting land back. Jews have had their idea changed. It's not their land. Our spirits are higher."

IBRAHIM SAMA'AN, Israel: "October war brought Israel back to its normal size, almost. The Arabs did not have a very tremendous military victory. They got back honour and dignity. Arab human beings are more respected now by the Jew, in the street and in the work. We used to be looked down upon."

INAM MUFTI, Occupied Palestine: "October war gave a little bit of self-confidence. We hate wars, but it helped to move towards the solution. People are becoming extremely tired of occupation. We had pride and strength also in front of Israelis."

* In this chapter, place names indicate location at time of interview.

FOUAD BAHNAN, Lebanon: "If the possibility was given for the oriental Jews now living in Palestine to give their honest and free opinion, they would say, especially after the October war, that they would rather live in the situation as it was prior to 1948 than the present situation which we are now in."

* * *

There is now among the Palestinians and among Arabs in general a whole spectrum of expectations. The least they expect is for Egypt to have all of Sinai back, and Syria the Golan Heights. The Palestinians themselves hope to have Israel withdraw from the West Bank, from East Jerusalem, and from Gaza in order to establish a Palestinian state.

Their greatest expectation or hope is that all the political and military boundaries will be erased, and a single state will be created in which all those who are there now and all those who are entitled to return will live together as equals and in peace. This state would be secular and democratic, or, to use once again the words of Nabeel A. Shaath, "a democratic, non-sectarian, secular, open, multiple, plural state" in lieu of "an expansionist, racist, ethnocentric, and closed state."

Not all those who hope and work for such a state are agreed on how it should happen, when, or how fast. Some see it as arriving in time as the natural outcome of an evolutionary process which will have its beginnings with the establishment of a state on the West Bank. Others see it as happening only as a consequence of a major war or revolutionary upheaval.

NAJIB, Lebanon: "We are building a new, progressive, democratic, and non-sectarian state where everybody, Jew, Muslim, and Christian, can practise whatever he wants but not practise it on others, I mean violently. I am free to be a Muslim, but I am not free to impose Islam on anybody, neither theologically nor by force. If somebody chooses to be a Muslim that is all right within a state that gives freedom to anyone. You can be a Muslim or Christian or Jew or atheist in Canada, can't you? We believe that this can take place only when the Zionist movement is destroyed."

IBRAHIM SAMA'AN, Israel: "I think the Palestinians should have their own state, not Jordan and not Israel, but part of what used to be Jordan. I mean the West Bank and part of what was under Egypt, that's the Gaza strip. This state that I have in mind for the Palestinians should have relations with Israel. In fact it cannot live on its own if it does not have a way to the sea. It should be given freeway to a port in Israel and normal relations should be reached between Israel and this Palestinian state. And I believe that there should be freedom for any Palestinian to live in Israel and for any Jew to live in the Arab Palestinian state. That is to say, there should be a confederation between Israel and this Palestinian state probably along with Jordan."

SAMIR, Syria: "I would be in favour of establishing a Palestine state on the West Bank. It should be on the original land."

ALBERT HADAWI, Canada: "They [the Israelis] come up with statements such as 'there isn't room enough for the Palestinians to come back,' and yet they claim that they want five million more Jews to come into the country. If there is room for those extra alien American, French, Russian, and German Jews, why not for the original people, the Palestinians, who have been living on the perimeters of their own country begging for all these 23 years? I am advocating as a peaceful solution the same proposal which the Palestinians have put forth: a pluralistic, democratic state of Palestine where both Arabs and Jews can live together in a Palestinian state. One man, one vote, simply that."

AREF AL-AREF, Occupied Palestine: "My suggestion would be to stop all actions that are being taken, deportation, arresting people, demolishing houses, and establishing a democratic Palestinian state in which all sections – Muslims, Christians, and Jews – live together under the same right and the same privileges."

ELIAS FREIJ, Occupied Palestine: "People say peace could come in one of three ways: the Jordanian government coming back to the West Bank; the Palestinians forming their own state; or complete annexation and integration by Israel. I personally have another solution. Israel should withdraw from the West Bank and the United Nations should create this as a UN trusteeship for five years. So, no to Jordan, no to Israel. We Palestinians would be under the jurisdiction and protection of the United Nations. Within five years, things would settle down. Then we would know what to decide, what to do, how to live. But you can't move from one occupation to another occupation."

SIMON, Occupied Palestine: "Peace can come by returning all Arab properties back to owners or compensation, by federation, and by making Jerusalem an open city – international."

RIBHI AWAD, Egypt: "I have become aware lately that there probably isn't a peaceful solution because once again our people are being swept under the rug. The whole issue is made to appear as though the struggle is between Israel and Jordan, when the crux of the matter is the Palestinian question. Our main objective is to establish the non-sectarian, democratic Palestine state where Jews, Muslims, Christians can live together in peaceful coexistence. It is a compromise. We are prepared to live with our killers and this is a great compromise to give them this proposal to live together. Those who killed us and those who are being there at our cost again we are ready to live with them but in a democratic Palestine state, with equal rights and on an equal basis."

FOUAD BAHNAN, Lebanon: "I fully endorse a social, democratic, and secular state for Palestine. If we are really honest and sincere, this is the only just and durable solution. An Israeli state, as it is today, will not give the Jews the security they are after. It is going to be a state that is going to be sustained indefinitely by power and military might, and I don't think this is the aim or the future destiny of the Jewish people. They have something more to contribute to the world than physical power and military ability.

"If we are really concerned enough for the Jews as Christians, it would be our Christian duty, in my way of thinking, to advocate this kind of situation, a secular state. Secondly, as Christians we should advocate this kind of state with reference to Islam and the Muslims. Islam has always been a theocracy, with no division between the state and religion. Here for the first time in the history of Islamic Palestinian people, the majority are recommending this kind of solution. Here are young people, who have been through the furnace of suffering and tribulation for the last quarter of a century. Out of this tribulation they have come into this deep insight and they are offering the world and even their staunchest enemies, who have expelled them, this approach, saying, 'Let's forget the past and live together, and together let's build this country of Palestine.'"

* * *

How realistic is it for the Palestinians to think of Arabs and Jews living together in the same land and in the same state? That there would be problems the Palestinians do not deny, but their optimism is also not without basis. They have lived together often, at many places, and over long periods of time in the past. Not a few Palestinians can give personal examples of a happy co-existence in the past. Furthermore they live together now in the Arab countries as well as in Israel. Besides, if reconciliation was possible between the Germans and the French and between other bitter racial or national enemies, why not also between Arabs and Jews? On this subject, we have first of all the words of Eliya Khoury, the deported priest and executive member of the PLO. Many others express similar opinions.

ELIYA KHOURY, Jordan: "I am sure that both the Jewish people and the Arab people can make Palestine a paradise. What is ruling Israel now is not the Jewish nation but the military institution. They have a very powerful military institution and this is the source of danger and this is actually causing the greatest obstacles in coexistence between the Arabs and the Jews. We are both semites, don't forget this, and we can coexist and live together beautifully, and in harmony.

"There is one thing that I fear actually, to be honest and truthful to myself and to you. Now the Arabs are very weak from a military point of view but they have the manpower and they have the money and perhaps there will come a day when the Arabs will be able to build up very powerful, very, very powerful military institutions. What will happen? Will three million be able to stand in front of say fifty million people? Then I am afraid, I am afraid that in that time the last Jewish child will be annihilated in Israel and for this I shall weep and cry if it happens. God forbid it, because they have a right to live, and I pray that they will come to their senses and to their reason. Eventually we could coexist beautifully."

ALBERT HADAWI, Canada: "Are the Arabs and the Jews more compatible than the French and the English? I think it is a matter of desire, not a matter of compatibility. I wouldn't have anything in common, for example, with a German Jew, or with a Russian Jew, but it is something that hopefully can come to pass with time. Who would have thought, for example, that Canada and the U.S. would be dealing with Germany today, after what happened in the Second World War – or with Japan? This is one of the major arguments that the Zionists put forth every time the Palestinian propositions for peace are made public. They say it is not realistic for Arabs and Jews to live together. They put forth this argument to maintain their own exclusive possession of Palestine. But there is absolutely no reason to suppose that the two communities cannot live together.

"Our history has been replete with incidents where all nationalities came to the Middle East as a haven from persecution. We have absorbed the Armenians and the Kurds. We have Turks among us. You name them, we have them. We even have some Mongols and Russians who have lived for centuries in peace and harmony with the Arabs. To suppose now that the Jews of Israel and the Palestinians cannot live harmoniously together is absurd.

"But I would like to ask this question. Which would be better for humanity, for us to try to live together for two or three generations knowing full well that it will be difficult after all that has happened, or to try and carry on the fight for two or three generations? As a Palestinian, I am sure most of my countrymen would opt for trying to live together. I would much rather live together for two or three generations than to carry on fighting for two or three generations. Any humanist, any moralist, anybody decent enough to be interested in justice and peace would opt for this kind of a solution."

SAMI EL-KARAMI, Canada: "Arabs and Jews can live together. The Arab people are not racist people. They don't have black and white discriminations. The Jewish people are not basically bad."

SHAKIB A. OTAQUI, Occupied Palestine: "Yes, I do believe Arab Muslims and Israeli Jews can embrace each other if conditions return to those that were there before 1948. I do believe normal life, peaceful life could be carried on amongst the three groups. But as things are now, it is impossible to call upon one group to live peacefully with the second, who has invaded her and robbed her of her properties and homes. If you read history, the Muslims in general and the Arabs in particular have been perhaps the most kind to the Jews in the last two thousand years. They've been the place to which the Jews have always gone for refuge whenever they were persecuted in Europe."

BISHOP CUBA'IN, Occupied Palestine: "The Arabs and the Jews lived together for centuries and they lived together peacefully."

AREF AL-AREF, Occupied Palestine: "Can the Arabs and Jews live together? Yes, they can. They lived together in the past. I myself was born in the old city of Jerusalem in a house where my parents and Jews lived together in the same house. And I have many, many Jewish friends. Two of my books were translated into Hebrew. I've learned Hebrew some fifty years ago. I have passed the Hebrew examination of the government. I lectured in the Hebrew University. I have many, many friends in among the Jews. And believe me, I don't hate the Jews and their nation but I hate the Zionists, particularly the extremists, who kick us out of our country and keep it purely for Jews. This I would never allow to happen even if they cut me into pieces."

FOUD DAJANI, Jordan: "I have Jewish friends at the University, and we have also a family doctor who is Jewish, who is living here and he refuses to go to Israel. He prefers to live here in Egypt and always says that this is his country, this is his homeland. Why shouldn't we live with them? We believe in one God, the same God. We are against the political regime, not against the Jews as a religion."

RAJA FARRAJ, Jordan: "We have many friends who remained in the West Bank and we hear stories from them that they have gone into competition with Jews, and that they have proved themselves. I don't think we will be afraid to start all over again there. I am sure of it. We can compete with the Jews. Definitely. Definitely."

ISHAEL ABED HUSSIM, Jordan: "It's not a matter of being among Jews or among Arabs. No, that's not the way we look at it. Jews are really not absolute enemies, no, I don't think so. The best proof is that the people on the West Bank are now living and merging with the Jews."

GEORGE FREIJ, Occupied Palestine: "Arab policemen and Jewish policemen work together."

AHMED ALI, Lebanon: "How do Arabs compete with the Jews in the same land? In Israel there are now two groups of people. There are European Jews, who are running the whole business, and there are the eastern Jews, North African Jews. The leadership is the Western Jew. I think most of the Palestinians are not worse than the North African Jews. Some of the educated Palestinians, at least on an education level, can compete with the educated Jew. The Palestinians might even be bridge-builders between the two groups of Jews. Or the oriental Jews might be bridge-builders between the Arabs and the Jews."

SAMI SALIM KHOURY, Jordan: "Can the Arab doctor compete with the Jewish doctor? Of course he can compete, if we are given the same opportunity, and if we have the Hadassah of America to send us millions and millions of dollars, to have our heart-lung machines and our equipment and so on and so forth. They always tell their tourists, look what we have done with Palestine. Let them go and see what the Kuwaiters have done with Kuwait in the desert. Give me money and I will show you what I can do."

RAJA FARRAJ, Jordan: "The average Arab is more superior than is recognized. Let me give you an example. Here, even in Jordan, our firm is established quite long. It's not easy for us to get a job from the government because we are a local firm. We do get around this by getting a foreign firm to stand in for us. We agree that we will be doing the job completely and we pay them an overriding commission maybe 10 per cent, maybe 20 per cent, to have them present the offer to the government. And this is done. A foreign firm will be accepted in here, but the foreign abilities are not applied. We the local people do the job. This is because of Arab lack of confidence in Arab know-how."

ELIAS FREIJ, Occupied Palestine: "As individuals we can compete successfully with the Israelis. There's no doubt. But we don't have money from Germany, from America, from England, from France."

LEILA NASSER, Occupied Palestine: "You see I was today at a Jewish lady. A very nice lady. The more I see her, the more I think she is a very nice lady. By chance she invited us to come to her home, and we went to visit her. Last week I went to see her, and she had a broken arm. I went today and took the needlework that she ordered. She is living in a home which used to be an Arab home, belonging to one of our friends, whose son, a driver, works with me. So I came and told my friends, and today I took the driver along for the first time to visit his father's former home. The Arab driver, he felt so badly, you know, in the beginning, but towards the end he liked it so well and he was talking to this lady and asked her if he could do anything for her. She says she wants the family to come up and help her with the garden. In future she wants to bring them in touch with the government and let them have part of the land, so they could live in their own home. I thought this was great."

AN ARAB IN ISRAEL, Israel: "The time will come when other Arab generations more honest, more brave will understand Israel. The time will come when other Jewish generations, more honest, more brave will understand the Arabs."

FUAD SAHKNINI, Israel: "The Jews have as much right to live and survive as the Arabs themselves. But there should be some kind of a plan where both of them could get along together instead of wasting most of the budget of the countries for war and weapons. I think the Near East can be one of the richest places in all the world."

IBRAHIM SAMA'AN, Israel: "I really don't want to talk about boundaries. I want to talk about good will. If good will proves to be there, the boundaries are not a problem. Good will is needed on both sides. Both are afraid of each other. Both do not trust each other. So this is the situation. If good will is proved to exist on both sides, believe me that several less kilometres or several more kilometres wouldn't make a bit of difference."

* * *

Can it happen? Will it happen? Feelings and thoughts about the future are mixed in the strongest of Palestinians. Hope is mixed with despair, optimism with realism and pessimism. But in the final analysis, the Palestinians feel that time is on their side. This is true in a double sense. Not only do they feel that ultimately the victory will be theirs, but also that the victory need not come in their own lifetime. Their concept of time is not a Western one. Indeed, for them it often seems that time does not exist, as the following conversations and statements illustrate.

BASIL SAHAR, Occupied Palestine: "The Palestinians have a story about Nixon, Brezhnev, and Sadat going to God and talking to him about their problems.

> Nixon: 'God, when will war in Vietnam end?'
> God: 'In two years, maybe.'
> Nixon (crying): 'Two years is too much.'

Brezhnev: 'God, when will all the world unite?'
God: 'In fifty years.'
Brezhnev: 'Long live . . . '
Sadat: 'God, when will Jews give back the land?'
God (Crying): . . .
Sadat: 'Why are you crying?'
God: 'Not in my time.' "

INAM YASIN, Egypt:
Q. "Mr. Yasin, how old are you?"
A. "About thirty."
Q. "You Palestinians don't measure time very exactly, do you?"
A. "It's important and unimportant."
Q. "Why important and unimportant?"
A. "Because we need time for our struggles. And unimportant because when you live as a refugee, time is a very bad thing to measure, you see. That's why we consider time very important and at the same time unimportant."

ELIAS ANDROUS DEEK, Lebanon:
Q. "How old are you?"
A. "About thirty-five years."
Q. "About thirty-five? You don't know for sure?"
A. "We left the real birth certificates in Palestine. These ages which we are saying are just approximate. The documents have been left behind. Now our ages are not very exact and not very important."

SALIM AHMED EL-NABULSI, Jordan: "I am about forty-nine years old. I don't know exactly because I have no certificate. I know I was born in the early 1920s."

HAZIM MAHMOUD EL-KHALIDI, Occupied Palestine: "I mean the whole universe is not built on that concept of time. It is based on the concept of immortality until God wills that there should be no longer life. And he has been unwilling for millions of years and may be unwilling to terminate this life for several millions of years to come, so why connect it with one's lifetime? One's lifetime is, I think, just a grain of sand in an ocean."

ISSA FARIS, Occupied Palestine: "Arabs have a different psychology and whole different approach to problems. There's a timelessness about them. Compromise isn't the most important issue. They don't even have the word in their language. They have learned patience."

SAID NASRALLA, Lebanon: "The obstacles are great and time required for reaching your goals is long. It is a long time, and we mean it, it is a long time."

NAJIB, Lebanon: "I will tell you a story. Maybe you have read it in a book by Mao Tse Tung. But this doesn't necessarily mean that I am a Maoist. I could be a Marxist. Let me tell you the story about a foolish Chinese man. This stupid man had a farm. He couldn't do anything about his farm because whenever he did the floods would come down the mountain and destroy his house and his crop and his rice and everything.

"Now, he undertook to remove the mountain lest a big storm kill him, his brothers, his sisters, and kill all his family, and all his village. So he started to remove the mountain a barrel load at a time. Now the wise white-bearded Chinese man of the village came to tell how stupid he was. The farmer replied: I think like you but with a different logic and towards different ends. If I don't do it my son will do it. If he doesn't do it his sons will do it. As high as the mountains are they cannot grow any higher, and yet with each wheelbarrow they are that much lower.

"Now to apply this story to our situation: it is inevitable that we fight. It is inevitable that liberation takes place. When or how much or how long is a question that we leave to the Zionists themselves."

* * *

As much as the October War may have changed the situation in their favour, the Palestinians still recognize that Israel is also stronger and more determined than ever to survive. The tightening of military occupation in Gaza and on the West Bank, the establishment of new settlements, the frequent bombing of refugee camps in Lebanon, and the expenditures on armaments, which Palestinians believe include nuclear weapons, are all signs that Israel will not change its position easily. But the Palestinian determination too has been reinforced, and consequently realism as frequently changes to optimism as it does to pessimism.

IBRAHIM AL-ABED, Lebanon: "The Palestinians are now facing a very critical position. On the one hand, Israel has declared its right openly and has emphasized its intention to wage a war of genocide against the Palestinians, to bombard and fight them no matter where they are."

GEORGES KHODR, Lebanon: "There is no hope for return, if we are realistic."

AHMED ALI, Lebanon: "The Israelis obviously have things under control. They have the support of the Americans. There is no real hope of going back in this generation."

ISMAIL SHAMOUT, Lebanon: "I tell you frankly, I believe I am not going to see free Palestine, but I am satisfied because I think we shall be successful in giving our children the flag of Palestine to carry on."

AREF AL-AREF, Occupied Palestine: "I anticipate more troubles, more unrest, more fighting. If the big powers and the United Nations don't find a way to stop the present atrocities that are being committed by the Israelis, there is no doubt that some more fighting will take place because the Palestinian Arabs are determined not to give up their country."

ANTON H. SAFIEH, Occupied Palestine: "An old man was once seen planting young olive trees. And you know it takes an olive tree thirty years to produce its first crop. And he was asked by this passerby, who said: 'Well, you fool! What are you doing? Will you ever eat from these olive trees?' And he said: 'No, I don't expect even to finish planting them. But they, meaning my ancestors, planted and I ate. And I will plant so that my sons and grandsons eat.'"

AHMED SALAN, Occupied Palestine: "The armed struggle will not be successful in the near future. At present the military machine of the Israelis is perfected to such a degree that I think the Palestinian commandos are no match for them. But eventually, I think, our cause will prevail, because if there is any justice in this world, then it should be directed our way, and I think the Palestinians will survive."

AYOUB, Occupied Palestine: "The Palestinian is not finished. Who is he to finish us? He is an agent, paid by the U.S.A. We have seen one defeat after another. We are still around. An agent will not always be an agent. The agents all die. Only the gold remains after going into fire."

ISSA FARIS, Occupied Palestine: "One cannot ignore history. The Crusaders came here with the support of all of Europe. They had this political feeling. After 100 years they were kicked out."

WADIE, commando in Lebanon: "We have never been defeated because we can afford many defeats. No doubt, we didn't win. But there is nothing that will make us lose."

* * *

A concluding assessment of the Middle East situation, including the conflicting emotions of the peoples involved, can lead the outsider also to very mixed feelings and much frustration. No resolution of the conflict seems in sight. The Palestinians for the most part are determined to die rather than to say good-bye forever to the land that once was theirs. The Israelis, with very few exceptions, are equally determined not to surrender an acre of the Palestinian area over which they have gained control. They would, they say, use nuclear weapons or re-enact Massada* before they reversed their policies.

Both sides are backed, perhaps equally, by the military, religious, and emotional energies of humanity. The stakes are very high. The conflict in the Middle East is constantly in danger of becoming not only an East-West confrontation of unprecedented magnitude, but a final round in the battles of the nations of all time.

It may, therefore, seem like an escape from reality to invoke the concept of miracles as the last remaining hope for peace. But that isn't necessarily the case, at least not if miracles are understood to mean a solution which is not now on the desks of diplomats, or if it implies that a rather drastic reorientation is necessary on the part of those involved. Or, if it is remembered that miracles themselves are an integral part of Middle East reality, in the present as well as in the past. Indeed, it is the Middle East which gave to the world not only the language but also the evidence of the miraculous.

Numerous Middle East miracles have already been reported in our lifetime: the creation of the state of Israel; the birth of a new cohesive society of Jews coming out of different cultures; the military victories of a young and untried state; the blossoming again of roses in the desert; the development of an agricultural economy where once were swamps or desert and of forests and woodlands where once the rocky hills stood naked.

Not all the miracles have been chronicled, however. Among the last places to be visited in pursuit of the material for this book was Kuneitra, the Syrian city totally destroyed in the wars of 1967 and 1973. The last blow came with the defiant Israeli departure in 1974 when a UN zone was set up between Israeli and Syrian lines. Of the 60,000 one-time residents only about ten had stayed through it all. Among them was the aged Wadid Nassif, a grandmother, who also identified herself as a Palestinian. Her story of unusual courage and remarkable survival symbolizes the best closing characterization of the Palestinian people while at the same time pointing to new Middle East possibilities. "The Israeli soldiers came to say goodbye," she said, pointing to the ruins around her. "Then they blew up what was left of the water system. But God provided for me in a miraculous way. A bomb fell nearby and opened up a spring of water."

The Wadid Nassif story is reminiscent of Genesis 21 and the account of Hagar (and thousands of similar Middle East stories). With her son Ishmael, Hagar wandered in the wilderness of Beersheba, expecting to die of hunger and thirst when the bread and skin of water, with which Abraham had sent them on their way, were gone. As Hagar cast her child into the

* The name of the Dead Sea fortress where 1,900 years ago the Jews committed suicide rather than surrender to the Romans.

bush, lest she see him die, a voice within encouraged her to pick him up again: "Arise, lift up the lad, and hold him fast in your hand; for I will make him a great nation." Doing as she was told, Hagar then looked around and beheld a well with water. Ishmael survived, not once but many times, and he became an expert in living in the wilderness, the father of twelve princes and tribes, and the revered patriarch of a large nation.

And so it has been with the Palestinians and their children in the desert. Wherever they have gone they have demonstrated a remarkable capacity for survival and for becoming expert in many things. Like Middle East plants surviving the parching summer on the morning dew, like roses blooming in a dry desert, like camels needing only the occasional oasis, like goats and sheep 'grazing' on barren hills, so also the Palestinians have lived miraculously in the deserts, in their horrible camps, and in the lonely diaspora of far-away countries. There are many miracle stories in the Middle East. The modern story of the Palestinians is not the least of them. Again and again, they have faced their impossible situation, and again and again they have discovered new possibilities for themselves. And whenever all hope was gone, another well opened up to water the desert in which they found themselves.

The experiences of the Israelis and of the Palestinians and of many peoples before them could be analogous. The terrible impasse confronting the Middle East is like a dry desert in which all of life is doomed. Yet, precisely where all prospects have vanished and when the elders are already turning their eyes away, less they see their children die, new possibilities may already be emerging. The same bush which hides the dying also shelters the well which gives them new life. The same bombs which smash the water systems open up new springs. The same explosion which brings Jews and Arabs together in bloody confrontation can also be the social shock treatment which unveils co-existence and human brotherhood as a real option for a new generation.

The miracle may actually already be in the making. Surely, at least some Palestinians realize that their much-touted secular Palestinian state, in which Jews, Christians, and Muslims will live at peace, must first of all be rooted firmly in the hearts and minds of their people before it can be agreed to on paper and implemented on the land. And that, therefore, conciliation and accommodation must begin in the camps as much as in the Knesset. And surely the Jews of Israel, and the nations of the world with them, have begun to conclude that 400,000 Arabs in Israel will not remain second-class citizens forever, that the additional 1,000,000 under Israeli control will not be driven out, and that another 1,000,000 pressing their claims from Jordan, Syria, and Lebanon cannot be bombed into submission or roasted with napalm without Israel itself going down to destruction.

As these conclusions become more general, the people will not only see an Israeli-Palestinian rapprochement, thinking negatively, as the only hope for survival, but also, thinking positively, as the great opportunity for both peoples to achieve their full genius and to make their much-needed contribution to the rest of humanity. When that begins to happen – and who is to say that it hasn't already begun – then the miracle will be on its way. Then men will understand the vision of Isaiah who saw Jerusalem becoming the mountain to which the peoples of the world would come to learn how not to make war any more. And then also the words of Yasir Arafat before the UN will be remembered: "War flares up in Palestine, and it is in Palestine where peace will be born."

Selected Readings

A. BOOKS

Abu-Lughod, Ibrahim. *The Transformation of Palestine.* Evanston: Northwestern University Press, 1974.

Al-Abed, Ibrahim. *A Handbook to the Palestine Question.* Beirut: Palestine Research Center, 1969.

Al Messiri, Abdul Wahab. *A Lover from Palestine and Other Poems: An Anthology of Palestinian Poetry.* Washington: Free Palestine Press, 1970.

Amad, Adnan (ed.). *Israeli League for Human and Civil Rights: The Shahak Papers.* Beirut: Near East Ecumenical Bureau of Information and Interpretation, 1974.

Antonius, George. *The Arab Awakening.* New York: Capricorn, 1965.

Epp, Frank H. *Whose Land is Palestine? The Middle East Problem in Historical Perspective.* Grand Rapids, Michigan: Wm. B. Eerdmans; and Toronto: McClelland and Stewart, 1970.

Forrest, A.C. *The Unholy Land.* Toronto: McClelland and Stewart, 1970.

Shazaleh, Adnan Abu. *Arab Cultural Nationalism in Palestine During the British Mandate.* Beirut. The Institute for Palestine Studies, 1974.

Hadawi, Sami, *Bitter Harvest: Palestine 1914-67.* New York: New World, 1967.

Jiryis, Sabri. *The Arabs in Israel.* Beirut: The Institute for Palestine Studies, 1968.

Khalidi, Walid and Jill Khadduri (eds). *Palestine and the Arab-Israeli Conflict: An Annotated Bibliography.* Beirut: The Institute of Palestine Studies, 1974.

Khurshid, Ghazi. *Human Rights in the Occupied Territories.* Beirut: Near East Ecumenical Bureau of Information and Interpretation.

Landau, Jacob M. *The Arabs in Israel: A Political Study.* New York: Oxford, 1969.

Laqueur, Walter. *The Israel-Arab Reader: A Documentary History of the Middle East Conflict.* New York: The Citadel Press. 1968.

Nasir, Musa. *Towards a Solution of the Palestine Problem: A Selection of Speeches and Writings 1946-66.* Bir Zait, 1966.

Nutting, Anthony. *The Arabs.* New York: New American Library, 1965.

Palestine Lives: Interviews With Leaders of the Resistance. Beirut: Palestine Research Center, 1973.

Parkes, James. *Whose Land? A History of the Peoples of Palestine.* Baltimore: Penguin Books, 1970.

Peretz, Don. *Israel and the Palestine Arabs.* Washington: The Middle East Institute, 1958.

Report of the Commissioner-General of the United Nations Relief and Works Agency for Palestine Refugees in the Near East. 1 July, 1966 — 30 June, 1967. New

York: United Nations, 1967. Also, same title, 1968, 1969, 1970, 1971, 1972, 1973, 1974, 1975.
Rodinson, Maxine. *Israel and the Arabs.* Baltimore: Penguin Books, 1968.

B. PERIODICALS

Journal of Palestine Studies: a Quarterly on Palestinian Affairs and the Arab-Israeli Conflict. The Institute for Palestine Studies, P.O. Box 7164, Beirut, Lebanon.
Palestine: Monthly PLO Information Bulletin. The Palestine Liberation Organization United Information, P.O. Box 8984, Beirut, Lebanon.

C. LITERATURE LISTS
Available from Addresses Below

Arab Information Center
747 Third Avenue
New York, N.Y. 10017

Arab Information Center
170 Laurier Ave. W. Suite 709
Ottawa, Ontario K1P 5V5

Near East Ecumenical Bureau of Information and Interpretation
P.O. Box 5376
Beirut, Lebanon

Palestine Liberation Research Center
P.O. Box 1691
Beirut, Lebanon

The Institute for Palestine Studies
Ashquar Bldg.
P.O. Box 7164
Beirut, Lebanon

The Lebanese Association for Information on Palestine
P.O. Box 11.7037
Beirut, Lebanon

Index of Interviews

(The following people were interviewed for this
book. Page references indicate quotation
in the text.)

Name or Pseudonym* and Page References	Occupational Identification	Origin in Palestine	Present Location
Abbasi, Isam, 168	Poet	Safad	Israel
Abbassi, Jabra, 114, 180	Medical doctor	West Bank	OP**
Abdelhadi, Khalil, 85, 183, 198, 205	Medical doctor	Shobeth	OP
Abdel-Jehil, Saleh, 19, 163	Teenager in orphanage	Baviksa	OP
Abdul, Massih, 198, 215	Commando editor	Acre	Lebanon
Abedilhadi, Isam, 93, 113, 125, 161, 164	Exiled women's movement president	Nablus	Jordan
Aboumar, Hanna Michel, 52	Professor	Haifa	Lebanon
Abu-Jawad, 125, 134, 169, 176, 178, 181, 191, 204	Commando officer	Jerusalem	Lebanon
Abullula, Yousif, 52	Camp administrator	Tiberias	Jordan
Akel, Isa, 190	Member of Parliament	Jerusalem	OP
Al-Abed, Ibrahim, 53, 63, 128, 225	Research director	Saforia	Lebanon
Al-Alami, Abdul Razzah, 56	Relative of Mufti	Jerusalem	OP
Al-Alami, Saladin, 202-4	Mufti of Jerusalem	Jerusalem	OP
Al-Araj, Farah, 55, 69, 78, 92, 179	Mayor	Beit Jala	OP
Al-Aref, Aref, 26-8, 81, 92, 95, 99, 113, 190, 218, 221, 226	Historian, former Jerusalem mayor	Jerusalem	OP
Al-Atawneh, Issat, 19, 85, 180, 191	Bedouin sheikh	Hebron	OP
Al-Atawneh, Maha, 21, 97	School teacher	Hebron	OP

*If requested by interviewee.

** Occupied Palestine – The part occupied by Israel in 1967, including East Jerusalem, Gaza, and West Bank.

Name or Pseudonym* and Page References	Occupational Identification	Origin in Palestine	Present Location
Al-Khateb, Mahmoud, 130	Camp resident	Zereau	Lebanon
Al-Khateeb, Hussam, 32	PLO leader	Tiberias	Syria
Alazeh, Muhammad, 19, 58, 63, 69, 183	Camp director	Beit Jibrin	Jordan
Ali, Ahmed, 44, 51, 56, 67, 124, 143, 174, 179, 183, 189, 199, 222, 225	Medical doctor	Acre	Lebanon
Ali, Ali Jamil	Muktar in camp	Ramallah	Jordan
Alwalid, Abu, 65, 179	Camp administrator	El-Kabri	Lebanon
Amad, Hajja Andalib, 19, 145	Leader of hospital auxiliary	Nablus	OP
'An Arab in Israel,' 21, 76, 180, 223	Lawyer-teacher	Tiberias	Israel
Asad, 190	Gardener	Bethany	OP
Asa's, Younes, 20, 64	Camp doctor	Jerusalem	Jordan
Assad, 113	Commando	Jerusalem	Lebanon
Atalla, Anton, 114	Banker, former foreign minister	Jerusalem	Jordan
Atalla, Foud, 34	Attorney	Nazareth	Jordan
Awad, Adla, 75	Author	Shafa Omr	OP
Awad, Arabi, 80, 146	Teacher	Nablus	Lebanon
Awad, Bishara, 78	Teacher	Jerusalem	OP
Awad, Ribhi, 218	Fatah representative	Beit-Safafa	Egypt
Aweida, Lina, 19	Student	Haifa	Lebanon
Ayoub, 77, 226	Retired school teacher	Haifa	OP
Ayoub, Musa, 32, 88	Camp chauffeur	Beersheba	OP
Aysheh, 85	Needlework lady	Jerusalem	OP
Azam, Marwan Abdalla, 125, 133, 142, 178	Radio announcer	Safa	Lebanon
Bahnan, Fouad, 47, 68, 215, 217, 219	Priest	Nusf-Jbeil	Lebanon
Bandek, Elias, 42, 182	Mayor of Bethlehem	Bethlehem	OP
Bandek, Leila, 193	Voluntary agency director	Jerusalem	OP
Bitar, Leila, 56, 63, 123, 136, 175	School teacher	Jaffa	Jordan

Name or Pseudonym* and Page References	Occupational Identification	Origin in Palestine	Present Location
El-Nabulsi, Salim Ahmed, 224	Painter	Hebron	Jordan
Es-Said, Nimreh Tannous, 16, 97, 135, 142, 162, 178	Refugee program director	Jerusalem	Jordan
El-Sourany, Gamal, 43, 86, 128, 179, 216	Diplomat	Gaza	Egypt
Farah, Leila, 58	Nurse	Nazareth	Lebanon
Farah, Sana, 129	Student	Nablus	Lebanon
Farah, Shafik, 43, 56, 63, 141, 171, 194, 205, 210	Education director	Shafa A'mr	Lebanon
Farbi, Ibrahim, 90, 197	Voluntary program administrator	Jericho	OP
Fariah, Ahmad, 11, 86, 183	Camp resident	Gaza	OP
Faris, Issa, 78, 113, 197, 224, 226	Priest	Tiberias	OP
Farraj, Fuad, 143, 175	Engineer	Jerusalem	Jordan
Farraj, Sr., Ms., 84	Grandmother	Jaffa	Jordan
Farraj, Raja, 39, 84, 142, 144, 221, 222	Businessman	Jerusalem	Jordan
Fatima, 208	School teacher and welfare worker	Jerusalem	OP
Freij, Elias, 19, 69, 89, 113, 180, 183, 218, 222	Business leader and exporter	Bethlehem	OP
Freij, George, 90, 222	Salesman	Bethlehem	OP
Georgieff, Nadejda, 55, 124	Seamstress	Jerusalem	Jordan
Ghuneini, Suleiman Abu, 58, 63, 175	Camp welfare officer	Jericho	Jordan
Giacaman, George, 57, 114, 197	College teacher	Bethlehem	OP
Gumri, Lily Tannous, 49, 68, 175	Homemaker	Jerusalem	Lebanon
Gumri, Wadie, 32, 43, 48, 58, 59, 129, 176, 181, 183	Chartered accountant	Jerusalem	Lebanon
Hadawi, Albert, 32, 34, 39, 85, 124, 174, 176, 193, 211, 218, 220	Graduate student	Jerusalem	Canada
Haifa, 130-2	Commando	Gaza	Lebanon

Name or Pseudonym* and Page References	Occupational Identification	Origin in Palestine	Present Location
Hamzeh, Ahmad, 63	Camp resident	Jericho	Jordan
Hatim, 134, 213	Commando	Jerusalem	Lebanon
Hazam, Nasr, 42	Restaurant owner	Bethlehem	OP
Hazbun, 91	Refugee at Allenby Bridge	Bethlehem	Jordan
Hikmat, 70, 172, 181, 206, 211	Needlework lady	Jerusalem	OP
Hussim, Ismail Abed El-Rahem Mousa, 221	Tourist guide	Lydda	Jordan
Issa, Adla, 216	Secretary	Ein Kerem	OP
Jabboud, Abbra, 75, 82, 173	Medical doctor	Haifa	Israel
Kanazeh, George J., 51	Businessman	Haifa	Lebanon
Kanazeh, Najla, 20, 143, 184, 199	Homemaker	Haifa	Lebanon
Kardosh, Monsour, 74, 93, 181	Businessman and activist	Nazareth	Israel
Kawas, Giries, 122, 146	Teacher	Gifna	Lebanon
Khader, Issa, 91, 208	Teacher	Ein-Arik	OP
Khamis, Hanna, 55	Engineer	Haifa	Jordan
Khodr, Georges, 171, 194, 197, 199, 211, 225	Church bishop	Syria	Lebanon
Khoury, Dalie Sami, 165, 176	Student	Jerusalem	Jordan
Khoury, Eliya, 33, 97, 118-21, 210, 219	Deported priest	Dothan	Jordan
Khoury, Margaret, 198	Homemaker	Acre	Jordan
Khoury, Najib, 193, 199, 204, 208, 210	Administrator	Jerusalem	OP
Khoury, Sami Salim, 59, 69, 163, 170, 180, 183, 194, 196, 198, 222	Chest surgeon	Nablus	Jordan
Leila	Commando	Safad	Lebanon
Majij, Amin, 78, 116	Medical doctor	Jerusalem	OP
Marouf, Othman, 49, 164	Camp resident	Acre	Lebanon
Mazem, Salama, 62, 114	Camp resident	Gaza	Jordan

Name or Pseudonym* and Page References	Occupational Identification	Origin in Palestine	Present Location
Mazen, Ahmad, 144	Refugee at Allenby Bridge	Hebron	Jordan
Mohammed, Ali, 49, 147	Cook	Beit Eksa	Jordan
Monsour, Sina, 77	School teacher	Ramallah	OP
Mouammar, Khaled, 42, 52, 84, 125, 176, 177, 179, 181, 193	Systems analyst	Nazareth	Canada
Mufti, Inam, 65, 216	Teacher	Safad	OP
Munzev, 20, 52, 77, 82, 178	Engineer	Jerusalem	OP
Musa, Muhammed Issa, 187	Taxi driver	Gaza	Jordan
Najib, 20, 48, 129, 133, 134, 171, 177, 189, 213, 217, 225	Commando	Gaza	Lebanon
Nasir, Hanna, 80, 92, 193	College president	Bir Zait	OP
Nasralla, Mary, 49, 51, 57, 62, 114, 190	Language teacher	Nazareth	Lebanon
Nasralla, Said, 33, 64, 142, 174, 181, 224	Businessman	Haifa	Lebanon
Nassar, Najib, 19, 136-9, 142	Father of imprisoned commando	Jerusalem	Jordan
Nasser, Leila, 23, 91, 114, 222	Needlework director	Jericho	OP
Nassif, Wadid, 227	Homemaker	Gaza	Syria
Nazer, Nizam, 56, 130	Camp doctor	Hebron	Jordan
Niga, Geffhah, 49, 52, 57, 62, 171	Needlework lady	Jericho	Jordan
Omar, 42, 123	Farmer	Jericho	Jordan
Omar, Mark, 43	Student	Jerusalem	OP
Osman, Fouad, 68	Teacher	Nablus	Lebanon
Otaqui, Shakib A., 37, 53, 69, 114, 124, 175, 208, 221	Graduate student	Jerusalem	OP
Otaqui, Salwa Khuri, 49, 67, 162, 195	Medical doctor	Jerusalem	OP

Name or Pseudonym* and Page References	Occupational Identification	Origin in Palestine	Present Location
Qamhawi, Abdul-Salam, 49	Medical doctor	Jaffa	Jordan
Ra'ii, Abdul-Rahman, 16, 49	Muktar in camp	Hebron	Jordan
Radani, Gerous Abou, 62, 64	Camp resident	Jaffa	Lebanon
Radani, Hoda Abo, 64	Camp resident	Jerusalem	Lebanon
Reema, 134, 161	Commando	Haifa	Lebanon
Safieh, Anton H., 226	Ex-mayor	Jerusalem	OP
Safieh, Emil, 94, 171	Accountant	Lydda	OP
Sahar, Basil, 58, 73, 78, 80, 82, 92, 223	Principal	Jerusalem	OP
Sahknini, Fuad, 39, 212, 223	Pastor	Nazareth	Israel
Said, Faoud, 43, 53, 130, 182, 190	Businessman	Jaffa	Lebanon
Said, Huda, 20	Homemaker	Jerusalem	Jordan
Sakkijha, Faizeh, 62, 85, 177	Women's movement volunteer	Gaza	Jordan
Salan, Ahmed, 226	Teacher	Jaffa	OP
Sama'an, Ibrahim, 70, 74, 76, 184, 189, 195, 211, 216, 217, 223	Journalist	Haifa	Israel
Samir, 19, 49, 62, 63, 70, 134, 142, 170, 180, 197, 198, 218	Military camp leader	Bel El-Shik	Syria
Salem, Ibrahim, 76	Teenager in orphanage	Jetha	OP
Sayegh, Gamil, 171	Chauffeur	Jerusalem	Jordan
Sayegh, Sami, 58, 62, 64, 181	Camp truck driver	Hebron	Jordan
Selim, Rahab, 144, 164, 190	Librarian	Jerusalem	Egypt
Shaath, Nabeel A., 37-9, 66, 125, 126, 144, 176, 178	Professor and PLO organizer	Safad	Lebanon
Shamout, Ismail, 67, 147, 165-7, 212, 225	Professional artist	Lydda	Lebanon

Name or Pseudonym* and Page References	Occupational Identification	Origin in Palestine	Present Location
Sharif, Bassam Abu	Commando leader	Koofr Akab	Lebanon
Shehadih, Asiz, 80, 82	Lawyer	Ramallah	OP
Shehadi, Foud, 81	Lawyer	Jerusalem	OP
Sima'an, Ne'Meh, 16, 32, 45, 75, 183, 194, 198, 205, 210	Church bishop	Nazareth	Jordan
Simon, 77, 218	Hotel employee	Ramallah	OP
Talep, Musa Abu, 16	Tourist guide	Jericho	Jordan
Tannous, Issat G., 28-31, 99, 163, 175, 194	Diplomat and doctor	Nablus	Lebanon
Tarak, 19, 132	Camp commando	Nablus	Lebanon
Tawfic, Khouder Abu, 165	Camp resident	Nablus	Lebanon
Thabet, Maher, 62, 88	Camp resident	Ashkelon	OP
Thurayia, Salama, 123	Refugee at Allenby Bridge	Hebron	Jordan
Tleel, Wadie, 32, 43, 56, 208, 213	Oil company representative	Jerusalem	Jordan
Toukan, Hanan	Women's movement secretary	Nablus	Jordan
Touma, Emile, 42, 44, 52, 184, 213	Editor	Haifa	Israel
Wadei, 226	Commando	Tulharem	Lebanon
Wasef, Abu, 83, 147	Muktar	Surif	OP
Yasin, Fouad, 52, 63, 124, 143	Radio director	Shagara	Egypt
Yasin, Inam, 62, 224	Priest	Nazareth	OP
Zananiri, Nazri, 65, 69, 98, 164, 171, 213	Administrator	Jerusalem	Jordan
Zananiri, Souad, 193	Homemaker	Ramallah	Jordan
Zananiri, Tawfic, 46	Grandfather	Micor Hayim	Jordan
Zigadeh, Younes, 180	Camp teacher	Hebron	Jordan

Frank H. Epp, a former journalist and
editor, is now president of Conrad Grebel
College at the University of Waterloo in
Ontario, Canada. His teaching concentration
is in the minorities field. In addition to his
other book on the Middle East, *Whose Land
Is Palestine: The Middle East Conflict
in Historical Perspective,* he has written
five books on the Mennonite minority. The
best known is *Mennonites in Canada,
1786-1920: The History of a Separate
People.*

John Goddard is a free-lance photographer
and writer from Peterborough, Ontario.
A graduate of the School of Journalism,
Carleton University, he has worked for
The Canadian Press in Toronto and Ottawa.
His career has taken him to the Middle
East three times and recently to Latin
America.